THE DEADLY SINS OF
ARISTOTLE ONASSIS
STUART M. SPEISER

ACW Press
Ozark, AL 36360

The Deadly Sins of Aristotle Onassis
Copyright ©2005 Stuart M. Speiser
All rights reserved

Cover Design by Alpha Advertising
Interior Design by Pine Hill Graphics

Published by ACW Press
1200 HWY 231 South #273
Ozark, AL 36360
www.acwpress.com
The views expressed or implied in this work do not necessarily reflect those of ACW Press.
Ultimate design, content, and editorial accuracy of this work is the responsibility of the
author(s).

Library of Congress Cataloging-in-Publication Data
(Provided by Cassidy Cataloguing Services, Inc.)

Speiser, Stuart M.

    The deadly sins of Aristotle Onassis : an international legal authority reveals
    the long-suppressed evidence of how the Greek tycoon's life
    of deceit caused the death of his son and brought on the
    overpowering guilt that ended his own life / Stuart M. Speiser. -- 1st
    ed. -- Ozark, AL : ACW Press, 2005.

      p. ; cm.

    Includes bibliographical references and index.
    ISBN: 1-932124-62-4

      1. Onassis, Aristotle Socrates, 1906-1975. 2. Shipowners--
    Greece--Biography. 3. Wealth--Moral and ethical aspects.
    4. Corporations--Corrupt practices--Greece. 5. Fraud--Greece.
    6. Avarice--Greece. I. Title.

HE569.O5 S74 2005
387.5/092--dc22   0506

Printed in the United States of America.

To Maxine Speiser

Table of Contents

Introduction

THIS BOOK PRESENTS THE STORY OF HOW THE DEADLY SINS of Aristotle Onassis—his arrogance, greed, and lifetime of deceit—led to the death of his son Alexander.

I learned these facts while acting as the lawyer for Don McCusker, an American whom Alexander was checking out for the job of piloting Aristotle's personal plane, a Piaggio amphibian which was carried aboard his opulent yacht *Christina*. When the plane crashed during the check-out flight, both pilots were injured, but McCusker survived and Alexander did not. Onassis publicly—and falsely—accused both McCusker and the C.I.A. of killing his son, causing a Greek court to indict McCusker for manslaughter.

It was my job to obtain evidence of Aristotle's own role in the death of Alexander, in support of our theory that it was Alexander's father rather than the pilot McCusker or the C.I.A. who caused the fatal plane crash. In the course of preparing for trial, I had to delve deeply into Ari's business operations and entire life history. I had to analyze his habitual frauds in detail, in order to understand their effects on his children and to prove how they caused his son to be trapped in the fatally defective Piaggio.

When I finally gained access to this evidence, it became clear to me that Ari understood how his deceitful manipulation of his yacht, his airline, and his Piaggio had trapped Alexander, and that he ended his own life voluntarily because he could not go on living with the burden of that guilt. His life story followed the pattern of

Greek tragedy, as though the great wealth and power he amassed led to the sin of hubris, which offended the gods and caused his downfall. In the contemporary setting, Ari's values clashed head-on with those of Don McCusker, his intended scapegoat.

The evidence I obtained, much of which was kept from public disclosure by Ari's bribery, intimidation, and media hype, is presented for the first time in this book. It leads me to suggest that this is the first definitive biographical analysis of Ari's life.

Ari maintained that his only rule was that "there are no rules, no right or wrong, there is only what is possible." It is a maxim often embraced by would-be imitators of Ari's success in glamorizing deceit by media hype, such as the perpetrators of the 2001 Enron disaster. It was enthusiastically adopted by Ari's Falstaffian media-hype expert and hatchet man, Johnny Meyer, whose true role in Ari's life is recounted here for the first time. I confess that I had some difficulty in remaining focused on searching for the truth when faced with the roguish fascination of the Ari-Johnny hype team.

What Ari did to Don McCusker demonstrates the damage that Ari's "no rules" principle can inflict on innocent victims, on the legal system, and on society. It is now my privilege to share with you my ringside seat at the clash between Ari's Rule and Don McCusker's quintessential Middle-American values.

Chapter One

From Smyrna to The Ritz Towers

SUCH WAS THE GUILE OF ARISTOTLE ONASSIS THAT EVEN his date of birth has escaped detection, despite relentless probing of his entire life history by swarms of prosecutors and journalists the world over, and an F.B.I. file that runs to 4,296 pages.

Aristotle Socrates Onassis was born in Smyrna (now known as Izmir), a city on Turkey's Aegean coast that was heavily populated by Greeks. At times, Ari claimed he arrived in this world on various dates between 1900 and 1906, depending upon whether he then considered it advantageous to appear younger or older. The official birth records were destroyed by fire when the Turkish army sacked Smyrna in 1922. The writer of his obituary in the *New York Times* (the newspaper of record) threw up his hands and declared that Ari's age depended upon "which of his birth dates he gave at various times." In later life, Ari joked about this deception, saying that his papers were so full of lies about his birth date that he did not know himself when he was born.

Probably the best we can do is to accept January 20, 1906, as his birth date, which would have made him seven years old when he began school in 1913, an event which was recalled by apparently credible contemporaries. Ari often used that birth date in passport applications, and it is the date adopted by the highly regarded four-man team of London *Sunday Times* investigative reporters in their 1977 biography, *Aristotle Onassis*.

Ari often claimed that he had risen from an impoverished childhood, his father hawking crude trinkets on the streets and his mother taking in laundry. In fact, the family lived very comfortably in Smyrna. Ari's father Socrates was a prosperous importer, tobacco merchant, and banker, one of the wealthiest of the Anatolian Greeks, named for their residence in Anatolia, the section of Asia Minor that had been fought over by Greece and Turkey since time immemorial.

Ari's father Socrates, stern and unaffectionate, was deeply immersed in his business and had little time for or interest in his only son. Ari's uncle Alexander was more of a kindred spirit, and Ari developed a loving relationship with him. When Ari was six, his mother Penelope died in the aftermath of kidney surgery. Socrates quickly remarried, but the stepmother relationship was a difficult one for Ari and his older sister Artemis. To bridge this gap, Socrates brought his mother Gethsemane into the household to raise Ari and Artemis, allowing Socrates's second wife Eleni to concentrate on her two new daughters, Ari's half-sisters Kalliroe and Merope. Gethsemane and Ari formed a loving relationship that was closer to a mother-son bond. In fact, Ari hardly remembered his mother and always thought of his grandmother Gethsemane in that role.

Gethsemane was a devoted substitute mother who doted on young Ari. She was also a religious zealot whose piety bordered on fanaticism. Each year she made a Greek Orthodox pilgrimage to the Holy Land and brought back mementos for the childrens' bedrooms. At home she subjected Ari and Artemis to nonstop religious instruction and insisted that Ari attend church and serve in the choir. Despite her dedication—or perhaps because of its intensity—Ari's potential interest in religious observance was turned off early in his life.

Ari's school career was a train wreck. He was a mischievous lad who embarrassed his father by causing disciplinary problems at every school he attended. Although he had a genuine gift for languages, he was not cut out for the regimen of the classroom. He was more interested in water sports (swimming, water polo, rowing, and sailing) and the pursuit of girls. He spent many afternoons swimming in Smyrna's harbor, where he first developed his love of boats. Despite his advantaged position and his quick mind, he never managed to finish high school.

Ari's carefree boyhood came to an abrupt ending in September 1922. In the aftermath of World War I, the Greek army had occupied Smyrna and marched inland from the Aegean coast, seeking to recover vast areas of Anatolia, which they had lost to the Turks five centuries earlier. The Greek forces held on until the summer of 1922, when the Turks launched a counteroffensive to retake Anatolia. The Turkish army commanded by Kemal Ataturk routed the Greek occupation forces and pushed them all the way westward to the coast at Smyrna. As the Greeks retreated, they slaughtered Turkish civilians in their path. By September 9 the remnants of the Greek occupation forces had been evacuated by the Greek navy, and the Turks marched into a defenseless Smyrna, spoiling to avenge the killing of their civilian compatriots. They did so without mercy, ravaging Smyrna, burning most of the buildings in the Greek quarter and butchering more than 120,000 Greek and Armenian civilians in one of history's bloodiest massacres.

The Turks rounded up all the male Greeks between the ages of seventeen and fifty. Ari escaped this dragnet because he was only sixteen, but his father and his uncles were arrested and seemed to be headed for quick execution. The details of what happened to Ari and his family during the five weeks following the Turkish army's return to Smyrna are lost in the mists of time, mainly because Ari himself told many conflicting versions of the story. Yet there is little doubt that Ari's precocious wheeler-dealer maneuvering, probably mixed in with some genuine heroics, helped to save his life and those of most of his relatives.

Ari was the only male member of his family who was not being held by the Turks. He wangled a pass which enabled him to visit his father in prison regularly. Socrates told Ari that the key to saving the family was to get his hands on the large cache of Turkish paper money that he had left in his office safes. Although the Onassis office had been wrecked by the marauding Turks, Ari managed to gain access to the safes and extract the money.

Socrates had enjoyed excellent relations with many of Smyrna's leading Turkish businessmen, as well as the American counsul. From his jail cell he gave Ari a crash course in how to use those contacts to perfect their escape. Ari's agile mind was up to this complicated task, and he managed to arrange passage to safety in Greece for himself and seventeen relatives. Socrates remained in the Smyrna prison but his life was spared. Ari's beloved uncle Alexander was not as fortunate. Identified as an activist for Greek separatism, he was quickly hanged. Seventy-five-year-old grandmother Gethsemane, who had become separated from Ari and the rest of the Onassis clan in the confusion of the exodus from Smyrna, reached Greece on her own, but died tragically at the dock in Piraeus (the port of Athens) when she was attacked by a gang of thieves.

When Ari arrived on Greek soil, he was carrying all that was left of the Onassis fortune. He quickly decided that he would use the remaining cash from the office safes to buy his father's release from the Smyrna prison. Still only sixteen, he sailed to Turkey in search of government officials who could be bribed to turn Socrates loose. Again the facts are blurred by conflicting recitations, but Socrates was released, either because of his good standing with the Turkish community of Smyrna, or the intervention of the Turkish officials bribed by Ari, or a combination of both.

Although the destruction of Smyrna had wiped out all his capital, Socrates quickly reestablished himself as a tobacco merchant in Athens. He wanted Ari to join him in the business, but they did not get along well enough for such a close relationship to work out. For nearly a year, Ari drifted restlessly about Athens, frustrated at the lack of opportunity that confronted him. The five million mainland Greeks made no secret of their disdain for the million and a half refugees from Anatolia, regarding them as little better than the hated Turks. This could only have made young Ari feel like a man without a country, and may have been at the root of his lifelong lack of allegiance to any nation. It would have been a natural reaction for Ari to make himself into a one-man nation, loyal only to himself, and needing to be in full control of his own destiny at all times.

Finally he decided to seek his fortune abroad. His first thought was to emigrate to the United States, but there was a quota system which would have blocked his entry for many years. In the end he chose Argentina, where he had some relatives and had heard that Greeks—even Anatolian Greeks like Ari who had never graduated from high school—might have opportunities to succeed.

His ship docked at Buenos Aires on September 21, 1923. Ari, then seventeen by our agreed count, walked down the gangplank and into his new life carrying the traditional battered suitcase and a few hundred dollars of borrowed money.

Let us give Ari a clean bill of health on his life up to that point. He had learned the value of keeping untaxed cash in a safe and of bribing government officials, but it would hardly be fair to condemn him for using such tactics to save his family and himself from the murderous Turks. He came to believe in himself, in his power to scheme and maneuver his way out of the most desperate predicaments by disdaining the rules that applied to ordinary people. Probably the myth of his invincibility was forming in his mind as he arrived in the Argentine and began his climb to legendary status.

Buenos Aires, 1923-1932

At first Ari found the going tough in Buenos Aires. He managed to eke out a living at menial jobs, from fruit peddler to hod carrier to dishwasher. In March 1924, he landed a job with the British United River Plate Telephone Company as an electrician. Noting that there was less telephone traffic at night, he got himself assigned to the night shift as a telephone operator. This was part of his emerging master plan to build his fortune by living a double life, for Ari became aware that he had extraordinary energy and stamina. He didn't really need a full night's sleep like other people. He worked at the phone company from 11 P.M. to 7 A.M., catching naps and doing a lot of educational reading during quiet spells. Then he would sleep for an hour or two after work, before beginning a full day in his second world.

Into that daytime world he managed to cram other jobs and experiments with entrepreneurial ideas, while also establishing a social presence at the swankiest of Buenos Aires country clubs. His first business foray was in tobacco, of which he had gained some knowledge through his father's operations in Smyrna and Athens. He observed that Argentinian cigarette manufacturers used strong tobacco imported from Cuba and Brazil, but hardly any of the milder Turkish brands. Spending much of his spare time in pursuit of women—especially well-to-do women—he also noticed that they were partial to the milder Turkish leaf, which they had difficulty finding. To fill this void, Ari arranged for his father to ship him high-grade Turkish tobacco on consignment. Ari sold the Turkish leaf to the Argentinian cigarette manufacturers, charging his father the standard 5 percent trade commission. These commissions produced enough income to enable Ari to retire from his night telephone job in May 1925, a little over a year after he had begun his double-shift business career.

While carrying on the tobacco importing business as his father's agent, Ari also launched his own cigarette manufacturing operation, focusing on the womens' luxury market. He employed Greek immigrants as piece workers to roll cigarettes by hand, a traditional Greek skill. Now, barely twenty years old, he began to exhibit the fraudulent streak that would characterize his rise to business stardom.

• *Tobacco Frauds:* To spice up his competition with the established Argentinian manufacturers, Ari would purchase a pack of their cigarettes, take it out of the store where he bought it, inject a chemical into the pack with a hypodermic syringe, and then return the unopened pack to the shopkeeper, claiming he had bought the wrong brand by mistake. The chemical injection gave the cigarettes a horrible taste, but the syringe left no marks and the unsuspecting shopkeeper would sell the pack to another customer, who would very nearly be overcome by the poisoned cigarettes and would thereby become a potential customer for Ari's brands. There is no record of how often Ari pulled this stunt, but he was fond of telling this story in later years after he had left the tobacco trade.

Taking more direct action against a major competitor, Ari marketed a new line of cigarettes under the brand name "Bis." This proved quite successful, as Bis happened to be the name of one of Argentina's best-selling brands. The proprietors of the real Bis brand took a dim view of this ploy, and hauled Ari into court. His defense, presented with a straight face, was that he had never heard of the "other" Bis brand. In the end he was forced to drop the bogus Bis brand, and he settled damages out of court for several thousand dollars.

• *Insurance Frauds:* The Turkish tobacco that Socrates Onassis sent to Ari was shipped via Genoa, Italy, where the bales were stored near the docks awaiting transshipment to Argentina. Sensing an opportunity for insurance fraud, Ari arranged to have some of the bales sprayed with salt water by his accomplices at Genoa. Ari then filed hefty claims for "sea damage," which were duly paid by the insurance underwriters. These payments were expedited by Ari's far-sighted recruiting of insurance company employees as collaborators. This scheme worked smoothly to bilk the insurers of substantial funds, until one of the crooked insurance company employees got caught cheating and gave the game away. Ari's cousin Nicolas Konialidis was a junior partner in the cigarette business, and had the bad luck to be in Genoa when the insurance scam exploded. Nicolas received a jail sentence, but Ari escaped punishment. This insurance fraud, and the probability that Ari bribed a Greek official to cover it up, is fully documented in a confidential memo sent to the F.B.I. by the U.S. Office of Naval Intelligence

(O.N.I.) in September 1943, which includes these observations: "The dossier appears to have been sent to Greece from Genoa, but is thought to have been lost owing to a close liaison between Onassis and one Michalakopoulos, a Greek minister at the time."

• **Black-Market Currency Frauds:** By the time the worldwide depression of the 1930s began, Ari had built a reputation as a remarkably agile entrepreneur, even though his limited capital restricted him to fringe businesses. He often employed other Greek expatriates, including as many as thirty cigarette-rollers at a time. He made a point of voluntarily keeping government officials in Athens apprised of favorable opportunities to increase Greek trade with Argentina. This enhanced his standing with the Greek government, and resulted in his being appointed Deputy Greek Consul in Buenos Aires in 1931. In addition to its prestige, this official position gave him access to large sums of Western currency at official exchange rates, which he proceeded to resell at much higher prices in the flourishing black market. Of course he paid no taxes on these illegal profits. This was the start of his career-long aversion to paying taxes of any kind to any country. The black market currency capers quickly multiplied his wealth.

During his Buenos Aires years, Ari first exhibited some of the unique traits that would characterize his reign as a world-class tycoon. Although short in stature and strikingly ugly by matinee-idol standards, his gifts of colorful conversation, rough-hewn charm, and unlimited gall (today it would be called *chutzpah*) brought him success in the pursuit of women. Not content to limit these skills to sexual conquests, from the beginning he used his women to gain financial leverage. As the normally stodgy shipping journal *Lloyd's List* later observed of Ari, "Putting to bed business deals and women were complementary thrills."

His earliest recorded bedmate-business colleague was an Italian soprano, Claudia Muzio, who sang in the first opera Ari ever attended, a 1924 performance of *La Boheme*. Although Claudia was then slightly past her prime at thirty-five, she had made recordings with Enrico Caruso and still enjoyed considerable celebrity in Buenos Aires. Ari wooed her relentlessly, and they became lovers. At that time women were just beginning to smoke cigarettes, and those who dared would only do so in private. Claudia smoked, but not in public. Ari quickly began a campaign to get her to smoke his Turkish cigarettes in public places, hoping that this endorsement would take the place of his nonexistent advertising budget. She resisted at first, but he convinced her that public smoking would be an act of emancipation. Claudia relented, and Ari had turned his lover to financial advantage.

In the end, despite Ari's heroic efforts to best the competition through counterfeiting and poisoning, his cigarette manufacturing business was not successful. He never built a sales staff, relying on one of his competitors, an established manufacturer, to distribute his brands. The clouds of Turkish smoke emanating from Claudia Murzo as they dined in Buenos Aires restaurants never did compensate for lack of advertising. After a couple of years, Ari shut down the manufacturing operations and focused on supplying his father's Turkish tobacco to the other manufacturers. Socrates continued to pay him the standard 5 percent commission, and this produced a steady if unspectacular income for Ari. While he could live well on his commission income, it was not "serious juice," Ari's term for real money. But to this mundane tobacco importing business he added the blossoming Onassis hype, which led to the consular appointment and the opportunity to make serious juice from the black market currency scam.

It has become part of the Onassis legend that by the age of twenty-five, he had made his first million dollars in the Argentinian tobacco business. The London *Sunday Times* biographers were more precise in their appraisal of Ari's F.B.I. file: "Other reports in the Onassis file comment censoriously on the insurance and currency swindles that assisted his rise to riches in the Argentine." By hook or by crook—mostly the latter—Ari had accumulated serious juice by 1932. His cash fortune then is estimated at $600,000 by the London *Sunday Times* biographers. In 1932, when ocean-going freighters could be bought for as little as $20,000, that kind of money was ample to fund the next step in his master plan: serious shipowning. This would require him to establish a working base in London, then the capital of the shipping world.

He would retain his Argentinian residence and passport, and would remain the Deputy Greek Consul in Buenos Aires, turning over the operation of the tobacco importing business to his cousins, the brothers Nicolas and Constantine Konialidis. In October 1932, with his South American safety net securely in place, the twenty-six-year-old Aristotle Onassis, who had arrived in Argentina nine years earlier as a steerage passenger, sailed first-class to England.

London, 1932-1940

In 1932, Greek shipowners dominated the tramp steamer market. The tramps were usually old, rickety vessels that operated without schedules or long-term contracts, picking up and delivering cargoes anywhere in the world where and when they could find customers. There were a handful of Greek shipowners operating out of London who had been able to establish more prestigious, more profitable operations. Livanos, Kulukundis, Goulandris were some of the prominent names. When the irrepressible Ari landed in

London, he established himself in the fashionable Savoy Hotel and headed straight for the upper-crust Greek shipowners, to learn how they operated and possibly pick up some of the crumbs from their tables to get himself started in serious shipping. Having gotten the taste of starting at the bottom in Buenos Aires, now in London he was going to start as close to the top as he could get.

Within a few weeks he found what he was looking for. The Canadian National Steamship Company had ten freighters for sale, all between 8,500 and 10,000 tons. They had been laid up in the Saint Lawrence River for two years when Ari arrived in Canada, accompanied by an engineer, to inspect them. The asking price was $30,000 each, about what they were worth for scrap metal. Ari drove a hard bargain and finally bought six of them for $20,000 each, paying cash, since the world shipping market was too depressed to make financing available. He renamed them with *Onassis* as the prefix. The first two were named *Onassis Socrates* and *Onassis Penelope* after his father and mother.

He opened an office in Buenos Aires to solicit cargoes, putting his Konialidis cousins in charge as he maintained his base in London. Tramp-steaming was a risky game, as the shipowner had to make a series of finely judged decisions to fix a rate that would yield a profit and yet be competitive. Mental agility was required to factor in the many variables for ports all over the world. The shipowner could lose his shirt if he guessed wrong on any of these variables. Ari had a natural talent for this kind of calculating, and he managed to keep his six ex-Canadian freighters moderately busy in the tramp market. He continued to commute between London and Buenos Aires, working day and night in offices, on the docks, in restaurants, country clubs, and nightclubs—endlessly talking, telephoning, making new contacts and massaging old ones, blending business and social life into a blur of frenetic activity.

Ari claimed to have pioneered an important innovation for shipowners during his London years: the flag of convenience. During the 1930s, he transferred his ex-Canadian freighters from Greek to Panamanian registry, thereby enabling him to operate his ships free of inconvenient government regulations such as safety standards, minimum crew wages, and taxes. Other shipowners also claimed to have been first into Panama registry, but there is no doubt that Ari was among the leaders who ultimately caused practically the entire industry to register in Panama or Liberia, regardless of the true situs.

In his first two London years, Ari did not make a big splash in the shipping world. The established London Greek shipowners were well aware of his brash presence, but until 1934 he was considered no more than a boisterous upstart. That year, on one of his regular voyages between Buenos Aires and London, this one on the Italian passenger liner *Augustus*, he met Ingeborg Dedichen.

Ari was instantly aroused by Ingeborg's blond, slim, Nordic beauty. To him she looked like Greta Garbo. His ardor was not dampened when he learned that she was a prominent socialite, the daughter of one of Norway's leading shipowners, and was traveling with a party of Norwegian maritime moguls.

During the voyage, Ari turned on all his charm in pursuit of Ingeborg. At first she and her Norwegian friends were derisive of Ari, this "little black man who looked like a simple Asiatic dockworker." They wondered how he had gotten into first class, speculating that he might be a gangster. But as he used his rich, husky voice and boundless energy to speak to them passionately for hours on end, he won over both Ingeborg and her snobbish Norwegian shipping friends.

The timing of their meeting proved ideal for Ari, since Ingeborg was at a low point emotionally, having recently lost her beloved father and then seen her second marriage disintegrate. They became lovers, and their affair was to span continents and last for more than a decade. No doubt there were strong physical and emotional attractions on both sides. The relationship with Ingeborg also raised Ari's social standing several notches. Beyond that, Ari used her as the wedge to make his breakthrough into big-time ship ownership.

During the 1934 voyage on the *Augustus*, Ari had learned that he could charm the cold-mannered Scandanavian shipping aristocracy, and it was in their direction he turned to make his breakthrough. Ari was farsighted enough to perceive that the independent shipowner's future prospects for serious juice lay in the hauling of oil in ocean-going tankers rather than the dry cargoes then carried by the Greeks and other independents. In the mid-1930s, coal was still king, supplying more than 75 percent of the world's energy, compared to 15 percent provided by oil. And the oil producers transported most of their crude in their own tanker fleets, leaving little potential business for independent shipowners. These facts of business life restrained the established shipowners from trying anything as radical as building oil tankers for speculative charter work. But such obstacles did not deter Ari, who foresaw both the emergence of oil as the leading fuel and the advantages of larger tankers.

Using Ingeborg's contacts, Ari sought to convince Gotaverken, a leading Swedish shipyard, to build him a tanker on liberal credit terms. At that time the largest tanker afloat was 12,000 tons, but Ari wanted Gotaverken to build him a 15,000-tonner. Despite his complete lack of experience, Ari had calculated that the larger tanker's economies of scale would make the difference between profit and loss in his envisioned oil charters.

The Swedes were skeptical about both the feasibility of such a large tanker and the wisdom of extending credit to this brash

Greek who was still in his twenties and had never owned or operated a tanker. Normally they required at least 50 percent in cash up front from any Greek buyer, and would not extend credit beyond five years. Bringing to bear all his charm, debating skills, and overpowering energy, he used Ingeborg's close contacts with Scandanavian shipping leaders to push through an unprecedented tanker deal. He overcame the Swedes' doubts about the feasibility of the large tanker, and their resistance to his proposed terms. The purchase price was set at $800,000, of which $200,000 was to be paid during construction, and the balance of $600,000 paid over ten years at 4.5 percent interest. This would enable the tanker to pay for itself out of its own charter earnings.

Ari named the ship *Ariston*, a play on Ari's name and the Greek word for "the best," a fitting title for the world's largest tanker. While the *Ariston* was under construction in 1937, Ari booked passage to Lakehurst, New Jersey, on the airship *Hindenburg*, to begin charter negotiations with American oil companies. Problems with the *Ariston's* construction forced him to cancel his flight. When the *Hindenburg* crashed in flames at Lakehurst, Ari concluded there was something mystical in his life being spared so dramatically.

Before construction was completed, Ari sailed to the United States and signed his first tanker charter, a nine-voyage contract (a full year's work) with J. Paul Getty's Tidewater Oil Company to transport their oil from San Fransisco to Yokohama. Thus did Ari combine romance, chutzpah, hype, and extraordinary business vision to pioneer the modern independent oil tanker business.

When the *Ariston* was launched in June 1938, Ari took Ingeborg and most of his own family on the maiden voyage to San Francisco, where the tanker was to begin its first charter for Getty's company. Ari had penciled in some personal conveniences, including a convertible swimming pool and two large staterooms, frills that were unheard of in merchant ships.

Not one to rest on his laurels, Ari quickly ordered two sister tankers from Gotaverken, the 15,000-ton *Aristophanes* and the 17,500-ton *Buenos Aires*. He was sitting pretty as the self-made leader of a new industry when Germany invaded Poland on September 1, 1939. Two of his tankers, the *Ariston* and the *Buenos Aires*, were in neutral Sweden, which quickly agreed with Germany that all such ships would be interned there for the duration of hositilities. His third tanker, the *Aristophanes*, was at sea under the Norwegian flag. When Norway's government went into London exile in 1940, it requisitioned the *Aristophanes*, leaving Ari without his tankers for the balance of World War II. He still controlled his six ex-Canadian freighters, two of which he was negotiating to sell to the Japanese.

As the war began to turn against Britain in 1940, most of the other London-based Greek shipowners hastily departed for New York. Ari was eager to follow but was stuck in London in the midst of negotiating the Japanese sale of the two freighters. Finally he completed the sale in June 1940 and booked passage to New York on the Cunard Line's SS *Samaria* departing July 1. He had to settle for a second-class berth.

The *Samaria*, unarmed and unescorted, was forced to zigzag in order to avoid U-boat attacks. Another liner ten miles away was torpedoed and sunk within sight of the *Samaria*. It finally arrived in New York after a hectic ten-day voyage. Due to what Ari called "a little technical irregularity," he was detained overnight on Ellis Island. He complained that this third-class facility, designed to process "all kinds of adventurers and dirty European immigrants of the old times," was entirely unsuitable for "first-class people," especially a rising shipowner whose destination was The Ritz Towers.

Chapter Two

The New York Years

SHAKING OFF THE THIRD-CLASS AROMA OF ELLIS ISLAND, Ari quickly ensconced himself in a thirty-seventh-floor residential suite at The Ritz Towers, in 1940 one of Manhattan's swankiest addresses. Awaiting his arrival was his cousin Nicolas Konialidis, who had sailed from Buenos Aires at Ari's direction. Ari now laid out a plan for what he called a "legal blitz"—a series of lawsuits that would squeeze the Norwegian government-in-exile into paying Ari for having commandeered his brand new tanker, the *Aristophanes*. The tanker was docked in Rio de Janeiro, and Ari knew that Brazil was not overly friendly toward the British cause. There was a large German expatriate community in Brazil, creating strong undercurrents of support for Hitler in those days when Britain stood alone against the Nazis.

The plan was for Ari's Brazilian lawyers to "arrest" the tanker in port, a maritime law maneuver that would prevent it from sailing until all claims were adjudicated. As the ship's owner, Ari had legal standing to arrest it and claim that it had been taken from him illegally. Cousin Nicolas protested that this plan was impractical, since the wartime Norwegian government had seized hundreds of ships and had never been forced to pay a dollar to anyone. Ari replied, "They'll squeal, but they'll pay. The *Aristophanes* is the largest tanker in service, and they can't afford to have it tied up in years of litigation."

Nicolas dutifully flew to Brazil, hired the lawyers to whom Ari had directed him, and got the *Aristophanes* arrested in Rio. Ari's price for allowing the tanker to continue its vital role in the war against Hitler was a million dollars in cash. Appeals to Ari's Greek patriotism fell on deaf ears, and the hard-pressed Norwegian exile government quickly paid the million dollars into Ari's account. Ari still owned the ship, and would either be able to reclaim it after the war or collect insurance proceeds if it was sunk.

Ari found New York an agreeable place to sit out the war. His remaining freighters were chartered to the U.S. Maritime Administration, netting him at least $250,000 a year without any risk or effort. His incisive knowledge of worldwide shipping enabled him to pick up other ships at bargain prices, and either resell them profitably or charter them to the U.S. war effort. In 1941, he bought what he described as "an old rust tub" for $350,000 while it was steaming off the east coast of South America, directing it to Florida for refitting. By the time it reached Florida, German U-boats were exacting such a fearful toll of merchant ships in the Atlantic that Ari was able to resell it for $1.2 million.

The wartime pickings were so easy for Ari that there was no need to employ fraud. The other expatriate Greek shipowners lost most of their ships in Atlantic U-boat attacks, and soon the insurance funds dried up, leaving them in a less advantageous position than Ari. They devoted much of their time to the Greek Shipowners' New York Committee, which barred Ari from membership because he had refused to turn over any of his profits to the Greek War Relief Association or otherwise demonstrate appropriate patriotic concern.

Ari's apparent lack of enthusiasm for the Allied war effort attracted the interest of J. Edgar Hoover, director of the F.B.I. In 1942, the U.S. embassy in Buenos Aires reported to Washington that they had "information that Onassis possessed fascist ideas and was considered shrewd and unscrupulous." In the same year, Hoover wrote to Admiral Emory S. Land, director of the War Shipping Administration, that an informant reported Onassis "has expressed sentiments inimical to the United States war effort." There were other informants who said Onassis was "pro-Axis." These vague reports resulted in the F.B.I. opening an espionage investigation, but by April 1944 the F.B.I. was not able to unearth any evidence of subversive activity, and the case against Ari was closed. Those who knew Ari well were certain that he was free of any political ideology. He was not pro-Axis or pro-anything other than pro-Onassis.

Ingeborg Dedichen had been trapped in France when Paris fell to the Nazis, but with Ari's help she managed to make her way to New York in November 1940. She moved into Ari's Ritz Towers apartment and the couple resumed their romance. But now her Scandinavian shipping connections were of no use to Ari, and the choices of female companionship for a wealthy bachelor in wartime would have been tempting even to a loyal lover. Ari and his Konialidis cousins had picked up two tankers which were carrying oil between the Los Angeles port of San Pedro and

Vancouver, British Columbia. Ari frequently flew to Los Angeles to inspect the ships and oversee the operation. During these West Coast visits, Ari moved into the Hollywood scene, staying at the Beverly Hills Hotel and dating such screen stars as Paulette Goddard, Veronica Lake, and Gloria Swanson.

In New York, Ari lived the Café Society lifestyle of the Stork Club and El Morocco. Gradually he and Ingeborg had grown apart, as Ari began to drink much more heavily than in prewar days. He took to beating Ingeborg savagely, kicking and hitting her until she looked like a boxer who had lost a fight. Ari sought to justify these beatings by his version of Greek tradition: "Every Greek, and there are no exceptions, beats his wife. It is good for them. It keeps them in line." Apart from the fact that Ingeborg was not his wife, she did not subscribe to this philosophy, and in the fall of 1944 she moved into her own apartment. Although they still saw each other and tried to remain friends, the long-running love affair was over. She decided to return to Norway in 1946. Ari rewarded her with a Paris apartment, $35,000 in cash, and a monthly payment of $500. For her voyage home, he put his ship *Aristophanes* at her disposal, so that she could stock it with food and luxuries that were still not available in war-ravaged Norway.

When the war ended, Ari found his shipping business in surprisingly good shape. His interned Swedish-built tankers were returned to him, and three of his other ships survived the hostilities. The other Greek owners did not fare that well, losing 360 of the 450 ships that participated. The Greek Insurance Fund had run out of money, delaying payment for the sunken ships. In 1946, Congress passed the Ship Sales Act, making U.S.-built Liberty ships and other war surplus vessels available to Greece and other war-devastated European nations. Greece was allocated one hundred ships, and Ari applied for thirteen of them. But the allocation was controlled by the Union of Greek Shipowners, which was dominated by Livanos, Kulukundis, and the other established operators. They shut Ari out with no ships, on the ground that the Liberties were made available to owners who had lost ships flying the Greek flag, a description that did not fit Ari because he operated under the Panamanian flag and in any event did not lose any ships to enemy action. Ari resented this treatment and vowed to get even in his own way.

One way that Ari could change his outsider status was to marry into one of the prominent Greek shipowning families. Their tight clique had a tradition of encouraging marriage among their own members, much in the manner of European royalty. Never one to sell himself short, the irrepressible Ari took aim at the family of the wealthiest and most prestigious Greek shipowner, Stavros Livanos, who had himself followed the Greek maritime tradition of uniting the most powerful families through a marriage alliance.

Stavros Livanos's grandfather (of the same name) had begun the family maritime tradition early in the nineteenth century as a simple seaman aboard a small sailing vessel based on the Greek island of Chios, which at the time was under Turkish rule. He never achieved his ambition of owning his own ship, but he passed to his son George (Stavros's father) his love of the sea. George managed to acquire a 2,800-ton steamship which he sailed from Chios, acting as captain and breaking in his four sons as crew officers. By 1911 Captain George owned a fleet of two large steamships and several sailing vessels, which became very profitable during the Balkan Wars of 1912-1913, when Chios broke away from Turkey and was reunited with Greece. George's third son, Stavros, studied engineering and at age nineteen became the

youngest chief engineer in the Greek merchant fleet. Like his
father and brothers, he manned the Livanos ships, which kept
down their labor costs and assured close family supervision of
their voyages. Soon after the outbreak of World War I in 1914,
Stavros was sent to London, the world center of shipping, to open
the family's office there.

Greece remained neutral during the first three years of the
war. This left the Livanos fleet free of British wartime controls
and taxes, and enhanced the profits earned by supplying crucial
shipping to the hard-pressed Allies. The Greeks—and especially
the Livanos family—were known for running their ships at the
lowest costs in the industry, largely through meager wages, horrible food, and family participation as crew members. Stavros was
a tireless worker and a hands-on manager who spent most of his
time on the London docks, checking every detail of the ships, the
crews, and their cargoes. He was also a shrewd businessman who
acquired eight more steamships at bargain prices.

When the war ended, the Livanos shipping business was near
the top of the Greek merchant operations. Following Captain
George's cardinal rule, they believed only in cash and ships. They
avoided the clutches (and the interest charges) of the bankers,
expanding by paying hard cash for ships, which could be bought
cheaper that way. This put the Livanos family in an advantageous
position when the collapse of the postwar shipping boom wiped
out many Greek shipowners who had leveraged their ship acqui-
sitions. When Captain George died on Chios in 1926, Stavros
and his brothers took over the fleet, with Michael operating from
Switzerland and Stavros remaining in London.

At the age of forty, Stavros married Arietta Zafirakis, the fifteen-year-old daughter of a wealthy Greek merchant. He brought
her to England to begin an unusually happy marriage. Their three

children were born in England: Eugenie in 1926, Tina in 1929, and George in 1935. Although Stavros had become one of the wealthiest Greek shipowners by the 1930s, the family's lifestyle remained modest. While many of the other Greek shipping magnates bought private yachts, Stavros considered this a waste of cash that could be better spent on a working ship. He was known as a tireless worker who was interested in little but ships, and he was as strict and tightfisted with his family as with his employees.

The worldwide Depression of the 1930s fell heavily on the shipping industry. Again the shipowners who had borrowed against their ships faced wholesale foreclosures, but for Stavros Livanos it was a time of great opportunity. Ships that had cost millions of dollars before the crash could be bought for less than $100,000, and Stavros used the hard-earned Livanos cash to snap them up. He even placed orders for new ships with the British shipyards that were practically shuttered. As a result, he made the most of what little shipping business was available, and he put the Livanos family in the ideal position to cash in on the coming resurgence. All the while he kept wages at the lowest level in the industry: one pound (about $5) per month for an able-bodied seaman, and 20 pounds ($100) per month for captains. By the end of the 1930s, the Livanos fleet was the leading Greek freighter line, and Stavros, his fortune enhanced by successful investments in securities and real estate, was considered one of the richest men in the world.

He continued to shun publicity and the trappings of great wealth. One exception was his chauffeured limousine, which he used mainly to transport his daughters Eugenie and Tina to King Arthur's Day School. As they matured, they went on to attend Heathfield, a fashionable girls' school in Ascot. They were growing up more as English sub-debutantes than Greek expatriates.

Each was a beauty in her way, Eugenie dark and sloe-eyed and Tina blonde with a peachy complexion.

The Livanos family history taught Stavros that wars create the greatest opportunity for shipping profits, and he was well-positioned when World War II began in 1939. The freighters he had built so cheaply in the Depression-ravaged shipyards soon were doing yeoman service as part of Britain's wartime lifeline. Stavros worked day and night to keep the ships working, often meeting with harried Naval officers at the Admiralty after spending twelve hours or more on the bomb-plagued docks. In the autumn of 1940, when he found he could no longer carry on efficiently under the Luftwaffe's bombardment, he sailed to Canada with his family.

Stavros ran his beleaguered fleet from Montreal until Pearl Harbor brought the United States into the war. Then there was only one place to be: New York. He moved the family to the Plaza Hotel, which had become a mecca for the London Greek shipowners, and he opened a downtown office at 24 Stone Street, to which he commuted by subway. The teenaged daughters quickly adjusted to this disruption of their lives. Eugenie attended Miss Hewitt's Classes, a toney girls' "finishing school," while Tina was enrolled in the equally fashionable Rosemary Hall in Connecticut before joining Eugenie at Miss Hewitt's.

Stavros was acknowledged as the leader of the expatriate Greek shipowners, and his suite at the Plaza became the site of many of their meetings. At one such meeting in 1943, Aristotle Onassis was introduced to Tina Livanos for the first time. The fourteen-year-old Tina had just suffered a horseback spill and was on crutches when they met. Ari was so taken with her that he recorded the time of the meeting in his diary: *Saturday, 7 p.m., 17 April 1943.*

At that point, Tina regarded Ari as just another of her father's business associates, without romantic attraction. She had a teenage crush on John Vatis, a tall, fair, lean, handsome heir to another Greek shipping fortune, much closer to her own age than was Ari. When the romance with Vatis showed signs of getting serious, Stavros put a stop to it. He felt that both Tina and John were too young to form a serious attachment, and he especially wanted to avoid a marriage that would violate Greek tradition by putting Tina ahead of her older sister Eugenie. Tina resisted at first, but when her domineering father forbade her to see John again, she reluctantly obeyed.

Ari made it a point to be on hand whenever the opportunity to socialize with the Livanos girls arose. While he often said that he had fallen in love with Tina at the first sight of her on crutches at the Plaza Hotel, his conduct indicates that he may have been willing to take either Livanos daughter as his bride. During the summer of 1945, Stavros's wife convinced him to loosen the purse-strings sufficiently to rent a house in Oyster Bay, Long Island. Ari materialized there as the summer resident of a nearby estate, and with the parents' permission, he often took Eugenie and Tina swimming, sailing, and waterskiing. Ari was good enough at these water sports to narrow the apparent age gap. In the fall, Ari continued his squiring of both daughters in Manhattan, taking them to the movies and to Rumpelmeyer's at the St. Moritz Hotel for hot fudge sundaes. Then early in 1946, having won Tina's love, Ari asked Stavros for her hand.

Livanos was furious that Ari would dare to ask him to bless the marriage of his younger daughter before Eugenie went to the altar. But underneath his gruff exterior, Stavros was a teddy bear when it came to his family. Tina and her mother played on his heartstrings to bless this love match with the most prominent member of the new wave of Greek shipowners, while Ari used all his vocal energy to persuade Stavros that times had changed and this was America, not ancient Greece. It was Tina's unhappy pouting that finally brought Stavros around, and the wedding was set for December 28, 1946.

It took place at the Greek Orthodox Cathedral of Holy Trinity on East Seventy-fourth Street. Archbishop Athenagoros, head clergyman of the Greek Orthodox Church in the Americas, presided over the two-hour ceremony. The seventeen-year-old Tina was attended by her sister Eugenie as maid of honor and four teen-age school mates from Social Register families as bridesmaids. The forty-year-old Ari's best man was his friend, André Embiricos, another Greek shipping magnate. The lavish wedding reception in the Terrace Room of the Plaza Hotel was one of New York's social events of the year. Ari presented Tina with a bracelet of ancient Greek coins engraved: *Saturday, 7 p.m. 17 April 1943, T.I.L.Y.* (for "Tina, I love you"), commemorating their first meeting.

Their honeymoon, which lasted for two months, began with a houseboat trip down the inland waterway to Palm Beach. Then on to Buenos Aires, where Ari had business interests to look after. Ari's friend, movie magnate Spyros Skouras, met them in Argentina and was quoted as saying, "They made a splendid pair, so much in love!" Then back to New York to begin married life in their new home, which was part of the dowry that came along with Tina.

Number 16 Sutton Square, the picturesque four-story townhouse overlooking the East River which would become Ari's first real home, had set Stavros back nearly half a million 1946 dollars. In a typical Greek shipowner's bargain, it was agreed that Ari would put another half million into remodeling and decorating, which turned it into the most talked-about house in Manhattan.

The Livanos daughters had attracted the eye of another ambitious Greek shipowner, Stavros Niarchos, Ari's contemporary who was to become his life-long rival. Niarchos had a different history and personality, but shared Ari's passion for becoming the world's leading shipowner. Niarchos was born to a prosperous Athens family in 1909, and did well in school, studying law at the University of Athens. He went to work for his uncles' flour-milling company, and in 1935 convinced his uncles they could cut their freight bills by buying their own ships to carry grain from Argentina. He soon was bitten by the maritime bug, and within a year he started his own shipping business.

While not a complete outsider like Ari, he was not able to crack the tight circle of the Livanos-dominated shipowner fraternity in the prewar years. He made the move from London to New York in 1940, and in 1942 he gave up the safety of New York to join the Greek Navy. Although he spent much of the war doing intelligence work in London, Alexandria, and Washington, he saw action in the Battle of the Altantic as an officer aboard a destroyer. The three ships he owned were chartered to the U.S. Maritime Administration, and two of them were lost in the Atlantic submarine warfare. Even with this pedigree, he was labeled a "parachutist" by the New York Greeks, the same derisive term they used to describe Ari's attempts to propel himself into their ranks from out of the blue.

In contrast to Ari's toad-like appearance, Niarchos cut an elegant figure. He was taller than Ari, handsome, and socially polished. His Saville Row suits always seemed freshly pressed, while Ari looked like he had slept in his cheaply made clothes. But compared to Ari he was an introvert, and was universally described as humorless and overly formal, if not downright boring. Although a serious, dedicated shipping executive, he was also an international playboy with a dazzling collection of mistresses. He had been through two divorces by the time Ari began wooing Tina.

Niarchos at first also seemed more attracted to Tina, but when Ari won her hand he quickly followed the cue and began courting Eugenie. They were married in November 1947 and moved into a townhouse at 25 Sutton Place, part of Eugenie's dowry which was just around the corner from Ari's 16 Sutton Square. This began their game of one-upmanship, since Niarchos boasted that his wedding gift was somewhat larger than Ari's.

His marriage into the Livanos dynasty immediately gave Ari a huge boost in prestige and enhanced his leverage for the acquisition of ships. To this he added his X-ray vision of the tanker industry, and his gifts of persuasion, to engineer the monumental breakthrough that revolutionized the tanker industry and built much of his great fortune.

To Ari's eyes, the pieces were lying there waiting to be put together. The major oil companies were facing the need for massive expansion in exploration, refining, and transportation to fuel the worldwide postwar recovery. Exploration and refining, which they could not farm out, consumed most of their capital. Transportation could be delegated to independent shipowners on long-term charters, relieving the oil companies of the capital outlays required for building large tankers. But where would the shipowners get the capital to build the tankers?

The answer was to use Other People's Money (shortened to OPM by Tina Onassis, who loved acronyms). Ari tried the major New York banks, but found (to nobody's surprise) that they were not interested in making such long-term loans. Some bankers told Ari he ought to try the life insurance companies, since they were regularly collecting money they would not have to pay out until the policyholder died. Ari zeroed in on the Metropolitan Life Insurance Company, the one with the most money in its coffers. Darting back and forth between the oil companies, Met Life, and the shipbuilders with the grace of a ballet dancer, Ari got the oil companies to agree to charter the ships for ten years, and then got Met Life to lend him sums equal to the charter payments, pledging the charter contract as well as the new tanker as collateral. The charter payments, which in total were sufficient to pay the cost of building the tanker, were assigned to Met Life and would not pass through Ari's hands. Thus he was actually riding on the credit of the major oil companies. It was, as Ari explained, "like lending money to someone who proposed to rent a house to the Rockefellers. It did not matter whether the house had holes in the roof or was gold-plated. If the Rockefellers agreed to pay the rent, that was good enough for anyone lending money on the house."

The logic appears self-evident in retrospect, but at the time it was revolutionary. To the established independent shipowners like Ari's father-in-law Stavros Livanos, such massive use of credit was a violation of their basic "cash and ships" philosophy, and an invitation to financial disaster. From the lender's standpoint, it was an untried scheme, and the standard charter clauses of the day did not satisfy the Met Life legal department that they were fully secured. It was there that Ari's vision, boundless energy, and irresistible salesmanship broke long-standing maritime and financial traditions, overcoming the resistance of conservative lawyers and accountants for the oil companies, the shipyards, the marine insurers, and the lender to create a new vehicle that assured the flow of the charter fees directly to Met Life until the shipbuilding loans were repaid in full. Many who observed this process firsthand believe that it happened only because of Ari's unique ability to combine complicated legal and financial innovations with the excitement of a great adventure that he conveyed through his charisma and his flamboyant lifestyle.

Using this new leveraging mechanism, Ari placed $40 million worth of orders in 1947 for one 18,000-ton tanker and five 28,000-ton tankers at the Bethlehem Steel yards in Maryland and Massachusetts. Ari was then on friendly terms with his new brother-in-law Stavros Niarchos, who quickly followed in Ari's footsteps by using Met Life credit to order two large tankers from Bethlehem. All these tankers sailed into a huge shipping boom that began in 1948 with implementation of the Marshall Plan. Ari noted that tankers "had become a sort of San Francisco gold rush." In the words of Henry Hagerty, the Met Life officer who first authorized the tanker loans, "The oil companies made the Greeks. We wouldn't have lent them a nickel without that connection."

Ari and Stavros Niarchos repeatedly used the Met Life formula to put themselves in the front rank of the world's shipowners. Meanwhile they sought every opportunity to acquire used freighters and tankers which were also capable of cashing in on the postwar shipping boom. Under the Ship Sales Act of 1946, the U.S. Maritime Administration was selling surplus tankers and freighters on very liberal terms, but was restricting ownership of those ships (which had potential wartime strategic value) to American citizens or companies controlled by American citizens. To Ari, Stavros, and other enterprising foreign shipowners, this was too juicy a deal to be passed up because of mere legal technicalities. Separately they consulted New York and Washington law firms, who assisted them in creating corporations that had the appearance of American ownership and control, but were actually controlled by the foreigners.

For this purpose they engaged high-priced American front men, many of whom were prestigious former government officials considered to be above reproach. The front men acted as shareholders, directors, and officers, to create the facade of American ownership and control. But behind the scenes, through an elaborate maze of paper corporations, leases, and secret agreements, Ari and Stavros controlled the surplus ships.

Ari proceeded to acquire a total of twenty-five surplus ships, fourteen of them T-2 tankers, which carried the highest strategic ranking. To avoid any doubt of its American character, Ari named his principal vehicle United States Petroleum Carriers, Inc. A subsidiary was dubbed Victory Carriers, Inc. Both of these companies were organized so that practically all the profit of operating the ships was funneled into Ari's pockets, through a web of Panamanian companies whose ownership was secret and undocumented.

As he sailed into the 1950s, everything was coming up roses for Ari. In 1948, his son Alexander was born in New York, followed by daughter Christina in 1950. In the shipping world, everything he touched seemed to turn to gold. His tankers and freighters, those he built with Met Life's money and those he acquired from the war surplus fleet, were plying the oceans laden with money-making cargoes. He was able to maintain control of the war surplus ships without any apparent legal problems. There was even time for some extracurricular fun.

In the summer of 1947, Ari and Tina were vacationing in the south of France, and when lunching at Monaco's Hôtel de Paris they encountered Ari's old friend from Argentina, Alberto Dodero, who was traveling as one of the escorts of Eva Perón, the glamorous wife of Argentine President Juan Perón. According to Ari, he took Alberto aside and asked him to arrange an introduction to Eva, which resulted in Ari being invited to a private luncheon at her villa at Santa Margherita on the Italian Riviera. Eva is said to have extended her hospitality to the bedroom, after which she cooked him an omelet for lunch. Ari bragged that he then gave Eva a check for $10,000 as a gift to one of her charities. As he told the story, Ari said that the omelet was "tasty, but the most expensive I have ever had." (While Ari is the only source for this story, it is accepted as true by most of the experienced Onassis-watchers.)

In those early days, Ari's rivalry with brother-in-law Stavros Niarchos, at least outwardly, was conducted in a friendly spirit of gamesmanship. At first the main contest was about who could collect the most spectacular homes. Ari maintained a beachfront house in Montevideo, a permanent suite in the Plaza Hotel in Buenos Aires, a seaside villa near Athens, and an apartment on the top floor of 88 Avenue Foch in Paris, in addition to the Sutton Square townhouse. He also rented the Château de la Croë at Cap D'Antibes on the Riviera, a magnificent twenty-five-acre estate that had previously been occupied at various times by King Leopold of Belgium, King Farouk of Egypt, and the Duke of Windsor. Stavros kept pace by adding palatial homes in London, St. Moritz, and Long Island, but he saved his trump card for the Riviera. Employing the stealth he had learned in wartime intelligence work, Stavros succeeded in buying the deed to the crown jewel of Ari's homes—the Château de la Croë—and had the pleasure of evicting his brother-in-law.

By 1953, Ari was spending more time in Europe than in New York. He had begun to find American shipyards rather expensive, and since his Met Life lenders did not care where his tankers were built, he believed he could do better in Germany. There he found that the German yards, reduced to rubble by Allied bombers, were eager to cut prices to the bone for the chance to revive their business. In 1950, Ari shifted most of his tanker orders to German shipbuilders, thereby becoming a local hero in Hamburg and later being credited with providing a decisive boost to the recovery of the entire German economy. As was his custom, Ari spent a lot of time in the yards that were building his ships, immersing himself in the design and construction details.

Since Ari was a global operator, he did not have to keep his headquarters in the United States, where he had come originally to escape the European war. With trans-Atlantic flights now a regular service, he could move his main base to Europe, where he could more effectively stifle government attempts to regulate his activities, and he could quickly hop back across the ocean to visit his financial colleagues at Met Life and his Café Society friends at El Morocco and the Stork Club.

He considered Athens, Paris, and London, but ultimately in 1953 he chose the one place in the world that was custom made for his headquarters. It was, in the words of Somerset Maugham, "a sunny place full of shady people": Monte Carlo.

Chapter Three

"The only rules are that there are no rules"

THERE WERE GOOD BUSINESS REASONS FOR ARI'S 1953 CHOICE of Monte Carlo for his new headquarters. Geographically it was in the perfect location, since it was halfway between the Middle Eastern oil fields and the great consumer markets of Europe. The balmy climate was also to Ari's liking. Even more attractive was the virtual absence of taxation, since the government of Monaco was designed to run on revenues from its gambling tables. As Ari told a *Fortune* magazine interviewer:

> *My favorite country is the one that grants the maximum immunity from taxes, trade restrictions, and unreasonable regulation. It is under that country's flag that I prefer to concentrate my profitable activities.*

Lunching in Paris with his French banker, Charles Audibert, Ari happened to mention that he was thinking of moving his headquarters to Monte Carlo. The astute Audibert pointed out that there was a publicly-traded company called SBM (Société des Bains de Mer et Cercle des Etrangers, literally the Sea Bathing and Foreigners Club) which owned most of Monte Carlo, including the casino, the Hôtel de Paris, and nearly all the important real estate. Audibert knew that SBM shares were then quoted very cheaply on the Paris Bourse. Scribbling on the proverbial napkin, he calculated that Ari could buy control of SBM for the equivalent of about $3 million. Ari's eyes lighted up at this price tag, which, he pointed out, was about the current value of each of his war-surplus T-2 tankers. Monte Carlo was surely worth the price of a small, aging tanker. It would be smarter, and more fun, to own Monte Carlo than to merely rent office space there. Before dessert was served, Ari ordered the banker to start buying up SBM shares, using the customary front men to avoid running up the price.

Prince Rainier III, Monaco's reigning monarch, owned about 20 percent of the SBM shares. Prince Rainier's ancestors, the family Grimaldi, had disguised themselves as monks and seized the 375-acre territory in 1297, and now he ruled it by means of an agreement with the French government. The twenty-nine-year-old unmarried prince was known more for his pursuit of actresses than for his business skills. After Ari bought up about a third of the shares in the market, he met with Rainier and won his support. The prince was delighted that the dynamic Onassis was willing to take control, for Monte Carlo had fallen on hard times and was losing its gambling and tourist clientele. Ari agreed to pump millions of dollars into restoring the resort to its Edwardian glory. Ari's own charisma, now redoubled by worldwide tabloid tales of

"The Man Who Bought the Bank at Monte Carlo," would in itself create a priceless public relations magnet.

So it was that in the summer of 1953, at the annual meeting of SBM, Ari voted his shares in concert with the prince, took over the company, and thereby assumed control of Monaco itself. Within a week, Ari's main company, Olympic Maritime S.A., moved its headquarters into the Old Sporting Club on the Avenue d'Ostende, overlooking Monte Carlo's spectacular harbor. Shortly thereafter, a sumptuous apartment was created for Ari in the same building.

This was a great personal triumph for Ari, as his name immediately became synonymous with the storybook splendor of Monte Carlo. He told an interviewer that as long as there were at least three thousand wealthy men left in the world, Monte Carlo should be very successful. He then launched a campaign to attract those three thousand multimillionaires—and more—to his new plaything. It was a hyping operation which, in Ari's hands, could not fail.

Ownership of Monte Carlo/Monaco was also important to Ari's business position. No other tycoon, however wealthy, could claim that he owned the country in which his business was headquartered. This coup appeared to make him practically immune from regulation by any government. Howard Hughes, with whom Ari exchanged what they called "intelligence," was highly envious of Ari's Monte Carlo arrangement, calling it "the perfect setup."

Ari often said that his lifetime motto was, "The only rules are that there are no rules." (Sometimes he put it more dramatically: "There is no right or wrong, there is only what is possible.") Emboldened by his unique Monte Carlo security blanket, Ari began to put into even more extensive practice his theory that the ordinary rules did not apply to him, no matter which nation sought to enforce them. The paint was hardly dry on Ari's new Monte Carlo offices in the summer of 1953 when he launched a scheme which only a person convinced of his own impunity would even contemplate. Ari would bribe high officials of Saudi Arabia to grant him an exclusive contract—the "Jiddah Agreement"—that would eventually put him in control of over 45 percent of the world's oil reserves.

Ari was led into the Jiddah Agreement by a shadowy Greek entrepreneur named Spyridon Catapodis, with whom Ari had minor business dealings prior to 1953. Catapodis was living in nearby Cannes when Ari took over Monte Carlo. In August 1953 they met to discuss a startling proposal. Catapodis, who had developed strong contacts in the Arab oil world, believed that high officials of Saudi Arabia could be induced to sign a contract which would eventually give Ari the exclusive right to transport all the oil produced in Saudi Arabia. Ari knew that the Arabian American Oil Company (ARAMCO), a consortium that included major American oil producers like Exxon (then called Esso), Mobil, and Texaco, already had the exclusive rights to both produce and transport Saudi oil, through an agreement with the king signed in 1933 and expiring in 2000. But a mere piece of paper would not prevent Ari from plotting to grab the richest business prize in history. He would find a way around it, even if this required bribery on a seven-figure scale.

Ari used Catapodis to make the first overtures to the Saudi regime, but later sidetracked Catapodis in favor of Dr. Hjalmar Schacht, Hitler's former finance minister, who had completed his prison sentence as a war criminal and now enjoyed excellent business relations in the Arab world.

In January 1954, Ari arrived in Jiddah aboard his newest tanker, the *Tina Onassis,* to sign the agreement. The signer for

Saudi Arabia was Sheikh Abdullah Al Suleiman, the minister of finance, subject to final ratification by King Saud. The key provisions gave Ari the mechanism to gain a monopoly over transportation of Saudi oil over a ten-year period. The vehicle was a new enterprise, the Saudi Arabian Maritime Company (SAMCO), chartered in Jiddah. Ari would supply the tankers and crews for SAMCO, ostensibly a Saudi Arabian government operation. Ari also agreed to establish a maritime training school for young Saudis, who would be employed as officers on SAMCO's tankers. At the outset, SAMCO would be given the privilege of transporting a guaranteed 10 percent of Saudi oil production. ARAMCO would not be permitted to expand their tonnage or renew their charters with new tankers when the existing ships became obsolete. Thus, by attrition, the ARAMCO transportation monopoly would run out within ten years, leaving Ari's SAMCO vehicle with a chokehold on transportation of all the oil of Saudi Arabia, estimated to comprise 45 percent of the world's reserves. In addition, because Ari was given the right to fix his shipping rates well above market level, his potential profits were astronomical.

The implications of the Jiddah Agreement were mind-boggling, even though the contract itself was not published. ARAMCO officials quickly perceived that it would lead to a complete monopoly on transportation of Saudi oil, which Ari could exploit in many ways. They also learned that Ari was preparing similar proposals to Kuwait, Iran, and other Middle Eastern oil-producing countries. ARAMCO protested vigorously to the Saudi government, charging that the Jiddah Agreement was a breach of their 1933 agreement. They announced that they would refuse to honor the Jiddah Agreement, so that when Ari's tankers arrived at the ARAMCO terminals to load ARAMCO oil, they would be turned away. ARAMCO's aggressive response served to inflame Arab pride and trigger increased resentment of the large American presence in Saudi Arabia. The U.S. State Department feared that ARAMCO's refusal to deal with SAMCO, which purported to be an operation of the Saudi government, might lead to repudiation of the 1933 agreement and nationalization of Saudi oil. Wars had been ignited by crises less volatile than this one.

Meanwhile there was great concern within the U.S. government, for the Eisenhower administration was well aware that American security and economic stability depended heavily on the uninterrupted flow of oil from the Middle East, especially Saudi Arabia. Officials of the C.I.A. and the State Department perceived the Jiddah Agreement as a wedge between the U.S.A. and the Saudi government, leading to erosion of American influence in the Middle East. In time of war or crisis, Onassis would have the power to turn off the oil spigot that America had to keep open. In 1954 the Cold War was being waged at high intensity. It was unthinkable that an international pirate like Onassis could be given the power to divert Saudi oil to the Soviet Union. But what could the United States do about it? Efforts by Secretary of State John Foster Dulles to convince King Saud to disavow the Jiddah Agreement met with failure when Ari flew to Saudi Arabia and agreed to some relatively minor changes. On May 18, 1954, King Saud formally ratified the agreement.

At this point Ari's archrival, Stavros Niarchos, stepped into the picture. By 1954, he did not need the money he was making by hauling Saudi oil in his tankers. He could have walked away from the shipping business and lived like a king for the rest of his life. But he was not about to let his brother-in-law trump him with this massive coup. So, in a scenario that would be rejected by most Hollywood studios as incredible, he proceeded to hire an American private eye to pull off the hatchet job that the United States government could not undertake.

The private eye was Robert Maheu, later to become famous as Howard Hughes's alter ego in Las Vegas. In 1954, Maheu, then aged thirty-six, had left the F.B.I. to establish a one-man private investigative office in Washington D.C. His first client was the C.I.A., who were frequently in need of "cut-out" agents to do jobs that the agency itself could not execute for fear of officially involving the government. (If anything went wrong, the C.I.A. would cut the agent out of their records so that it would appear he was acting on his own.) There were many former F.B.I. agents in the C.I.A., and they naturally turned to their old-boy network when they needed a private cut-out operative.

Robert Maheu told his portion of the Saudi story firsthand in his 1992 autobiography, *Next to Hughes.* One day in 1954, a secretive London solicitor (lawyer) named L.E.P. Taylor appeared in Maheu's new office and, without identifying his client, described the Jiddah Agreement and asked if Maheu could find a way to kill it. For a $500 retainer, Maheu agreed to look into the prospects.

Maheu quickly realized that the only way he could pull off what the English lawyer wanted was to get the U.S. government behind him and make it a C.I.A. cut-out operation. Maheu spoke to Jim O'Connell, an old F.B.I. friend who was his contact at the C.I.A. O'Connell was intrigued but concluded that before the C.I.A. was asked to get involved, Maheu should seek backing from the National Security Council.

Maheu reported this to Taylor and said he would take on the job. Taylor paid him $6,000 in cash and gave him a copy of the Jiddah Agreement. When Maheu read it, he could hardly believe his eyes. As he put it, "By regulating the chief source of energy in an oil-dependent world, Onassis would become one of the most powerful men alive, capable of bringing whole governments to their knees." A week later Taylor finally identified his client as Stavros Niarchos, a name that meant nothing to Maheu.

Maheu began by placing (illegal) wiretaps on the phones in Ari's New York office and his Paris apartment. Then he hired researchers to help him present the proposal to the National Security Council (N.S.C.). Four weeks later the proposal was ready, and Maheu was told that he had to sell it to Vice-President Richard Nixon, the main player on the N.S.C. An appointment with Nixon was quickly arranged. To Maheu's delight, Nixon realized at once that "there was no way we could let this agreement stand," and said he would present it to the next N.S.C. meeting with his support. As Maheu left Nixon's office, the vice-president said to him, in hushed tones, "If it turns out that we have to kill the bastard, just don't do it on American soil." This was a shock to Maheu, but he was not about to turn down the crucial support of the vice-president.

Soon Maheu received word that the Company (code for the C.I.A.) would be clandestinely involved, but he would have to work strictly as a cut-out, affording the U.S. "full deniability, because if our government was seen acting against the Saudis, ARAMCO might be thrown out of the country." Maheu then flew to London for his first meeting with Niarchos, held in the shipowner's suite at Claridge's Hotel. Niarchos was certain that Ari had obtained the contract by bribing a high Saudi official, for otherwise it made no sense. Niarchos felt that if Maheu could find out who took the bribe and prove it to the satisfaction of King Saud, the king might well decide to cancel the contract.

Maheu agreed with this analysis, and brought into play all the available behind-the-scenes resources of the C.I.A. to determine who took the bribe. He also enlisted the aid of Spyridon Catapodis, the Greek entrepreneur who had originally broached the idea to Ari but by this time had been cut out himself and was angry enough to sabotage the Jiddah Agreement. Catapodis swore that there was a written agreement to cut him in on the profits, which he claimed Ari had signed in disappearing ink.

Maheu was able to gather enough documentation to prove that the bribed official was Ali Alireza, brother of the Saudi minister of commerce and a close friend of the finance minister who negotiated and signed the agreement, Sheikh Abdullah Al Suleiman. The amount of the bribe was "a cool million." That was just for procuring the contract. There would be ongoing bribes in the form of huge kickbacks based on every SAMCO tanker that sailed from a Saudi port in the future.

Still being financed solely by Niarchos and holding no official instructions or authority from the U.S. government, Maheu flew to Jiddah to present the evidence of bribery to King Saud. There he met with the king's personal assistant, who spoke perfect English. Maheu argued his case for four hours, interrupted frequently by the assistant stepping out of the room and returning with new questions. Maheu believed that the king was eavesdropping in an adjacent room, and that the new questions were coming from him. At the end of the meeting, the assistant told Maheu that the king was most grateful for the information, and that he would come to Maheu's hotel the next day with the king's decision.

Maheu was somewhat uneasy since the Saudi procedure was to grant only an entry visa in advance, with the exit visa remaining at the discretion of the king after arrival. Maheu was attacking powerful forces within the Saudi government. He had no exit visa, and had been told that as far as support from the U.S. government was concerned, he was on his own.

After a sleepless night, he was relieved when the king's assistant came to his hotel at noon the next day. He handed Maheu the exit visa and said, "His Excellency also instructed me to tell you that he would be pleased if this story about the payoff were to become known in the world press. But it must begin in a foreign country, neutral to both the United States and Saudi Arabia."

Clearly the king was going to use the press reports of bribery as the basis for nullifying the Jiddah Agreement. Maheu was delighted, and thought it would be very easy to get the story published in the European press. But here he was to be disappointed: "No news agency or magazine in Europe would touch it. Onassis was known as a man who got back at those who crossed him, and no one in the media wanted to take that chance."

Stavros Niarchos was up to this challenge. He provided a "loan" of $75,000 to an Athens newspaper, which broke the story. Soon it was reprinted all over the world, and King Saud then had to act to preserve the honor of his country. That was the end of the Jiddah Agreement, as well as the reign of Sheikh Abdullah Al Suleiman as finance minister.

It was also the end of Ari's most audacious power grab, which failed only by a photo finish. The next attempt to gain such a stranglehold on strategic oil supplies did not occur until 1990, some thirty-six years after Ari put the Jiddah Agreement into motion. In contrast to the unarmed Aristotle Onassis giving the marching orders from his ornate office in Monte Carlo's Old Sporting Club, the 1990 attempt by Iraqi ruler Saddam Hussein required deployment of the world's fifth largest army—a million strong—and an arsenal that included ballistic missiles. At that, Saddam Hussein targeted Kuwait, whose oil reserves paled in comparison with those of Saudi Arabia.

In retrospect it appears that Ari must have been drunk with power to attempt the Saudi coup, for it put him into explosive conflict with his leading customers, the major oil producers who were then chartering his profitable tankers. He tried to dance his way out of this predicament by claiming that the whole thing was the Saudis' idea, and that he stepped in only to assure that the SAMCO tankers would be in trustworthy hands. This ploy was not well received, and as current charters expired, Ari found half of his tankers idled. His core business was saved from ruin by the Suez crisis of 1956, in which Egyptian President Nasser shut down the Suez Canal and thereby blocked oil shipments from the Middle East, forcing the oil producers to charter any tanker that would float in order to transport oil on the much longer route around the Cape of Good Hope.

While Ari directed the Saudi caper from Monte Carlo in 1954, he was also commanding his private navy in a whaling war which brought his ships under attack by bombs and bullets. In 1949 Ari incorporated the Olympic Whaling Company in Panama, converting one of his war-surplus T-2 tankers to the factory ship *Olympic Challenger* and commissioning German shipyards to convert seventeen war-surplus corvettes into hunter-killer catching ships. The *Olympic Challenger* was well named, since Ari used it to challenge every regulation then in effect to assure humane practices in whaling.

Success in whaling depended largely on the harpooning skills of the gunners. Ari proved to be an equal opportunity employer, taking on the notorious Lars Andersen, a convicted "Quisling" (traitor) who had collaborated with the German occupiers of his native Norway. Andersen, a world-class harpooner, helped Ari to sign up another fourteen exiled Norwegian gunners, thus assuring that his whaling operations would not be impeded by pangs of conscience.

Through the International Whaling Convention, the whaling nations agreed to limit the worldwide kill to sixteen thousand whales per year in order to preserve the species, with each nation accepting a maximum quota. The convention established strict rules about the killing of whales, including the length of the hunting season, minimum size, and protected species. Ari made a mockery of all these rules, claiming that they did not apply to his operations since his ships were registered in Panama, a nation which had not adopted the International Whaling Convention.

This behavior went unpunished in his first few seasons, mainly because the international whaling community was not organized well enough to enforce the rules against illegal slaughter on the scale conducted by Ari. Evidence was difficult to come by, even though it was later shown that on every voyage, Ari's whalers had killed well before and well after the season officially began, and had slaughtered *thousands* of whales which were too young, too small, pregnant, or members of protected species. In fact, Ari turned whaling into a spectator sport, installing luxurious living quarters on the *Olympic Challenger* so that he could invite special guests to witness the bloody harpooning.

During the 1954 season, Ari came into conflict with the most bellicose whaling nation, Peru. Tired of having to fight off illegal whalers who plundered the large groups of sperm whales found off its shores, Peru enacted a decree that established a protective zone of two hundred miles from its shores, within which it claimed the right to exercise "military administration and fiscal jurisdiction." From the shelter of the Old Sporting Club, Ari decided to test the resolve of the Peruvian Navy. In late August 1954, the *Olympic Challenger* and fifteen catching ships sailed into the protected area and prepared to defy the decree. As they approached, the headline story in Peru's leading newspaper, *La Nación*, demanded action:

The whaling pirate Onassis insists on disregarding our national sovereignty. This will not be tolerated. His ships must be seized by our Navy.

Ari replied that the Peruvian two-hundred-mile limit was illegal, and that he reserved the right to arm his ships for self-defense. This defiant proclamation caused disquiet among the families of the six hundred German seamen who manned Ari's whaling fleet, since the seamen had not signed on for a war. When Ari's crews began killing whales within the two-hundred-mile limit, Peruvian President Manuel Odria ordered his navy into action. Prize crews from Peruvian destroyers boarded two catchers, *Olympic Victory* and *Olympic Lightning*, and sailed them back to Lima. Then Peruvian Air Force planes spotted the factory ship, *Olympic Challenger*, and ordered her by radio to proceed to Lima. Ari's crew responded by heading in the opposite direction at top speed. Then the whaling war turned into a shooting war, as the planes fired machine gun bursts close to the ship and dropped several small bombs which exploded nearby in the water. That was enough to persuade the captain to turn around and proceed peacefully to Lima. In all, five ships and four hundred German sailors of Ari's whaling fleet were held in captivity.

Ari managed to wriggle out of this debacle, even though a Peruvian naval court held an inquiry and found that Ari's German sailors had killed as many as three thousand whales off Peru before the seizures. The court levied a fine of $2.8 million, which Ari was able to get Lloyd's of London to pay under his insurance policies. Since Norway suffered most from Ari's illegal whaling, the Norwegian Whaling Association conducted a further investigation, including testimony from some of Ari's former crewmen.

One of them, Bruno Schlaghecke, had kept a diary of the 1954 season which included these chilling entries:

> *Killed almost all [prohibited] blue whales today. Woe if that leaks out.... Killed only small sperm whales today. The sight of these small animals, which had not even grown teeth, makes me inwardly dumb and empty.... Shreds of meat from the 124 whales killed yesterday are still lying on the deck. Scarcely one of them was full grown. Unaffected and in cold blood everything is killed that comes before the gun.*

Soon after the Peruvian naval engagement, Ari sold his whaling fleet to a Japanese operator, and emerged from his illegal plundering with a handsome profit. The London *Times* observed, "Certainly, although he makes no claims for statehood, he does not disguise his international influence." This showed Ari in a modest light, for he could easily have claimed statehood as the owner of Monaco.

While Ari was fighting these comic opera battles in Saudi Arabia and Peru, he came up against a trickier problem in the United States. The twenty-five war-surplus ships he had bought very cheaply under the 1946 Ship Sales Act had been operating profitably for nearly seven years, and no questions had been raised concerning their ownership or control. It appeared that the Maritime Administration officials had not been concerned about who actually controlled the ships, so long as their ownership at the time of purchase was in the hands of companies whose majority shareholders were American citizens. Ari, like Stavros Niarchos and other foreigners who bought ships under the act, had followed expensive legal advice in constructing a façade of American ownership through highly-paid front men whose presence appeared to satisfy the limited curiosity of the government officials. But into this tranquil picture strode the tempestuous Senator Joseph McCarthy, caring nothing about the smooth functioning of the international shipping industry, bent only on exposing Communist spies.

In 1952, McCarthy's Senate Subcommittee on Investigations held hearings on the alleged use of war-surplus ships in trade with Communist nations. The Department of Defense was asked to investigate, and they reported that ships of two of the Greek owners—Livanos and Kulukundis—had on a few occasions visited Communist ports. There was nothing illegal about this, since the ban on trading with Communist nations applied only to Americans, not to foreigners like the Greek shipowners. But if they were foreigners, what were they doing owning or operating war-surplus ships? Both the Senate committee and the Department of Defense concluded that enforcement of the Ships Sales Act was a matter for the Department of Justice, to whom they sent their files on the foreign shipowners. Livanos and Kulukundis quietly agreed to stop trading with the Communists. This satisfied Senator McCarthy, whose career was to self-destruct in 1954, long before Justice took definitive court action on the question of whether any of the foreign purchasers had committed fraud under the Ships Sales Act.

The Justice Department found the surplus ships case extremely complicated, since it involved an intricate web of dummy corporations and financial sleight-of-hand. The Onassis investigation alone required the services of forty F.B.I. agents, all of whom were either lawyers or accountants. Finally in 1954 a federal grand jury in the District of Columbia returned a criminal indictment charging Ari, his American front men, and six of his corporations with fraud against the government. The eighteen-page indictment contained eight counts and listed many "overt acts" that were fraudulent, including secret agreements to transfer stock from the American shareholders to Ari after the government had allocated the ships to purportedly American-owned corporations; chartering of the ships to Ari's Panamanian corporations, which gave him actual control; and filing false financial statements which disguised the fact that Ari was the real source of the money used to buy the ships. Since all of these allegations were undeniable, Ari told his lawyers to seek the softest plea bargain that the government was willing to entertain.

The negotiations went on for nearly two years before a deal was struck in December 1955. The government was not eager to prosecute the case because the Ship Sales Act was loosely drafted and leniently enforced against other foreign shipowners. By 1955 Ari's war-surplus ships were practically at the end of their useful years. The purpose of the American-ownership provision was to assure that the ships would be available in the event of war or other crisis. Ari had offered to turn them over to the U.S. during the Korean War, but they were not needed. Therefore, his violations of the Ship Sales Act had not caused the nation any direct harm. Also, many of Ari's frauds had occurred far enough back in time to bar prosecution because the statute of limitations had run out.

For these reasons, Ari's lawyers were able to get him off with a fine of $7 million, which was only a fraction of the profits he pocketed from operating the surplus ships. His corporations pleaded guilty to fraud, but the charges against him personally were dropped. While being arraigned and fingerprinted on the fraud charges, he was forced to spend ten minutes in jail (in the company of the Puerto Rican nationalists who had attempted to bomb Congress) before his lawyers bailed him out. Ari laughed off this indignity as part of the game.

The three monumental frauds we have examined—bribing the Saudis, slaughtering the whales, and duping the U.S. Maritime Administration—were extensively covered by the worldwide media. Such exposure would probably have crimped the style of most confidence men, but Ari took this notoriety in stride. Escaping with total punishment of ten minutes in jail renewed his faith in the credo that the ordinary rules did not apply to him.

Back in the shelter of Monte Carlo, not a day passed without Ari enriching himself by tax fraud. By the late 1950s his fortune was estimated at $300 million. He continued to benefit financially from the marriage to Tina Livanos, even though he considered himself free to play the field in extramarital affairs. He and Tina had an arrangement which permitted both of them to indulge in sexual play with others, provided it was kept out of the media. Ari became an expert at such concealment, but in July 1959 this proved to be beyond even his legendary powers, when Maria Callas and her husband boarded the *Christina* at Monte Carlo for what turned out to be its most historic cruise.

Chapter Four

The Two Most Famous Living Greeks

BY THE TIME MARIA CALLAS ENTERED ARI'S LIFE IN 1959, she was firmly established at the pinnacle of grand opera, worshipped as the world's greatest soprano and the most famous living female Greek. Like Ari, her rise had not been easy and did not follow the traditional path to greatness.

Maria's parents emigrated from Greece to New York in 1923. She was born there in December of that year and so became an American citizen. Her father, George Calogeropoulos, owned and operated a small pharmacy business in Manhattan, and adopted the name Callas because it fit more easily on his business sign. In the wake of the 1929 stock market crash he lost his business and took a job as a traveling salesman. His wife Evangelia was a domineering and boisterous woman who was unsympathetic with George's business reverses. Their endless shouting matches turned the small family apartment into a Bedlam for Maria and her older sister Jackie.

In 1929, six-year-old Maria suffered serious injuries in an auto accident, after which she gained so much weight that she became almost grotesquely fat. Her ambitious mother soon noticed that Maria had an extraordinary singing voice, and forced her to perform publicly despite her extreme shyness and sensitivity to the inevitable audience snickering at her obesity. In 1934, despite her excess poundage and thick glasses, her voice won her second place in a nationwide radio contest hosted by Jack Benny.

Evangelia managed to scrape up enough money to provide rudimentary singing lessons for Maria and piano training for Jackie. In 1937, after Maria finished the eighth grade, Evangelia put the whole family out of their misery by leaving her (grateful) husband George in New York, sailing to Athens with her two daughters to begin a new life in her native country. In 1939, sixteen-year-old Maria's amazing voice gained her a scholarship to the leading Greek music school, the Ethnikon Athenon, where she became a pupil of the renowned coloratura soprano, Elvira de Hidalgo. Maria put all her time and energy into learning from Elvira, and by 1940 she was ready for her professional opera debut as Beatrice in *Boccaccio*. While her voice dazzled the audience and the critics, its extraordinary range was not yet appreciated, and her rise was hampered by the two hundred pounds she brought on stage. Her first major role came in 1942, when on short notice she substituted for the Athens National Opera Company's leading singer as the star of *Tosca*. Surviving taunts from stagehands about her massive weight, she captivated the audience and earned rave reviews.

Greece was then occupied by German and Italian troops, and food for the populace was scarce. Often Maria was paid in food rather than in money, and her singing helped her mother and sister to survive the war. Greece then fell into civil war between the communists and those supporting the monarchy. In 1946, her long-estranged father, now working as a pharmacist, took pity on Maria and sent her a steamship ticket to New York, which she was able to use because she was still an American citizen.

She spent nearly two years with her father, but was unable to land any singing roles. She blamed her weight, which she had managed to maintain in the heavyweight class despite wartime food shortages. Still determined to become an opera star, she gave up on America and sailed to Italy. She had an unsuccessful audition at Milan's La Scala, and finally settled for a role in *La Gioconda* at the lesser opera house in Verona, opening in August 1947. In the audience was Giovanni Battista Meneghini, a wealthy Italian building-materials manufacturer who was instantly smitten by Maria and her voice. Although he was more than twice her age, they were married in April 1949, when Maria was twenty-five and tipped the scales at 230.

Meneghini sold his business so he could devote all his time to building Maria's career. He proved an able manager as well as a dedicated husband, and is generally credited with enabling Maria to develop her great talent, despite her later charges that he mishandled some of the proceeds. He persuaded the noted conductor Tullio Serafin to coach her, and Serafin discovered that she was that extreme rarity, the unlimited soprano, her extraordinary voice bursting the conventional boundaries between soprano, mezzo-soprano, and contralto.

During the 1950s, she captivated the opera world with one stunning triumph after another, from Europe to Latin America to the United States, where she earned sixteen curtain calls in her debut at New York's Metropolitan Opera. Finally she erased the memory of her earlier rebuff at Milan's La Scala by drawing unprecedented praise for her performances there. The Italian press dubbed her "La Divina." Such was her impact on the opera world that works by Bellini and Rossini which had not been performed for a century were revived to satisfy the mania for Maria's magic touch. Although her recordings were also very successful, it was her ability to dramatize her roles that set her live performances apart from those of the other opera superstars.

Although Maria reduced her weight to 140, she exhibited a temperament befitting the self-indulgent diva. There were frequent battles with opera house managers, some of which were intensified by her husband's haughty attitude. But she gave Meneghini much of the credit for her success, telling the press that "my career would not exist were it not for my husband." By 1959, when Ari stepped into the picture, the gloss had worn off their ten-year marriage, and the age difference was beginning to draw them apart. Yet there had never been a hint of an extramarital affair.

Ari and Tina were in their thirteenth year of marriage, and were spending much of their time apart, partly because of Ari's incessant business travels. Also, their recreational interests were rarely in harmony, as Tina was dedicated to winter sports in the Alps, which Ari despised. Ari's parties were usually boring for Tina, since they were largely populated by Ari's business cronies with whom he would talk shop far into the early morning hours. Tina was not enamored of Monte Carlo's social whirl, and she preferred to spend her time at their Paris apartment on Avenue Foch. Ari was always more comfortable aboard the yacht *Christina*, which he now regarded as his real home.

It was apparent to Tina that her father's prestige was at least a major reason why Ari had married her, and by this time both of them were seeking other liaisons, albeit relatively discreet ones. Tina was often seen in the company of Reinaldo Herrera, a dashing young Venezuelan oil magnate, while Ari was partial to Jeanne Rhinelander, a school-days friend of Tina's who now lived in the south of France. Once Tina angrily interrupted a tryst between Ari and Jeanne, but mostly the couple tolerated such side affairs as part of their life in the fast lane of the 1950s.

Maria and Ari first met in 1957, introduced to each other by the celebrity gossip columnist Elsa Maxwell at the annual ball which Elsa gave at the Venice film festival, this one in honor of Maria, who had become her protégé. Ari and Maria had an innocuous conversation, but he must have felt some attraction, at least to her great celebrity. Maria and her husband spent the next few days with Ari and Tina, visiting aboard the *Christina*, motor-boating around Venice, and attending other parties as a foursome.

They met again in Venice in 1959, where the *Christina* was docked to enable Ari and Tina to attend the highlight of the summer social season, the annual ball at Countess Castelbarco's palace. Again the guest of honor at the ball was Maria Callas. This time her conversation with Ari was more animated, and their obvious interest in each other soon caused their spouses to join them. Ari extended the customary yachting invitation to the Meneghinis, but Maria said that her opera calendar was too crowded. She mentioned that she would be opening in *Medea* at London's Covent Garden in June. Ari quickly replied, "We shall be there!" This astounded Tina, since Ari had made no secret of his inability to stomach opera.

Not content with merely showing up for Maria's Covent Garden *Medea*, Ari insisted that he and Tina throw the London party of the year in her honor, inviting over 150 people to supper at the Dorchester following the opening performance on June 17.

At the party, Ari made no effort to conceal his excitement at being in Maria's company, and Meneghini struggled to keep their effusive togetherness from dominating the party. This resulted in a famous photograph *(Figure 4)* in which the two men appear to be maneuvering to embrace Maria (who towered over both of them), only to wind up clasping each other's hands around her.

Ari persuaded Maria and her husband to accept an invitation for the *Christina*'s next cruise, which departed Monte Carlo on July 22, 1959. In addition to the Meneghinis, the guests included Sir Winston and Lady Churchill; their daughter, Diana Sandys; Churchill's doctor, Lord Moran; and Churchill's secretary, Anthony Montague-Brown and his wife Noni. The famous yacht would make its way through the Gulf of Corinth, on to Smyrna, up the Dardanelles to Istanbul, and back to Monte Carlo on August 13. During those three weeks, Ari and Maria spent much time together, including long conversations at night when all the others were asleep, but they did not engage in lovemaking on board the yacht. When they docked at Istanbul, Ari and Maria disappeared for several hours. After they returned to the *Christina*, Maria told her hapless husband, already devastated by seasickness, "It is all over. I love Ari."

The paparazzi who hounded Ari's every public move had picked up the scent of scandal emanating from this voyage, and they intensified their pursuit after the *Christina* docked at Monte Carlo. Maria returned to Milan, where Ari joined her twice in late August. On August 31, he sent his Piaggio plane to pick her up and fly her to the Riviera where the couple spent three days. They returned to Milan together in the Piaggio, where the paparazzi discovered and photographed them. On September 5, Ari flew in the Piaggio to Venice, where he was to meet Tina. He remained there only that night, flying out the next day in the Piaggio to pick up Maria in Turin, from where they flew to Nice. Ari's over-worked personal pilot, Angelo Pirotti, was quoted as saying, "The Piaggio has never flown so much since Mr. Onassis bought it."

Ari and Maria spent a few more days trying to keep their trysts concealed. Finally both Callas and Meneghini publicly announced that their marriage was over and that he was no longer her business manager. Ari was cornered by reporters in his Milan hotel, where he managed to trash his wife, his children, and his lover with the machismo announcement, "I am a sailor, and these are things which may happen to a sailor." Tina and her furious father remembered that when Ari was wooing Tina, he had presented himself as a rising shipowner rather than as a sailor with a girl in every port. They were particularly outraged at what they considered Ari's public pursuit of Maria. Ari protested that he could not control the rantings of the tabloid press, but he was aware that some paparazzi would willingly risk their lives to get a good shot of the two most famous living Greeks in each other's company.

Ari's method of cooling down this firestorm was to arrange another two-week cruise on the *Christina,* with only one guest aboard: Maria herself. When they arrived back in Monte Carlo, they found that Meneghini had talked freely to the press, accusing Ari of seeking to marry Callas because "he wants to glamorize his grimy tankers with the name of a great diva." Meneghini then filed suit for a legal separation from Maria in Italy, where divorce did not exist. Tina refused interviews, but she fled to New York with the children, Alexander and Christina.

Outraged that his wife would dare to react so unsportingly, Ari deluged the media with derogatory hype about Tina, claiming (along with allegations unprintable even in the tabloids) that she had kidnapped his children and was demanding a $20 million ransom. Although he wanted to carry on the affair with Maria on his own terms and under his own (nonexistent) rules, he did not want Tina to divorce him. That would be a slap in the face and a challenge to his manly dominance. There was also the prospective loss of the Livanos cachet which had helped to propel his rapid rise in the worlds of shipping and finance. He decided that the best way to avoid a divorce was to intimidate Tina, continuing to trash her and the Livanos family in the media so that they would be forced to accept his lifestyle. Apparently he gave no thought to the effects of this poisonous hype on the eleven-year-old Alexander or Christina, aged eight, both of whom had been aboard the *Christina* throughout the fateful Callas cruise. But Tina, supported by her powerful father, filed in New York for divorce and custody of the children.

Since the sole ground for divorce in New York at that time was adultery, Tina's suit alleged that Ari had committed adultery "by land and sea" with a "Mrs. J.R.," whom the journalists were quick to identify as Tina's old friend Jeanne Rhinelander. Thus Tina deprived Maria of whatever satisfaction she might have derived from an admission that she had stolen Ari away.

Ari made frantic efforts to get Tina to drop the suit, recruiting friends like Sir Winston Churchill, Elsa Maxwell, and Spyros Skouras to assist in reconciliation, and of course leaking this news to the media to increase the pressure on Tina. But Tina had taken enough. She was still young and attractive, did not need Ari's money, and did not want to be part of his circus-style life any longer. She did spare the children a New York adultery trial by agreeing to a quickie Alabama divorce on grounds of mental cruelty in June 1960. She was granted custody of the children, whose support was assured through the American trust which Ari had established for them as part of the earlier war-surplus ship scheme, in which he had used their American citizenship to enhance the illusion of compliance with the Ship Sales Act. Ari was granted liberal visiting rights, and Tina waived alimony.

Although Ari claimed to the end that he did not want the divorce, it opened the way for a comparatively peaceful continuation of the affair with Maria. Since he was now a bachelor cohabiting with a legally separated woman, their romance was considered slightly less salacious by the tabloids, although the paparazzi continued to click away with abandon whenever they caught the two together. For half a dozen years after the 1960 divorce, Ari and Maria continued their storybook romance, punctuated by his peripatetic business trips and her singing engagements. She shared his suite aboard the *Christina*, but Ari established prudish rules which excluded her from some of the cruises, such as those carrying the Churchills as guests, since both had been close friends of Tina. Somehow Ari convinced Maria that her presence would be embarrassing, even though the Churchills had been aboard the 1959 cruise that ended the Onassis and Meneghini marriages.

Until the affair with Ari, Maria had considered sex an unpleasant wifely chore. She reported that she had experienced her first orgasm during the Istanbul rendezvous with Ari, and from that moment on she was hopelessly in love with him. He was the only man who had made her feel like a whole woman, and despite her conventional attitude toward marital fidelity, she decided in Instanbul to walk away from her past life and dedicate herself to Ari. There is every indication that she believed Ari felt the same way, and that he would divorce Tina and marry her.

Although Ari told Maria whatever was necessary to take possession of her life, he fought against the divorce in the hope of retaining his prestigious Livanos wife along with his celebrity mistress. Immediately after the 1960 divorce, Maria was ecstatically happy, and her actions showed that she was expecting Ari to marry her as soon as she could obtain legal freedom from her husband. He named his Monte Carlo nightclub Maona, a combination of her first name and his last. At the Maona on August 10, 1960, Maria made a public announcement that they intended to marry soon. The next day, Ari announced that the marriage talk was a fantasy and that Maria had only been joking. Despite this public humiliation—the first of many to come—Maria talked herself into believing in Ari's good intentions.

That same year, Ari made a show of taking Maria to inspect the Château du Jonchet in Euer-et-Loir, France, and they let it be known that it was their prospective marriage home. But he never bought it, and Maria had to settle for living with Ari, mostly aboard the *Christina*. As the years went by, Maria often told her friends that she was still expecting him to marry her, but when the question was raised by the media, Ari always said that they were simply "close, good friends."

There was an obstacle presented by the Italian courts, which sustained Meneghini indefinitely as Maria's legal husband under the separation decree. But other subjects of Italian separation decrees had found ways to marry, and for Ari this legal problem was miniscule compared to others he circumvented every day. Maria took steps to remove it by renouncing her American citizenship in 1966, following legal advice that by becoming a Greek citizen she could claim that the marriage to Meneghini was invalid because Greek law recognized only marriages performed in the Greek Orthodox church. This meant that her marriage to Ari would be recognized everywhere outside of Italy. But when reporters questioned Ari about whether Maria's change of citizenship signaled that they were heading to the altar, he responded:

"We have explained that we are very close, good friends. This new event changes nothing."

Ari and Maria were kindred spirits who were proud of their Greek heritage even though neither had lived long in Greece. Ari always said he could talk to Maria—about his problems, his desires, even business—more freely than to any other woman. Yet they seemed to enjoy fighting with each other as much as making love. They had many noisy arguments (some punctuated by mutual slapping and punching), leading to bitter separations and then to passionate reunions, usually sweetened by Ari providing gifts of expensive jewelry, real estate, and even ship ownership.

The question of Ari's effect on Maria's career is a complicated one. When they began living together in 1960, Maria was so enthralled that she no longer desired to perform. She was perfectly content to give up opera so she could devote all her time and energy to being Ari's lover. It was mostly at the urging of her friends, and of Ari himself, that she accepted an engagement in Greece for August 1960, and one at La Scala in December. Despite its brilliance, her voice had always been somewhat erratic and difficult to control. Now with singing only the second most important activity in her life, the drive to control and perfect her performances was no longer there, and it was noticeable. Living on the *Christina* with Ari and dancing with him at Maona was much more enjoyable for her, and she did not perform again until August 1961.

Ari expressed his annoyance at the prospect that Maria's fame might be fading. While he was obviously attracted to her physically and emotionally, for him it was vital that she also remain the most famous living Greek female. Otherwise his indispensable mystique would be diminished. When it became apparent that her voice was faltering and that she lacked the will to rehabilitate it, he tried to push her into a movie career. Carl Foreman, producer of the 1961 film *The Guns of Navarone*, was a guest on the *Christina*. Ari prodded him to offer Maria a leading role, offering to underwrite the costs if it did not work out. But to Ari's great displeasure, Maria turned down the part, which eventually was filled by the prominent Greek actress Irene Papas.

Between 1962 and 1965, Maria performed occasionally and erratically, sometimes scoring triumphs as of old, and other times almost losing her voice entirely. In a 1965 Paris performance before an audience that turned hostile, she collapsed on stage and the final act was cancelled. Her final engagement of the year was for four performances of *Tosca* at Covent Garden, but she was able to sing for only one night, at nothing approaching her peak form. By that time she had lost her confidence, and would not even attempt to perform again for eight years. For this blow to his mystique, Ari turned on her viciously, berating her in front of visitors to the *Christina* with tirades like the widely quoted gem: "What are you? Nothing! You just have a whistle in your throat that no longer works!"

Determined to maintain the public's adulation of Maria even against her wishes, in the summer of 1965 Ari tried to package a film version of *Tosca* starring her, to be directed by Franco Zeffirelli. This led to many heated battles which finally sank the project, and left the relationship between Ari and Maria in a deteriorating state from which it never recovered.

Thus it cannot be said that Ari deliberately damaged Maria's career. But his cavalier treatment of their relationship, which kept her in a constant state of insecurity, damaged her physically and emotionally, eventually leading to dependency on prescription drugs which robbed her of any chance to sing again as Maria Callas.

Ari was not given to carrying on numerous affairs at the same time, and so he remained (at least outwardly) faithful to Maria, up to a point. That crossing point came in 1963, when Princess Lee Radziwill, sister of first lady Jackie Kennedy, came into Ari's sights. She and her husband, Prince Stas, had become part of the set that clustered around Ari in Monte Carlo. Ari invited the Radziwills to join a *Christina* cruise from which Maria was barred because the Churchills were again the principal guests. When the beautiful Lee Radziwill stepped into the tabloid photos with Ari, journalists such as Drew Pearson began publishing rumors (floated by Ari's hypesters) that Ari might become the brother-in-law of President Kennedy, a prospect that could not help but enhance Ari's mystique. The rumors picked up momentum when Ari made it clear that Stas would not be an obstacle to such a union. Ari appointed the penniless Polish prince a director of Olympic Airways, thus putting him on the payroll of the government-subsidized airline to facilitate Ari's trysts with his wife. When Ari wanted to be alone with Lee during a *Christina* cruise, he would arrange to have Stas called to an urgent Olympic directors' meeting in Athens.

Maria kept a worried eye on Ari's ongoing relationship with Lee Radziwill, but was soon to learn that she was focusing on the wrong Bouvier sister.

The Return of Ulysses

In the 1960s, Ari's relationship with the maturing Prince Rainier III began to change. During Rainier's bachelorhood, Ari had tried to arrange a royal marriage with Marilyn Monroe, which Ari felt would greatly increase tourist traffic. Marilyn was willing to audition, but the prince had ideas of his own. In 1956 he gave Ari the tourist attraction he was seeking by marrying Grace Kelly.

At first the prince was content to bask in the glow of her beauty and fame, but after a few years he began to show displeasure at his image of Mr. Grace Kelly and the compliant silent partner of Aristotle Onassis. He started to meddle in Ari's business plans, pressuring Ari to plough back casino profits into construction of hotels, apartments, and public amenities in Monaco.

Ari pretended to go along, but to assure control he secretly bought up enough SBM shares to give him an outright voting majority. He thought this would quiet Rainier, but the prince was determined to regain control of his country. In 1966, Rainier adopted a plan devised by his brother-in-law, Paris lawyer Jean-Charles Rey. Monaco would create and acquire 600,000 new shares in SBM, which gave the state a clear majority. It would offer to purchase the old shares at a price halfway between the SBM market high and low during 1966.

Ari did his best to undermine this decree, but in the end he had to settle for selling his SBM shares, which had cost him $3 million thirteen years earlier, for a total of $10 million. He thought he had been gypped, since he had revived an almost moribund Monte Carlo, but in the end he was forced to sell lest he be left in a minority position that denied him any real voice in running Monte Carlo. He retained his Olympic Maritime headquarters in the Old Sporting Club, leaving his 180 employees (including his son Alexander) there. This would continue to provide the desired tax and regulatory shelter for his shipping enterprises. But it was time for Ari himself to move on.

Ari visualized himself as the reincarnation of the mythological hero Ulysses, the ancient Greek monarch who returned to reclaim his island kingdom after years of wandering and trials. After his wartime residence in New York, Ari had reestablished contact with Greece, buying two adjacent seaside villas in the

Athens suburb of Glyfada. He installed his sister Artemis in one of the villas and used the other one as his residence during visits to Greece. But with greener business pastures in New York, Monte Carlo, London, and Paris, the modern Ulysses was in no hurry to fulfill the legend by returning to a Greece which held no financial attractions for him.

This began to change in 1956, when newly elected Prime Minister Constantine Karamanlis decided it was time to attract the expatriate Greek shipowners back home and get them involved in reviving the Greek economy. He reached out to Ari and to Stavros Niarchos, asking them to submit competing bids for building a shipyard and taking over operation of the state-owned airline, T.A.E. (for Technical and Air Exploitation Company). Ari's proposals for both projects were more attractive, but the wily Karamanlis saw more leverage in splitting them up, hoping thereby to attract more expatriate investment in the Greek economy. So it was that Ari was awarded the airline, which he renamed Olympic, and Stavros was permitted to build the Hellenic Shipyards at Skaramanga.

The intensive rivalry between Ari and Stavros continued, in business and in extravagant lifestyles. When Stavros bought the five-thousand-acre island of Spetsopoula and turned it into a luxurious private manor and hunting paradise, Ari felt the need to follow suit. In 1963 he bought the four-hundred-acre Ionian island of Skorpios and hatched plans to make it his personal kingdom. Maria Callas spent much of her time on Skorpios when she was not aboard the *Christina* with Ari. When the Greek military coup of April 1967 toppled the democratic regime in favor of the dictatorship of the Colonels, Ari became more serious about making Greece his main base. He was more comfortable working with dictators or monarchs than with starry-eyed democrats who inevitably wanted to collect taxes from the wealthy. While he continued to commute to Paris and New York, he began to spend most of his time in Greece, using as homes his Glyfada villa near Athens, his island of Skorpios, and the *Christina.*

Ari was sixty years old when he left Monaco in 1966. With his shipping empire safely sheltered in Monte Carlo, he began to focus more on his personal life. He continued the long-running affair with Maria Callas but as we have seen, he kept stringing her along without making any marital commitment. For that he had bigger plans: Jackie Kennedy.

Chapter Five

Enter Jackie—and Johnny

IT WAS ARI'S AFFAIR WITH LEE RADZIWILL THAT FIRST brought her sister Jackie Kennedy into his life. In August 1963, Jackie was deeply depressed after the death of her three-day-old son Patrick. Lee was scheduled to take a cruise with Ari on his yacht *Christina* in October, and she thought that inviting Jackie would lift her sister's spirits. Ari eagerly agreed, and Lee sent word of the invitation to Jackie. She decided to accept, but had to clear it with her husband.

The invitation was greeted by the White House staffers as enthusiastically as if it had been an incoming Soviet missile. Given Ari's sleazy reputation, the president's closest advisors were wary of the political repercussions with an election year coming up. But Jackie wanted to go, and JFK felt it would do her a lot of good. He agreed to the elaborate pretexts designed by his staff.

Jackie's vacation was described to the media as "a visit to Greece with her brother-in-law and sister, Prince and Princess Stanislaus Radziwill." Going along as chaperones were Secretary of Commerce Franklin D. Roosevelt Jr. and his wife Suzanne. There was no mention of Ari or the *Christina*.

According to most accounts, Ari was a gracious host who succeeded in getting Jackie's mind off her loss, playing the role of a friend in need, making no attempt to court her. The yachting party docked at Smyrna, where Ari, with others present, told Jackie the then current story of his boyhood there. The photographers who dogged Jackie's every move took many pictures of Jackie and Ari walking through the streets of Smyrna. Even though they were not alone, Maria Callas was infuriated by the photos. She sensed that Ari was attracted to Jackie. The photos also caused President Kennedy to phone his wife and insist that Jackie return on the agreed date of October 17. At the urging of his political advisors, he also told her to make sure that Ari did not come to the United States until after the 1964 election. Apart from the potential political fallout from Jackie being seen with Ari, there was the sticky problem of Lee Radziwill's apparent interest in divorcing Stas to marry Ari.

It was only a few weeks after her return from the cruise that Jackie accompanied Jack to Texas on his tragic final trip. In the wake of the Dallas assassination, Lee flew to Washington to be with her widowed sister. She was still carrying on the affair with Ari, and she invited him to join the family group (including her husband Stas) at the White House. With the nation in chaos, Ari's presence at the White House was hardly noticed by the media.

In 1963 and 1964, Ari phoned Jackie often, again in the role of the consoling friend. Jackie did not resume her social life until

1964, when she moved to New York in search of privacy for herself and her children. Such was her status as a national icon that she could be escorted in public by married men (including the film director Mike Nichols and the economist John Kenneth Galbraith) without raising eyebrows. She also began dating single men, and at various times between 1965 and 1967 was rumored by gossip columnists to be on the verge of marrying the noted architect Jack Warneke, the former British ambassador to Washington Lord Harlech (a close friend of JFK), and the former Deputy Secretary of Defense Roswell Gilpatric. Meanwhile Ari seemed to have his hands full with the game of musical chairs he was playing at the expense of the long-suffering Maria Callas and the ever-hopeful Princess Lee Radziwill. While Jackie was reported to have been spotted visting Skorpios in the summer of 1967, it was not until 1968 that rumors of an affair with Ari began to surface.

By the early spring of 1968, Jackie had been seeing more of Ari and was seriously considering the marriage proposal that he now pressed with vigor. Jackie and Lee had been taught by their socialite parents to be very conscious of money and luxury, and Jackie had been left with surprisingly little of the Kennedy fortune. Obviously Ari could afford to cure this deficiency. Also, Jackie felt vulnerable to the threats—spoken and unspoken—of making her and her children the next Kennedy assassination targets. Ari's team of bodyguards would provide physical security. Beyond that, he brought more excitement into her life than any of her other suitors.

For Ari, Jackie was the ultimate trophy wife, one whom Stavros Niarchos could never possibly top. She also conformed to the pattern of Ari's prior romantic attachments. In addition to her glamour, which formed the basis for a strong emotional bond, she would enhance his mystique, which Ari always considered crucial to success at the highest level of business. The Gallup Poll reported for five consecutive years that the American people considered Jackie "the most admired woman in the world." What banker, business leader, or even head of state would turn down an invitation to dine with Ari and Jackie aboard the *Christina*?

In April 1968, when Jackie decided she wanted to marry Ari, she sought the confidential advice of Bobby Kennedy, who had become the closest Kennedy to her and tried to be a father to her children after Jack's assassination. Bobby was horrified, mostly because he was then a candidate for the Democratic presidential nomination, and felt that his former sister-in-law's marriage to the likes of Ari would hurt his chances. Bobby believed that Ari was one of the biggest crooks in the world, an assessment that gains significance from the fact that as attorney general, he had access to the confidential government files on Ari. Bobby told Jackie that if she married Ari before the election, "it could cost me five states." At Bobby's insistence, Jackie agreed to say nothing about her marriage plans until the 1968 election was over.

While Bobby's campaign was picking up steam on the West Coast in May, Jackie was cruising the Virgin Islands on the *Christina* with Ari. On June 5, a few days after she disembarked and returned to New York, she was awakened by a call from London. It was Stas Radziwill, asking if she'd heard about Bobby. "Isn't it wonderful?" she said. "He's won—he's got California!" Stas asked, "How is he?" Jackie asked, "What do you mean?" Stas replied, "Why, he's been shot!"

Bobby Kennedy's death freed Jackie from her commitment to delay the marriage until after the election, and it also strengthened her resolve to remove her children from the violence of America to accept the shelter that Ari promised. As she put it, "If they're killing Kennedys, my children are next!"

Ari flew over in June to console her on the loss of Bobby. She took him to her mother's home in Newport and to the Kennedy compound in Hyannis Port. Nearly all of her relatives, except for Rose Kennedy, were opposed to the marriage. Her mother and stepfather, Hughdie and Janet Auchincloss, tried especially hard to talk her out of it. But none of this opposition shook Jackie's resolve. She was weary of giving priority to serving the political causes of the Kennedys and determined now to do what was best for her and her children. For his part, Ari kept quiet about the marriage plans, especially since he was still regularly consorting with Maria Callas at the Paris apartment he had bought for her in 1966.

Another hurdle for Jackie was the effect of marrying a divorced man on her standing as a Roman Catholic. She sought the aid of Richard Cardinal Cushing, the aged Boston prelate who had presided at her wedding to Jack, Jack's inauguration, and the funerals of Jack and Bobby. Although members of the Kennedy family brought pressure on Cardinal Cushing to dissuade her from the marriage, he refused to do so. He told her that such a marriage would force the Church to bar her from the sacraments, but if she decided to go ahead, he would personally support her publicly. For this decision he was to receive so much hate mail that he retired from his post in disgust some months earlier than he had planned.

By August the wedding plans were firming up, but the public was still in the dark. When society columnist Doris Lilly predicted the marriage on the Merv Griffin TV talk show, she was denounced by other writers and Jackie's fans as a purveyor of rubbish, for they were unable to believe that the saintly Jackie would marry anyone like Ari.

Behind the scenes, the financial arrangements were being discussed. First Teddy Kennedy flew to Greece in August, meeting with Ari on Skorpios to negotiate a prenuptial agreement that would protect Jackie and her children. Teddy pointed out that Jackie would lose her income from the Kennedy Trust (about $175,000 per year) if she remarried. Ari promised to replace that income, and also that he would provide Jackie with a sizable (but unspecified) additional monthly stipend. He gave Teddy a draft of his prenuptial proposals. Teddy found it rather vague, and sent it on to the New York financier André Meyer, who had been acting as Jackie's financial advisor.

André found it completely inadequate and he telephoned Ari in Greece to tell him so. They made an appointment to meet in André's apartment at the Carlyle Hotel on September 25. At the meeting André told Ari that he should present Jackie with $20 million before the wedding. This infuriated Ari, who stormed back to his Fifth Avenue office and dictated a memorandum of the meeting, making a point of his feeling that the $20 million proposal "might easily lead to the thought of an acquisition instead of a marriage."

In the end, Ari agreed to give Jackie $3 million outright, plus the annual interest on a $1 million trust established for each of Jackie's children, John F. Kennedy Jr. and Caroline, until they reached age twenty-one. In the event of divorce or Ari's death, Jackie would also receive $150,000 per year for life. In exchange, Jackie was required to execute a waiver of the 12.5 percent share of his estate to which his widow would be entitled under Greek law. This financial package was, of course, chicken feed for the wife of one of the world's wealthiest men, but Jackie was naively induced to sign it without the benefit of legal advice. In fact, waiver of the 12.5 percent share was prohibited by Greek law, but Ari was already planning to bribe his friends, the corrupt Greek Colonels, to enact a special provision making such an agreement valid if executed outside of Greece by a foreign spouse.

The financial arrangements concluded, the way was opened for the wedding of the year, if not the era, on October 20, 1968. Skorpios was the logical site for the ceremony, since it had a small private chapel and would be the most difficult place for the media representatives to overrun. Jackie and Ari pleaded with the media to let them get married in peace, but the army of journalists and photographers assigned to the story tried every conceivable trick to gain access to the private island on the wedding night. More than three hundred of them climbed aboard hired boats and surrounded the island, creating such chaos that the Greek navy was called in with orders to sink any vessel that came within 1,000 meters of Skorpios. Finally it was agreed that four journalists would be allowed to attend the wedding as a pool for the world's media.

Jackie was resplendent in a two-piece beige chiffon Valentino dress. Ari wore a blue double-breasted business suit. Her mother, Janet Auchincloss, had never ceased her efforts to talk Jackie out of the wedding, and she continued to whisper this demand in Jackie's ear even as her daughter began her walk toward the altar. The ornate Greek Orthodox ceremony was chanted in Greek and in English. Jackie (then thirty-nine) and Ari (then sixty-two) took three sips of wine from a silver chalice and circled the altar three times, sealing their union. The wedding reception was held on the *Christina*, where the couple spent their wedding night.

Public reaction to the wedding was almost entirely negative. Many Americans were aghast at the spectacle of Aristotle Onassis taking the place of the beloved Jack Kennedy as the husband of "Our Lady of Camelot." The tabloids had a field day, with headlines like "JACKIE WEDS BLANK CHECK" and "JACKIE, HOW COULD YOU?" Even *The New York Times* reported, "The reaction here is anger, shock, and dismay." But by Jackie's account, she was strongly attracted to Ari sexually and emotionally. Ignoring the media outcry, the newlyweds publicly demonstrated their love for each other as they set about the formidable task of making the marriage work. With his customary braggadocio about sexual prowess, Ari leaked the story that they had made love five times on their wedding night.

Despite Ari's obvious infatuation with Jackie the trophy and Jackie the woman, he could not bring himself to break off the long-standing relationship with Maria Callas. Indeed, there is every indication that in 1968 Ari believed he could and should have Jackie and Maria, just as in 1959 he believed he could and should have Tina and Maria. Within days after the wedding he was at Callas's Paris apartment. At first Ari did his best to conceal his meetings with Maria, but Jackie was soon to learn the secret. Although it hurt her, she was no stranger to such problems, and she resolved to keep the marriage going. She focused on the positive aspects: Ari's lavish gifts of jewelry, his tolerance of her extravagant shopping bills, and his courtly notes inviting her to dinner, touches that were missing from her marriage to Jack. She immersed herself in Greek life, learning the language and teaching it to John and Caroline. She absorbed generous portions of Greek philosophy and literature from Ari's friend and mentor, Professor Yanni Georgakis.

In 1969, Jackie threw herself into decorating the Pink House on Skorpios which Ari had turned over to her. She brought in several decorators, including her old friend Billy Baldwin from New York. Ari didn't care much for Jackie's taste but he indulged her on the Pink House, since he spent most of his time on the *Christina,* with which he did not permit Jackie to tamper. Ari continued the heavy traveling which he felt was necessary to maintain his business empire. In that first year of marriage, Jackie began to get bored with Ari's long and frequent absences. She missed the circle of friends she was accustomed to in Washington and New York. She befriended Ari's sister Artemis, but the two had little in common other than their regard for Ari.

While Jackie's initial reaction to Bobby Kennedy's assassination had been to flee from the violence of the United States, she modified that stance by retaining her fifteen-room Fifth Avenue cooperative apartment and keeping her children in American schools. They continued to be guarded around the clock by Secret Service agents. The children had already been uprooted several times, and she felt it would be unwise to force them to grow up in a foreign country. Since they were in school for nine months of the year, Jackie spent close to half of her time in New York. Ari was often in New York, but did not move into Jackie's apartment, preferring to keep his suite at the Pierre, a hotel address that expedited his avoidance of American taxes.

While Ari's children Alexander and Christina ignored Jackie, Ari tried to establish a warm relationship with Jackie's children. He bought them many gifts—Shetland ponies, a jukebox, a sailboat—and he spent time with them, taking John to the movies in Athens and baseball games in New York, and attending Caroline's school plays and horseback-riding lessons. The Kennedy children enjoyed their summer vacations on Skorpios and appreciated Ari's interest in them. Ari was also attentive to Rose Kennedy, inviting her on three *Christina* cruises during 1969.

Although Ari wanted a compliant Greek wife and was somewhat miffed by Jackie's insistence on putting her children first, the couple managed to get through the first two years without signs of serious trouble, thanks largely to Jackie's silent acceptance of Ari's visits to Maria's Paris apartment. Their first major crisis arose from the relentless media pursuit of Jackie's private life rather than any fault on the part of Ari or Jackie. Jackie had a lifetime habit of writing gushing letters. In February 1970, four letters she had written to Roswell Gilpatric between 1963 and 1968 were put up for sale at the Hamilton Galleries in New York. Three of them were written before Ari began courting Jackie, but she wrote the last one while she was on her honeymoon with Ari. It read:

> *Dearest Ros, I would have told you before I left [about her plans to marry Ari]—but everything happened so much more quickly than I'd planned.*
>
> *I saw somewhere what you had said [wishing Jackie happiness] and was very touched—dear Ros—I hope you know all you are and ever will be to me—with my love, Jackie.*

The letter was innocent enough to those familiar with Jackie's effusive style, but the media had a field day with it, augmented by the contemporaneous filing of a divorce suit by Gilpatric's estranged third wife and her colorful description of the relationship between Jackie and Ros. Ari's machismo was deeply disturbed by the worldwide publicity, especially the disclosure that his wife was thinking endearing thoughts about another man while on the honeymoon with him. He told friends that the letter made it look like she was playing him for a fool. In May 1970, he took his revenge by playing the Callas card, posing for photos with Maria at Maxim's and allowing himself to be seen leaving her apartment.

Jackie flew to Paris and fought back. Ari squired her to Maxim's and they were duly photographed there. This gave Maria sleepless nights which resulted in an overdose of sleeping pills, although she denied it was a suicide attempt.

Jackie and Ari reached a temporary truce, but there were more public sightings of Ari and Maria which put the marriage under continuous strain. Their differences began to overshadow their common interests and regard for each other. Ari liked to be on his yacht, while Jackie preferred dry land. Ari looked forward to spending late nights and early mornings in nightclubs, while Jackie was more inclined to curl up with a book. Ari sought the company of media celebrities, while Jackie was more comfortable with intellectuals.

Ari continued to pout about the way that Jackie's separate life was tarnishing his image as the macho man in control of his wife. He went out of his way to humiliate and criticize Jackie in front of other people, and as his verbal tirades became louder and uglier, Jackie began to spend more time in New York with the children and her friends. Her reaction to his abuse was to simply ignore it and carry on with the marriage. She realized that the price she had to pay for Ari's protection was to put up with his need to control her life, a need which forced Jackie's strong streak of independence into an ongoing conflict that neither spouse would be able to win.

Ari's mania for total control was also tested by his unstable daughter Christina. Ari had warned her and his son Alexander that he would not hestitate to destroy any romance involving his children which did not suit his own agenda. If any proof were needed, Ari provided it when Christina had the temerity to marry a Beverly Hills businessman named Joseph Bolker without consulting him, thus challenging Ari's long-standing preference for a merger with the scion of one of the wealthy Greek shipping families.

Christina met Joe Bolker in 1971 when he was visiting Monte Carlo for a convention of the Young Presidents Association, an American group that honored business executives who reached the top rung of management before age fifty. Joe was forty-eight at the time and barely qualified as a young president. Christina was then just twenty. Joe was divorced from savings and loan heiress Janice Taper, with whom he had four daughters close to Christina's age. The two hit it off during his Monte Carlo stay and arranged to see each other again during trips to Europe which he had planned for that summer. They became intimate during these visits. While Bolker enjoyed the brief fling and was flattered by the attention of a younger woman who was also famous, he became uneasy at the intensity of Christina's passion for him. He shortened his stay in Europe and returned to California, expecting that this would be the end of the affair.

Bolker had misjudged Christina. She was something like her father in this respect: when she wanted something badly she spent every waking hour contriving to get it. She besieged Bolker with phone calls, letters, and cables. He began to duck her phone calls. Finally in July 1971 she appeared on the doorstep of his apartment at Century Towers West. In panic, Joe asked her whether her mother knew she was there. When she said no, he phoned Tina, who had long since divorced Ari. Tina agreed with Joe that the visit was entirely inappropriate, and said that Christina either had to return to England "or make it legal." This was more than Joe bargained for, since he had no interest in marrying Christina.

Christina had been listening on an extension phone in another room, and came out screaming at Bolker, "Why don't you want to marry me? Am I not good enough for you?" Joe tried to quiet her down, but later he found her unconscious in the bedroom. She had taken some pills and it was clear to the panic-stricken Bolker that she had tried to kill herself. He quickly summoned a doctor who brought her around, whereupon she told Bolker, "I'm going to keep on doing this until you marry me!"

In this unromantic fashion, Joe Bolker was hijacked into marrying Christina. The civil ceremony took place in Las Vegas on July 27, 1971. Ari, summering on Skorpios, got the news when the rest of the world did. He went ballistic at the thought of Christina defying his authority. He was also much put out by the failure of his intelligence system to provide advance warning of the marriage plans. He berated his head spy, Johnny Meyer, from whom he had reason to expect a stronger surveillance performance.

Johnny (Pick Up the Check) Meyer

Johnny Meyer was a character right out of a Harold Robbins novel, and it was appropriate that he first came to public notice in Hollywood. He began his California career in the late 1930s in the service of Tony Conero, a leading racketeer who operated gambling ships at a sufficient distance from the coast of Santa Monica to thwart both federal and local law enforcement authorities. According to Johnny's F.B.I. file, "He had acted as master of ceremonies and saw that lone men and women gambling on the ship became acquainted." This was the first public recognition of Johnny's talent for procuring women, which was to earn him the F.B.I.'s ranking of Hollywood's Number One Pimp.

Johnny moved from the gambling ships to Hollywood's Trocadero nightclub, where he served as what was then called a press agent. In 1938 he was befriended by Erroll Flynn, Warner Brothers' biggest star, which led to his employment as a press agent by that studio. One of his major assignments there was to get favorable media coverage for the off-screen antics of Flynn, who was often accused of statutory rape and other practices which were considered unsavory at that time. The F.B.I.'s informants believed that Johnny's press-agent job at Warner's was mostly a front for his real function: procurement of women for studio big-wigs and their business associates.

Johnny's sterling performance in these assignments brought him to the attention of Howard Hughes, who hired him away from Warners in 1941, and used him mainly to procure dates with Hollywood starlets for high-ranking military officers who were responsible for placing large orders for wartime aircraft from Hughes's factories. Hughes also made liberal use of Johnny's talents to arrange introductions to Hollywood actresses who excited Howard's own fancy.

According to the F.B.I. file, Johnny "graduated from pimp to business associate in 1941" under Hughes. Johnny proved himself so valuable that Hughes Aircraft Company insisted he was essential to the war effort, thus enabling him to avoid military service.

One of his trickier assignments was to obtain some five million feet of raw film which Hughes needed to release his movie production, *The Outlaw*. It was 1944, and film was rationed under wartime restrictions which limited its availability to movies holding the industry's seal of approval, for which *The Outlaw* did not qualify. Johnny somehow found the necessary five million feet of film and so made possible the contribution of Jane Russell's cleavage to American culture.

Meyer's biggest success for Hughes came in 1942, when he managed to corrupt the Army Air Forces procurement program so thoroughly that they gave Hughes a $43 million contract to build 100 highly questionable all-wooden XF-11 photo-reconnaissance planes. Johnny accomplished this feat by procuring Hollywood starlets and picking up large entertainment tabs for the key officers in the contract decision: Colonel Elliott Roosevelt (the president's son), and Major General Bennett Meyers.

Johnny Meyer and Elliott Roosevelt became fast friends, as Johnny continued to pick up all the entertainment checks and even supplied cash loans. This friendship brought Johnny into the inner circle of the White House, especially after his introduction had led to Elliott's marriage to film star Faye Emerson. According to the F.B.I. file, Johnny was an overnight guest at the White House, and "had been known to make telephone calls from the White House to his friends" which "enhanced his prestige in Hollywood as the operator would get the individual on the phone and state that the White House was calling." Another F.B.I. informant related that Elliott had introduced Johnny to his father, and that Johnny had ingratiated himself with the president by telling him off-color stories about the Roosevelts, which ordinarily annoyed FDR, "but he was amused when Johnny told them the latest ones and apparently believed that Johnny was a very bright young man."

Despite these colorful adventures, the F.B.I. showed a marked lack of respect for Johnny, based on the appraisals of informants whom the bureau considered reliable. They were concerned about his "possession of substantial sums of money which he did not earn through his studio salary," noting indications that Johnny had come by this cash—and the ownership of homes with fancy Beverly Hills addresses—"by arranging shake-downs by compromising certain men and then collecting pay-off money" which he shared with "the girls used in these schemes."

The F.B.I. file is studded with other uncomplimentary evaluations, such as "Meyer is a gentleman blackmailer," "a corrupt and unscrupulous individual," and "a complete scoundrel." Despite these put-downs, the F.B.I. found that Johnny had faced criminal charges only once, a 1938 arrest by the Beverly Hills police for "suspicion of kidnap and hit and run," the disposition of which was not recorded in Johnny's file.

Johnny became a national icon in July 1947, when he and Elliott Roosevelt, along with Hughes, were summoned to testify before a U.S. Senate committee investigating alleged irregularities in wartime aircraft contracts. The committee included Senator Joe McCarthy of Wisconsin. All the newsreels ran footage of the corpulent, apple-cheeked, affable Johnny Meyer, who befuddled the senatorial inquisitors with his glib testimony and thereby brought unprecedented prestige to the pimping profession. His testimony, and that of Roosevelt and Hughes which he helped to orchestrate, got Hughes off scot-free with the image of a patriotic national hero bedeviled by corrupt witch-hunters. At the same time the public learned from the unflappable Johnny (Pick Up the Check) Meyer just how life on the fast track was supposed to be lived.

By the time of Christina's affair with Joe Bolker in 1971, Ari had spirited Johnny Meyer away from the increasingly reclusive Hughes, and put him in charge of the Onassis dirty tricks department. Johnny was adept at arranging all kinds of surveillance, including tapping of telephones. Laws against such activities did not deter him, especially now that he was working for an international tycoon who lived outside the law and had an unlimited budget for bribery and the planting of false media stories.

On Ari's instructions, Meyer had arranged to bug the phones in Christina's London mews flat. Johnny overstated the position somewhat by boasting that "Ari had a file on Bolker before Bolker had finished his soup on the very first date with Christina." Johnny's wiretaps revealed Christina's infatuation with Bolker, but she did not mention any marriage plans on that phone line. Nor did it ever occur to Ari that his daughter would want to marry a middle-aged Jewish businessman whose comparatively small real estate fortune would do nothing to enhance the worldwide Onassis empire.

When Ari learned of the marriage through the news media, he did not give a thought to the possibility that his neurotic daughter had at last found someone who might make her happy. He immediately plotted with Johnny Meyer to find the quickest way to destroy the marriage. He dispatched Meyer to California to have a quiet talk with the newlyweds.

The meeting took place in the Polo Lounge of the Beverly Hills Hotel. The perceptive Christina had known Meyer since her childhood, and was aware that despite his Falstaffian appearance, Johnny was a perfect fit for her father's needs, taking care of a lot of dirty jobs that went far beyond the bounds of public relations and female procurement. She increased Joe Bolker's discomfort by informing him that Ari and his henchman Meyer were capable of "having people assassinated, having your legs broken or something." Joe would have been even more concerned had he learned that Fiona Thyssen, girlfriend of Christina's brother Alexander, had stumbled across a typewritten memo (which was not intended for her perusal) revealing that Johnny and another Onassis employee were actually plotting, on Ari's orders, to have Bolker worked over by professional hit men.

Johnny Meyer was right at home in the Polo Lounge, where he had been a fixture during his Hollywood days. On Ari's orders, Johnny began the summit meeting by using a carrot instead of a stick. There was a $75 million trust fund coming to Christina when she reached her twenty-first birthday, just a few months away. Meyer informed the couple that Ari had already rewritten the trust so that the $75 million would be withheld as long as she remained married to Bolker. He made it clear that the money was hers the day she divorced Joe.

Then Meyer used all his roughish charms to detach himself from his obnoxious mission. He feigned great personal concern about Christina's happiness, and tried to reason with Bolker's business sense. "You see, Joe," he said, "Ari has a lot of dealings with the Saudis. They won't like the idea of a Jew in the family. If they pulled out of their contracts with Olympic, the bankers would get nervous. If they called in their loans, Ari would have a lot of unnecessary headaches to deal with." Obviously Christina could not have a happy marriage if it was threatening the destruction of the Onassis empire.

Meyer was surprised to find that Bolker was not rocked by this statement. Joe insisted that he had plenty of Saudi friends himself, and had no reason to believe that they harbored animosity toward him or other American Jews. Johnny was also surprised that Joe did not seem to be interested in Christina's $75 million trust fund. Concluding that the carrot was not going to do the trick, Meyer knew that he would have to wield the stick. But it was not his style to confront his victims directly. Instead, in his affable way, he proceeded to take the Bolkers into his confidence, assuring them that he was rooting for them, and that he would plead their case personally to Ari, telling Ari that they were the picture of wedded bliss and that he should give them his blessings.

When they left the Polo Lounge meeting on this upbeat note, the Bolkers hoped for the best. But the devious Meyer was only lulling them into complacency so that they would do nothing to impede his underhanded activities, which in this case would take the form of a vicious smear campaign in the press. Johnny knew which tabloid reporters could be turned with money or other illicit incentives. Secretly the Onassis coffers were opened to procure a first-class hatchet job on Joe Bolker.

Within days of the Polo Lounge meeting, Christina began to receive phone calls from people bought by Meyer for Onassis, informing her that Joe Bolker was a secret collaborator with organized crime and urging her to get a quick divorce. Similar calls were made to Christina's friends. The whispered charge was that Joe was the front man for a mob operation that supplied rigged gambling equipment to casinos all over the world. Since Ari had owned and operated the Monte Carlo casinos and Johnny had worked on Tony Cornero's gambling ships, they had the technical knowledge to lend some authenticity to this story. Quickly these false allegations found their way into print, first in American tabloids and then in London and Paris. In less than three weeks, Joe Bolker's reputation was blackened as thoroughly as if his name had been Joe Bonnano.

Whether Joe could have stood up to this barrage of Johnny Meyer's smears much longer is problematical. Considering that he had not been eager to marry Christina in the first place, he showed considerable spunk in refusing to cave in to Meyer at the Polo Lounge meeting. Now he found that Meyer/Onassis were (in his words) "systematically nullifying" him, his business, and his marriage. Yet he did not throw in the towel immediately. But as her father well knew, Christina's fragile emotional underpinning was not up to this kind of attack. She returned to her self-destructive pattern of drug abuse, bringing herself to the brink of suicide. Finally she caved in and agreed to end the marriage.

When the divorce was arranged, there was no payment asked for or received by Bolker, who thereby proved that he had never been interested in the Onassis money. Ari was ecstatic that his customary strongarm tactics had won the day. For icing on his cake, he flaunted his power by dispatching Johnny Meyer to California to bring Christina back. This time Johnny was accompanied by two armed thugs, just in case Joe Bolker got any foolish ideas about changing his mind at the last minute. Christina's departure from Los Angeles was turned into a public spectacle when the captain of the TWA plane refused to take off until Meyer's henchmen turned in their 45-caliber hardware.

In the fall of 1972, Ari decided to dissolve the four-year-old marriage to Jackie. Officially he complained that Jackie's runaway spending had reduced the marriage to a monthly argument over her shopping bills, and he had Johnny Meyer spread the story that he had found it necessary to reduce her shopping allowance from $30,000 to $20,000 per month. But this made no sense, as Ari had always bragged about the millions of dollars worth of jewelry he showered on Jackie, and how well he could afford to indulge her rich tastes. It was certainly not news to him that Jackie was a world-class shopper. It is apparent that the story of reducing Jackie's allowance was designed to restore the image that Ari was in full control.

But Ari had underestimated the difficulty of appearing to be in control of a woman whose every public move was photographed. Through the coverage of the paparazzi and the worldwide media, it was clear that Jackie was living her own life at her own homes and devoting herself to her own children, beyond Ari's control. Now Ari was dogged by the perception that his independent wife was playing him for a sucker. This was an image that his ego and machismo could not bear.

To end the marriage, Ari engaged the crookedest lawyer available, Roy Cohn of New York. Ari also ordered the faithful Johnny Meyer to put Jackie under surveillance, including the use of illegal wiretaps, to gather evidence with which Ari and Cohn planned to intimidate Jackie into accepting a niggardly financial settlement. Cohn, no stranger to illegal strong-arm tactics, was greatly impressed by Johnny's underworld connections. It was quite a trick to put Jackie under close surveillance when her children were guarded around the clock by Secret Service agents. The surveillance proved only that Jackie was not engaged in any extramarital affair, a highly predictable finding considering the slim chances of conducting such a relationship in secret.

By 1973, Ari had half a century of successful business fraud behind him, and had employed the same tactics—indeed, the same personnel, such as Johnny Meyer and his stable of thugs—in his private life, including relations with his own family. (We are using "fraud" in the broad sense of dishonesty and deception, rather than restricting it to the narrower legal definition, although we have seen that Ari's major deceptions provided ample grounds for prosecution.)

There was no reason to believe that Ari would suddenly turn honest in either branch of life. Both in business and in private affairs, he was driven by the craving to show up Stavros Niarchos; the desire to project the image of invincibility; and the need to maintain absolute control of everything that was important to him.

These forces came together in the transcendent fraud of Ari's life: his beloved yacht *Christina*.

Chapter Six

Christina vs. Creole

The Rivalry

WE HAVE SEEN THAT WHEN ARI AND STAVROS NIARCHOS
married the daughters of Stavros Livanos in the late 1940s, their
first rivalry involved the plush Sutton Place townhouses which
Livanos had given each of them as wedding presents. Niarchos
gained the upper hand there, for he always placed more emphasis on impressive homes than did Ari, who characterized himself
as a lifelong sailor. As time went by, this difference of emphasis
continued, with the temporary exception of the sumptuous
twenty-five-acre Château de la Croë at Cap D'Antibes on the
Riviera, which Ari rented for a few years before Stavros swooped
down and bought the deed. Stavros did not use the Château often,
but he derived continuing pleasure from the feat of evicting Ari.

The real estate rivalry switched to Greek islands, and there again Stavros had the upper hand, for Ari's Skorpios was no match for Stavros's Spetsopoula. Apart from the difference in size—five thousand acres compared to four hundred—Stavros's island came equipped with a stately home and many luxurious amenities when he bought it. Ari had to start from scratch at Skorpios, and it never approached the level of splendor at Spetsopoula.

The same was true of fine art. While Ari acquired a few paintings which may or may not have been done by El Greco, he did not pretend to be a serious collector. Stavros stocked his homes with authentic Renoirs, Van Goghs, Gauguins, and Cézannes. In 1957 he scored a coup by buying, sight unseen, the renowned fifty-nine-piece art collection of the actor Edward G. Robinson, who was forced to sell in a division of community property. Stavros acquired many old masters, of which his favorite was the true *Pietà* of El Greco. In addition to his own world-class collection, he gained stature in the art world by making generous cash donations to museums such as the Louvre for maintenance of their masterpieces.

In the never-ending game of topping each other, they devoted appropriate effort to collecting women. Here Ari, with Tina Livanos as his first wife, Jackie Kennedy as his second, and Maria Callas in between and amongst, was difficult to top. But Stavros did not fail to try. His collection of stunning mistresses was the envy of the world's playboys. His marriage to Eugenie Livanos took a strange detour in 1965, when he divorced her in Mexico in order to provide a legitimate birth for his expected child by Charlotte Ford, glamorous daughter of Henry Ford II. Stavros was eight years older than his new father-in-law. Early in 1967, Charlotte Ford returned to Mexico to divorce Stavros, who promptly went back to Eugenie. He did not remarry Eugenie because he took the position that the Mexican divorce and the marriage to Charlotte were nullities in the eyes of the Greek Orthodox church, so that he had always remained married to Eugenie.

In the early morning hours of May 4, 1970, on Stavros's private island of Spetsopoula, the all-forgiving forty-four-year-old Eugenie died under mysterious circumstances. According to Stavros, he went into her bedroom at 10:25 P.M. to explain why he had invited his ex-wife Charlotte Ford and their daughter to visit the island, a subject about which they had quarreled earlier that evening. He found Eugenie lying on her bed with her eyes closed. He tried to revive her by vigorous shaking and slapping, but she fell to the floor without showing any signs of life. He then sent for coffee, which he and his valet attempted to force between Eugenie's clenched teeth. He took his time in summoning a doctor, who did not arrive until 12:25 A.M., a full two hours after Stavros had entered her bedroom. The doctor pronounced her dead.

A series of investigations produced conflicting medical reports, some attributing the death to an overdose of barbiturates and others blaming the physical injuries caused by the alleged attempts to revive her. At one point the investigating magistrate, Constantine Fafoutis, recommended that Stavros be charged with inflicting injuries leading to Eugenie's death, which could have resulted in a five-to-ten-year prison sentence. At first, Ari Onassis appeared to believe that Stavros had killed Eugenie, either accidentally or on purpose. But his view was not shared by Arietta Livanos, Eugenie's surviving parent, nor by Eugenie's sister Tina, who by then was Ari's ex-wife. When a panel of three judges rejected the proposed indictment and found that Eugenie had committed suicide, Ari decided not to add to the family's anguish by intervening. That put a formal end to the investigations, but Stavros was never able to completely dispel the clouds of suspicion.

In 1971, eighteen months after Eugenie's death, Tina divorced her second husband, the Marquis of Blanchford, and married Stavros Niarchos in Paris. This news drove Ari to distraction, for Stavros had topped him by taking over Tina, whom Ari still considered to be his rightful possession. Ari had forged ahead with his 1968 marriage to Jackie Kennedy, the ultimate trophy wife, but as we have seen, by 1972 he perceived that he had lost control over her and was plotting with Roy Cohn and Johnny Meyer to dump her as cheaply as possible. Thus Ari dissipated his once commanding lead over Stavros in the wife department.

In business, the longest and most intense Ari-Stavros rivalry was in the ownership of tankers. While Ari took the early lead in the 1940s, Stavros overtook Ari after the 1954 Saudi misadventure had temporarily put Ari on the oil producers' blacklist. Of course, it was Stavros who thwarted Ari's SAMCO scheme by calling in Maheu and the C.I.A., which earned Stavros the gratitude—and the increased tanker charters—of the major oil producers. Ari made a strong comeback thanks to the 1956 Suez crisis, and then they slugged it out year after year. When Ari built a 28,000 ton tanker, Stavros topped it with a 32,000-tonner. Ari regained the heavyweight title with a 46,500-tonner, only to be dethroned by Stavros's 47,750-tonner. So it went, blow-for-blow, into the 1970s, when the insatiable rivals pushed the tanker size up to 400,000 tons.

They competed in two other businesses, shipbuilding and oil refining. Stavros made a success of his Hellenic Shipyards, which he had been permitted to build in compensation for Ari's takeover of Olympic Airways. Ari was always jealous of Hellenic Shipyards, and made many attempts to acquire rival shipbuilding firms, notably Harland and Wolff of Belfast, but without success. Stavros, on the other hand, was always envious of Ari's ownership of Olympic Airways, even though it was not highly profitable. Whether it was because of the prestige of owning his country's airline, or simply because Ari owned it, Stavros made several attempts to pluck it away from Ari. Whenever Ari sought additional subsidies or financial concessions for the airline from the Greek government, Stavros stepped in and offered to operate it without such help. This resulted in Ari being forced to continue operating it on the old terms.

In oil refining, Stavros got the jump by arranging a partnership with Mobil to operate the profitable Aspropyrgos refinery. Ari countered by seeking a concession from the Greek Colonels to build a larger refinery, slipping generous bribes to the dictator, Colonel George Papadopoulos. Stavros fought Ari's proposal tooth and nail, trumping every bid that Ari made and providing incentives to his own friends in the Greek dictatorship. Finally Ari's Omega project won the concession, but Stavros's intervention had made the scheme so convoluted that Ari was not able to carry it out. Thus in oil refining as in shipbuilding, the final score was Stavros 1, Ari 0.

In tax evasion, Ari proved more skilful. Here the main hazard was the U.S. Internal Revenue Service, practically the only agency which had the facilities and determination to enforce tax collection on a large scale. To evade U.S. taxes, both men employed the device of multiple lease agreements which shifted charter income actually earned in the United States to their sham Panamanian corporations. Ari got away with this, but Stavros was caught in 1965 by the zealous prosecutor Robert M. Morgenthau, who obtained judgments for more than $25 million in unpaid taxes against six Niarchos corporations domiciled in New York. Stavros avoided visiting the United States for several years, until his lawyers were able to settle this tax liability.

Both men were dedicated to hiding their true wealth lest it be subjected to the indignity of taxation. Therefore it is impossible to compare the grand totals of their holdings. On the surface, it appears likely that Stavros accumulated a higher net worth because he was more focused on pure money-making. Apart from his tightly-managed businesses, his prudently-acquired art collection was on track to appreciate by hundreds of millions of dollars before the century ended. Ari spent time and money on such enterprises as Monte Carlo and Olympic Airways, which indulged his egotism and enhanced his mystique but did not swell the coffers the way that Stavros's shipyard and refinery did. There are published estimates that in the early 1970s, Stavros was worth $750 million to Ari's $500 million, but the evidence was so laboriously concealed that it is more judicious to conclude the race was too close to call.

Helen Vlachos, editor and publisher of the highly-regarded Athens newspaper *Kathimerini,* was the only newspaper owner who refused to publish under censorship when the Greek Colonels came into power. This led to harassment, house arrest, and finally the threat of jailing by the Colonels, which drove her to escape to London. She knew Ari and Stavros very well, and wrote about their rivalry in her 1970 book *House Arrest.* She likened the rivalry to a giant chess game—"my move, your move"—where the pieces were wives, islands, and yachts, as well as tankers, shipyards, and airlines.

While she evinced more respect for Stavros, she wrote that Ari was much more interesting, more charming, and more amusing than Stavros, whom she described as "one of the few genuinely boring clever men I have ever met." She went on to comment that Stavros

...basically is a serious, solid, responsible man, much more old-fashioned than his fooling around and trying to beat the authentic adventurer, Onassis, allows him to appear....

These [Onassis] successes were the origin of Niarchos' obsession. He always felt he was worth more than Onassis, that he was more solid, more serious, more important, richer. But he was not content to keep this knowledge to himself, he wanted the world to know about it and Onassis to hear about it. If only Onassis had been a different man, Niarchos might have developed into the kind of benefactor that Greece knew in the past century, generous, protective, patriotic. He had it in him.

Thus Helen Vlachos lamented the lost opportunity to harness the energy of the Onassis/Niarchos rivalry for the benefit of the Greek nation, in a way which might have hastened the return to democracy instead of strengthening the grip of the dictators. She went on to explain that Stavros at least volunteered in the wartime Greek Navy, "a gesture which probably never even crossed Onassis' mind." But with the coming of the Colonels, "the worst traits of both the top star shipowners" took over and dominated their rivalry. Here she was highlighting the fact that Ari and Stavros took turns in bribing the Greek Colonels to feed their own insatiable traits of greed and one-upmanship. Her 1970 book thus identified the seeds of self-destruction that the rivalry nurtured.

It is clear that by the 1970s, Ari was hard pressed to keep pace with Stavros in every phase of their rivalry. But if he had to concede to Stavros the edge in houses, art, and wealth, there was one race Ari had to win at all costs: the ongoing contest between his *Christina* and Stavros's yacht *Creole*.

The Battle of the Yachts

The 190-foot *Creole*, acclaimed as the world's largest and most beautiful privately owned sailing ship, began life as the *Viva*, built by the distinguished British firm of Nicholson & Cooper. She was turned over to the Royal Navy during World World II and used as an anchorage for barrage balloons that helped to defend British ports against attacks by low-flying aircraft. After the war, Stavros picked her up for an undisclosed price and had her refurbished in a German shipyard at the then unprecedented cost of $2 million.

Stavros maintained a captain and a thirty-two-man-crew, but he was happiest when he took the helm himself. He was a serious sailor who loved the sea for itself. He often captained the *Creole* in international championships, such as the demanding Torquay-Lisbon race.

The *Creole* could entertain large parties in great comfort, but it was not designed to compete with Ari's *Christina* in eye-catching furnishings. It was done in the classic understated style of the great British yachts, its interior resembling that of a Pall Mall men's club.

Helen Vlachos wrote that the *Creole* was

...a dream of a three-master, a living ghost from a splendid past, and there was no more beautiful sight on the Aegean waters than her, flying past under full sail. There was the sobriety of perfection in her pale ashen teak decks, her warm, gleaming mahoganies, her gay golden brasses.

Helen Vlachos found that while there was no valid way of comparing the *Creole* with Ari's *Christina*, the two yachts epitomized the contrasts in the owners' personalities. She wrote of Ari:

[He] is certainly the top public relations genius in the world, and he concentrates on one client, himself.

His greatest asset is his connections. The rest—houses, art collections, properties—has always been a little nebulous. He has had no real home other than the Christina....

In that yacht, if everything is not gold, it is certainly gold-plated, and sumptuous enough to satisfy the soul of the most exacting and voluptuous potentate. The swimming pool on the afterdeck, lined with beautiful mosaic work, not only empties at the flick of a switch, but slowly rises up at another, and at floor level it becomes a gleaming dance floor. Multicolored lights flicker, soft music fills the air, caviar is passed around, champagne bubbles and flows, and Ari Onassis sits down to talk to his guests.

In 1953, Ari purchased the *Stormont*, a 322-foot war-surplus Canadian Navy frigate, for $50,000. He then deposited it in the Hamburg shipyard which was building his latest tankers, with instructions to make *Christina* the most spectacular yacht the world had ever seen. No expense was spared. Wherever marble or gold could be fitted in, they were used. The added weight of an extra deck and all of Ari's indulgences made the yacht top-heavy and slow, with a maximum safe cruising speed of only 14 knots. The final makeover bill was $4 million, a king's ransom in the 1950s.

While the bronze-bordered mosaic swimming pool that converted to a dance floor was noticed by every observer, it had to compete with many other lavish appointments. As reconstructed, the *Christina* was on five levels, starting with a newly inserted bridge deck, below which were the boat deck, the main deck, the tween deck, and the hold. Ari's own spacious four-room suite was on the bridge deck. It had a sunken blue Siena marble bathtub patterned after one built for the palace of King Minos, ruler of ancient Crete. There were nine luxurious guest suites on the boat deck, each named after a Greek island and each decorated in the specific wood or stone native to that island. The Ithaca suite was usually reserved for a special guest, like Greta Garbo, Marlene Dietrich, or the pre-Onassis Jackie Kennedy.

Also on the boat deck was a large oak-paneled game room which included a grand piano that Frank Sinatra enjoyed playing, and a working fireplace covered in deep blue gemstones. Then there was the bar room, the like of which could not be found outside of the Onassis empire. Despite Ari's difficulties with whaling authorities, he proudly announced to the world that the bar stools were upholstered with the foreskins of whales, and the footrests were of whales' teeth. One of the bar's walls was covered with a large map, on which models of Ari's tankers could be moved around by electromagnets. He usually arranged the models so that the sun never set on the Onassis fleet. Along the bar there were engraved scenes from Ari's favorite story, Homer's *Odyssey*.

On the main deck (the third level) was an oval dining room, seating twenty for formal dinners. Nearby was a reception hall that could accommodate two hundred people and Monte Carlo's Hôtel de Paris orchestra. The crew of forty-two included the sailing personnel as well as valets, masseurs, stewards, bartenders, maids, and seamstresses. There were always two chefs, one French and one Greek. The 24-hour food and beverage service was commensurate with the yacht's living style. Ari would proudly tick off the countries from which various gourmet delicacies had been flown.

Everywhere there were specially commissioned murals, down to nursery scenes by Ludwig Bemelmans in the children's suites, first occupied by Alexander and Christina and later by Jackie's children, Caroline and John Jr. There were two paintings which Ari claimed were done by El Greco, and a dazzling jade Buddha encrusted with rubies.

Other distinctive features were a small hospital which included an operating room and X-ray machine, and a movie theatre in the style of a Hollywood mogul's screening room. Perhaps it was this touch which caused the producer Daryl Zanuck to label Ari "the Greek Gatsby" after he visited the yacht.

Guests did not feel trapped on the *Christina,* for it was equipped with no less than four large Chris-Craft speedboats, a hydrofoil speedboat, lifeboats, kayaks, and a glass-bottomed boat for viewing marine life. There was also a white Fiat auto for land transport. And the crowning touch was the five-place Piaggio amphibian airplane lashed to the back end of the boat deck.

The overall impact of the *Christina* was powerful enough to draw the observation by Egypt's King Farouk that it was "the last word in opulence." The docking of the *Christina* created traffic jams of gawking spectators even in such blasé ports as Palm Beach. Richard Burton, who was a guest along with his then wife Elizabeth Taylor, remarked, "I don't think there is a man or woman on earth who would not be seduced by the sheer shameless narcissism of this boat." Ari took this as a compliment.

As Helen Vlachos noted, the *Christina* served as the stage setting for Ari's conversation with his guests. Ari was considered a founder of the Jet Set, successors to Café Society, consisting of the people who were too important to be in only one place at a time. His Olympic Airways was among the first airlines to provide international jet service in the pioneering De Havilland Comet. London's *Sunday Times* reported that Elsa Maxwell, then the *grand dame* of international society, "claimed that any film star, head of state or captain of industry who had not been up the [*Christina's*] gangplank at least once would have suffered a serious inferiority complex." Of those who had been up the gangplank, no guest was more treasured than Sir Winston Churchill, Britain's wartime prime minister, considered by many to be the twentieth century's leading statesman.

After completing his second stint as prime minister in 1955, Churchill loved to winter on the French Riviera. In January 1956 he was staying at the Riviera villa of his literary agent, Emery Reves, when his son Randolph brought Ari there for dinner. Ari had done some favors for the carousing Randolph Churchill in the hope of arranging such a meeting. Ari was able to charm Sir Winston with his conversation, which Randolph described in these terms:

> *He is a born orator with a poetic sense and can build up a list of adjectives in an ascending order of emphasis and weight which are as perfect as a phrase of music. Just as his listener is caught by the spell, he will suddenly bring the edifice tumbling down by a deliberate piece of comic bathos. He will burst into laughter at the very moment when almost any other man would be exploding into passion.*

Soon after that dinner, Churchill, with his wife Lady Clementine and his pet parakeet Toby, moved from his agent's villa to the penthouse of Ari's Hôtel de Paris in Monte Carlo. He was to spend his remaining eight winters there as Ari's guest, interspersed with long cruises on the *Christina*. Ari coddled the octogenarian Sir Winston, often turning his own bridge-deck suite over to the Churchills, and providing another suite for Anthony Montague Browne, Sir Winston's private secretary. Ari and Sir Winston drank champagne and brandy and talked history and philosophy for hours on end. Churchill was the *Christina's* prize catch and a magnet for other celebrity guests. In 1957, the then Senator John F. Kennedy and his wife Jackie came aboard for a cocktail party in the harbor of Monte Carlo, attracted mainly by the opportunity to meet Churchill for the first time. Ari made sure they did not abuse his hospitality, telling the Kennedys, "I must ask you to leave by seven-thirty, as Sir Winston dines sharply at eight-fifteen."

By January 1973, Ari had lost Monte Carlo and was in the process of shedding Jackie. Thus the *Christina* became his defining possession, the essence of his all-important image. Stavros Niarchos could keep his silent possessions like the big island, the art collection, the refinery and shipyard. *Christina* spoke with Ari's voice. She was a living, breathing part of Ari's mystique, his signature, his stage, even his sex symbol. The stuffy sailing ship *Creole*, which wasn't even named after a human being, could not come close to matching her.

This made it all the more urgent for Ari to maintain the advantages that *Christina* gave him over Stavros. Beyond the one-upmanship—which was to continue even after death so that each dominated the other's newspaper obituary—there was Ari's ongoing need to maintain absolute control of everything that was important to him. The control mania came into play strongly because *Christina* served as Ari's floating office as well as his home.

One of the four rooms in Ari's bridge-deck suite was his study, from which he conducted his worldwide business operations by phone. Ari kept his important business data in a red leather pocket notebook, no larger than the address book in a woman's purse. He prided himself on being able to store most of his vital business information in his head. Unlike ordinary executives, he did not require a conventional office staff or even a personal office, preferring to use the rooms of his subordinates when in Athens or New York. But Ari felt it was essential to demonstrate to the world that he was in full control of his business operations while in residence on the yacht. Since many of his cruises kept him at sea for weeks at a stretch, he needed to guard against being perceived as isolated or out of the loop.

The society columnist Doris Lilly, author of *Those Fabulous Greeks* (1970) and contributor to *Look* magazine, visited the *Christina* and was given a guided tour by Ari. Although Doris was more interested in the sensuous features of the yacht, Ari insisted on showing her the telephone system, and boasted that the forty-two radio-telephones on board gave him communicating ability "as powerful and as complicated as that of the flagship of the U.S. Atlantic Fleet." In fact, the radio-telephone equipment of that time was erratic enough to cause some of Ari's subordinates in New York to complain that they were often unable to understand what he was saying from the yacht. But to Ari it was crucial to show the world that he was always in control, never out of touch.

This compulsion to demonstrate control was not limited to the forty-two radio-telephones. It encompassed Ari's purported ability to depart the *Christina* in mid-ocean and materialize anywhere in the world he might be needed, to close a deal or relieve an emergency. Thus he would always be in personal control of his business, and neither Niarchos nor any other opponent could take advantage of his temporary physical absence to outmaneuver him. This magic-carpet quality was ascribed to the Piaggio airplane, classified as an amphibian because it could operate on land or water, depending on the position of its retractable wheels. Ari's authorized biographer Willi Frischauer recounted this boast in *Onassis* (1968):

Altogether, the Christina *is a fine home even at her remote moorings, particularly for her owner who can leave her by boat, motorcar, or airplane at a moment's notice and be in Athens, Rome, Paris, or London as quickly as a commuter reaches New York City from his home in Connecticut.*

The media, for whom Ari was always great copy, never challenged this claim. After all, it was made by the tycoon who founded the Jet Set, the only man who owned his nation's airline. It was reported as fact by journalists all over the world and persisted in later biographies, as in Frank Brady's *Onassis: An Extravagant Life* (1977):

In case the telephone should ever prove insufficient to his need to communicate at high speed, Onassis kept aboard...an Italian amphibious seaplane with a range of 1,200 miles...which could be lifted off and onto the deck by a huge, self-contained crane.

In his 1991 book, *All the Pain that Money Can Buy: The Life of Christina Onassis,* William Wright was even more specific:

With the Piaggio, Onassis could leave a yacht party in mid-Mediterranean, fly to London for a meeting, and be back in time for dinner with his guests.

Ari himself often reiterated this claim. He was fond of bragging that he used the Piaggio "in all the seas of the world." This was intended to solidify the established legend that the Piaggio could be put over the side by the *Christina's* deck crane anywhere in the world, whether on the Mediterranean or the Atlantic Ocean, and be ready to whisk Ari to wherever he needed to be.

This celebrated boast, as we shall see, was 100 percent false, a monumental fraud, as deceitful as Ari's 1926 claim that he had never heard of the leading Argentine cigarette whose brand name he had stolen—but far more deadly.

Chapter Seven

Prelude to the Downfall

THE TURNING POINT OF ARISTOTLE ONASSIS'S LIFE CAN BE tracked to the minute. It came at 3:19 P.M. on January 22, 1973, when Ari's son Alexander, sitting in the cockpit of Ari's famous Piaggio amphibian, received clearance for takeoff from the tower at Athens International Airport. The twenty-four-year-old Alexander was on the brink of completing his last chore before breaking away from the father who had dominated his life.

Alexander Socrates Onassis was born in New York City on April 30, 1948, when Ari and Tina were living in the Sutton Square townhouse that Stavros Livanos had given them as a wedding present. He was named after Ari's martyred uncle Alexander and also the legendary Greek hero Alexander the Great. He spent his childhood in a succession of locales, as Ari's business interests spread around the globe.

Alexander and his sister Christina, younger by nearly three years, were raised largely by nannies, governesses, and employees of the Onassis business empire. Their parents were too busy living the lives of international Jet-Setters to devote much time to their upbringing. Ari and Tina would be away from their children for weeks and months at a time, often on separate itineraries.

Traditionally, Greek sons are the alter egos of the father, the most important thing in the world to them. In most Greek families at that time, the son was valued much higher than the daughter, and whatever resources were available to the family for rearing children were concentrated on the son, who would carry on in the footsteps of the father, illustrious or not. So it was with Alex and Christina. In the little time that Ari spent with the children, he showed favoritism to Alex, teaching him Greek, which Christina never really mastered.

Despite his obvious pride in having produced a son, Ari went about fatherhood in a strange way. It appeared that he did not know how to raise a son, and he was not inclined to seek or accept anyone's advice on this subject. For the most part he either ignored Alexander or attacked him verbally, driving his son away from him and at the same time creating a strong incentive for Alexander to seek his attention.

The daughter Christina suffered even more acutely from parental malpractice. She had inherited the unmistakable Levantine countenance of her father, complete with a very prominent nose, a swarthy complexion, and pronounced circles under her eyes. Tina, who had delicately beautiful features framed by a fair skin, did little to hide her revulsion at having produced such an unattractive daughter. The mature Christina often told her friends that she had been made to feel like the ugly duckling of the family.

This devastating lack of regard for the children's development ruined their childhood. It was inevitable that Alex and Christina suffered from inferiority complexes, based on their feeling that because their parents were not interested in being with them, they did not measure up to the exalted Onassis standards. Alex followed the classic pattern of the neglected son by seeking attention through reckless behavior, especially in speedboats and powerful sports cars. In Christina, initially it took the form of autism. She stopped talking temporarily at age three, finally getting her mother's attention, but planting the seed of deep emotional illness which was to bedevil her until her mysterious death at age thirty-seven.

While Ari went out of his way to loudly criticize Alex's every failing, at other times he lavished extravagant affection on his son. He especially sought to nurture in Alex the feeling that as an Onassis he was unique, and that the rest of the people in the world were inferior and could be bought at a price.

By age six, Alex had more than fifty military and sailor uniforms. He also had a toy gasoline-powered racing car which could speed at twenty-five miles an hour, as guests of Onassis found out when the neglected son aimed the menacing car at them with the throttle wide open. Before turning seven, Alex experienced the power and prestige of being an Onassis by pressing the button that launched the biggest oil tanker built up to that time.

In 1956, when Alex was eight, Ari took a few stabs at teaching him to swim, but soon gave the chore over to crewhands of the *Christina*, who became his surrogate family. Yorgos Zakarias, the youngest member of the crew, became Alex's closest friend. They met when Alex was eight and Yorgos was sixteen, and they hit it off immediately, because Alex was starving for friendship. Soon Yorgo assumed the job of acting as companion to Alex whenever he was on board the *Christina.* Yorgo helped Alex to indulge his passion for motors and mechanical gadgets. They would spend hours dismantling radio equipment and other devices aboard the yacht, putting most of it back together successfully. Since Alex grew up without real friends apart from the mechanics and deckhands of the *Christina,* he had great diffculty conducting a conversation about anything other than machinery, for which he seemed to have a natural instinct.

Because Ari did not believe in sheltering Alex, he was allowed to have his own powerful Chris-Craft speedboat at the age of nine. Alex showed his innate mechanical talent by maintaining the boat and souping up the engine himself. Soon he was running it at full throttle. One day he pushed it to the speed of forty-five knots, at which point it somersaulted three times. Luckily Alex was thrown clear of the boat on the first somersault. Ari promptly replaced the wrecked speedboat. Alex soon disposed of the replacement boat by ramming it into one of the yacht *Christina's* metal lifeboats at high speed.

In 1960, at age twelve, Alex coaxed his father into taking a ride in the boy's latest personal speedboat. Alex drove it like a madman, prompting Ari to realize that Alex's recklessness was a threat to himself and those around him. Ari's solution was to assign Costa Koutsouvelia, brother of the *Christina's* captain, to take charge of Alex as a sort of special guardian. This changed nothing.

Aboard the *Christina,* Ari would occasionally introduce his children to famous guests. Ari advised Alex to spend as much time as possible around Winston Churchill, from whom he could learn "more in a few hours than through years of university courses." But Alex was more attracted to Gianni Agnelli, who built motor cars. At the age of ten, Alex bombarded Agnelli with surprisingly sophisticated questions about automobiles.

The beautiful Tina was delicate and childlike herself and therefore ill-equipped for parenting. When Ari started courting her she was only fourteen. She married him at seventeen, and at nineteen she bore Alexander. Now she was absorbed in her own high society life which left little time or energy for the children.

Thus Alex and Christina entered their teenage years detached from reality, because of Ari's crushing egocentrism and Tina's indifference. The children's lives were shaped by their father's money, ambition, and values. To the extent that those values could be perceived, they revolved around the principles that wealth, power, and possessions were everything, and that there were no restrictions on how an Onassis went about obtaining them.

Yet Ari insisted that he loved Alex, and he probably did, to the extent that his egotism permitted him to love anyone. And despite the difficulties of his childhood, Alex admired his father in some ways. Two of Alex's childhood heroes were Ari and Ari's friend Howard Hughes, but it was clear that he admired them for their wealth and power rather than their personal qualities. Ari often spoke of his dealings with Howard Hughes and how they saw eye to eye on important principles of business. Alex pumped Ari for details of his meetings with Hughes, whose aviation exploits Alex greatly admired. Alex was becoming an aviation buff himself, and he read everything he could get his hands on about Hughes's adventures as a daredevil pilot and aviation pioneer. Ari was more articulate about Hughes's unorthodox business methods, which fitted the Onassis mold in their defiance of the rules that governed ordinary people.

As if poor little rich Alex and Christina did not have enough emotional challenges, in 1960 they were subjected to the trauma of the divorce that followed in the wake of the Ari-Callas affair. Neither child would ever fully recover from this blow to their security.

As we have seen, Tina received custody of both children, but freely granted Ari all the visiting time he wanted. The children's visits to Ari were frequently made unpleasant by the presence of Maria Callas, especially when they were forced to cohabit the yacht *Christina* with her. Both children blamed Callas for the breakup of the marriage and the thwarting of their ongoing hopes that the parents would reconcile.

After the divorce, Tina lived in Paris and St. Moritz. Both children were enrolled in Paris day schools. Because Tina resumed the high society lifestyle which left little time for Alex and Christina, they lived much of the time in the Paris apartment of their Livanos grandparents on Avenue George V. In 1961, Tina married a titled Englishman, John "Sunny" Spencer-Churchill, Marquis of Blanchford, heir to the Duke of Marlborough, and kinsman of Sir Winston Churchill. She moved into the Marquis's country home at Lee Place, near the Marlborough seat of Blenheim Palace. Christina spent much of her time with Tina at Lee Place, but Alex remained based in Paris where he unenthusiastically attended school and lived mainly in the grandparents' apartment.

Both Alex and Christina spent long summer vacations on Skorpios. In 1963, when he was fifteen, Alex was given the honor of throwing the switch on the island's new electrical plant. These Skorpios visits were marred for the children by the ongoing presence of the despised Maria Callas. Alex took to baiting her to the point of incurring his father's wrath. His favorite trick on the yacht *Christina* was to wait until Callas was rehearsing at the piano or napping in her stateroom, whereupon he would take to his Chris-Craft speedboat and rev up the engines to create a deafening roar.

As Alex's sixteenth birthday approached in 1964, he was growing up in Paris, mostly alone. He spent some time in Ari's penthouse on Avenue Foch when Ari was there, but lived mainly in the grandparents' apartment, now occupied by the surviving maternal grandmother, Arietta Livanos. During one of his Paris visits, Ari decided Alex should begin his sex life, which he duly launched by treating him to a rollicking evening at the famed establishment of Madame Claude.

Ari was dertermined to put a stop to Alex's harassment of Maria Callas. To accomplish this, he proposed a typical Onassis deal: Ari would give Alex his own luxurious Paris apartment, and supply him with other trappings with which to enjoy bachelor-hood, provided that Alex treated Callas with respect. When Alex agreed, Ari attached another condition: that Alex would apply himself to his studies and make every effort to improve his rather dismal school performance.

Alex agreed to that condition too, but did little to comply with his father's demands for better grades. Although highly intelli-gent, Alex had always done poorly at school, largely because he lacked motivation and parental guidance. Ari, a self-made school dropout, had a low opinion of formal education, and Tina could not be bothered. Ari did insist that Alex attend school, but when the results were negative he was more concerned about Alex dar-ing to flout his parental authority than about his son's need for proper incentives.

Finally in 1964, despite the fact that he had a private tutor, Alex flunked his exams at a Paris lycée after a wild weekend in St. Tropez. Infuriated at this defiance of his wishes, Ari refused to support his sixteen-year old son in school any longer and directed that he go to work for Olympic Maritime (Ari's main shipping company) in Monte Carlo. There would be no salary, since Ari made it clear that Alex could not possibly justify receiving even a lowly beginner's wage. Instead, since he was still Ari's son, he would be given an allowance of $12,000 a year. This demeaning gesture only increased Alex's frustration and the hostility he felt toward his father.

Ari made certain that Alex never had much cash, so that he would always be dependent on his father. But Ari arranged matters so that to the outside world, Alex looked like an Onassis. He showered Alex with expensive toys, like Ferraris, gold watches, and the use of luxurious houses, but gave Alex nothing that he could own or turn into independence-producing cash.

At the Olympic Maritime headquarters in Monte Carlo's former Old Sporting Club, Ari appropriated for his personal office the cavernous chamber that had once been a gambling casino, outfitting it like a war room complete with a magnetic wall map that showed the disposition of his tanker fleet throughout the world. Alex was now trapped in Ari's sights because his desk was also in the war room. More than ever, Ari took advantage of this arrangement to loudly belittle Alex in front of others, and to demonstrate that only Ari could rule the Onassis empire. This pushed Alex into venting his frustrations by speeding his powerful Ferrari around the Riviera's hazardous hairpin curves, usually at night.

Ari's bad-mouthing often took the form of publicly stating that Christina should have been the boy, since she seemed to have more of a head for business than did Alex. This was the unkindest cut of all, since it drove a wedge between his children. Christina, neurotic about her appearance, was not interested in being told she would make a good businessman. Alex, while respectful of his father's business accomplishments, did not relish being told that he wasn't fit to emulate them. Alex brooded over these oft-repeated insults which Ari bellowed in public with the obvious intention of downgrading Alex's self-esteem. Perhaps this was Ari's way of seeking to toughen Alex for the challenges of doing business in the world of the Greek shipowners, but it had an almost entirely negative effect.

The proximity of their desks in the large office chamber at Monte Carlo caused Alex to try to avoid his father whenever possible. At this point it seemed to those around Alex that his whole life was dedicated to eluding Ari. Alex devised elaborate schemes to avoid being in the same place as Ari, especially when the place was the stultifying confines of the yacht *Christina*. Yet they spoke on the phone as often as twenty times a day, since Ari insisted that Alex get his approval for anything he wanted to do, whether business or personal.

Alex's social life was also warped. By age eighteen, he had come through his Paris period, when his female companions were often the girlfriends of the older Onassis employees assigned to keeping him out of trouble. Now he lived alone in Monte Carlo at the Hermitage, one of the hotels which Ari owned. Ari had encouraged him to have affairs with the likes of Odile Rubirosa, widow of the late Dominican playboy Porforio Rubirosa. Odile was a good ten years older than Alex.

Alex clearly preferred the company of older women, probably because of his experience with the girlfriends of his chaperones, as well as his need for a parent-friend-confidante. So it should have been no surprise that he was attracted to Fiona Thyssen. When their paths crossed at St. Moritz in 1967, he considered his life to be empty, and felt many needs which Fiona was uniquely equipped to fill.

The former Fiona Campbell-Walter, after her marriage known formally as the Baroness Thyssen-Bornemisza, was renowned as a world-class fashion model and one of the great beauties of her time. She came from a socially prominent British family. Her father was a rear admiral in the Royal Navy, and her mother devoted herself to promoting Fiona's career. Born in 1932, Fiona reached the pinnacle of the modeling profession in the early 1950s.

A photographic as well as a fashion show model, she became a favorite subject of London's renowned Cecil Beaton, the official photographer of the Royal Family. She joined the top-drawer Lucie Clayton Agency and was the star of many editions of *Vogue*. In 1953, she achieved a level of recognition which was rare even for a cover-girl model: she appeared on the cover of *Life* magazine.

In 1955, at the height of her modeling career, she retired to marry Baron Hans Heinrich ("Heini") Thyssen, who at thirty-three was the handsome heir to one of Europe's largest steel fortunes. Young Baron Heini was noted for his cultivation of the Thyssen family's world famous art collection. They seemed the ideal Jet-Set couple, combining beauty and culture with riches and fame. Thyssen had several homes, but they chose to live at the Villa Favorita in Lugano, Switzerland, which included several palatial houses as well as a large museum to display the art collection.

Heini and Fiona frequently hosted parties for their favorites among the Beautiful People, including Prince Rainier and Princess Grace of Monaco; the Agnellis (Fiat automobiles); actress Joan Collins; the Guinness family (beer); the Niarchos family, whom we have met; and Princess Lee Radziwill.

Fiona's marriage to Thyssen produced two children: a daughter, Francesca ("Chessie") born in 1958, and a son, Lorne, born in 1963. Despite Fiona's devotion to the marriage and the unfading beauty which continued to gain her mention by leading professional photographers as one of the loveliest women in the world, the Thyssens were divorced in 1964. Fiona was then thirty-two.

She insisted upon and received sole custody of the children and moved from Switzerland to London. Baron Thyssen was not stingy with the financial arrangements, so Fiona continued to live in the style of high society, dividing her time between London and St. Moritz.

Although she remained a prominent member of international society, Fiona's main interest was her children, followed closely by charitable and cultural activities, and skiing.

It was not until 1967 that Fiona, still single three years after the divorce, became involved in another serious love affair. This time her lover was Alexander Onassis. Fiona was then thirty-five and Alexander was eighteen.

Alexander had first laid eyes on Fiona during a St. Moritz snowstorm in the winter of 1960. As Fiona climbed out of her sports car and tossed back her long red hair, the twelve-year-old Alex fell in love with her on the spot. That she was still married to Baron Heini Thyssen and she was only three years younger than his own mother did nothing to dampen Alex's infatuation for her.

As Alex's teenage years went by, he kept track of Fiona from a distance, reading everything he could find about her in the society pages and catching an occasional glimpse of her on the streets of St. Moritz. For six years he worshipped her from afar, indulging himself in adolescent fantasies of possessing her.

Then early in 1967 during the winter skiing season at St. Moritz came the opportunity that Alex had been awaiting. His mother Tina was giving a dinner party and asked Alex to attend. He found these affairs boring and normally shunned them, even though his mother was eager to show off her blossoming eighteen-year-old son. But this time he played his cards like a true Onassis: he would come to the party if Tina invited Fiona

Thyssen and seated Alex next to her. Tina was taken aback, but since Fiona was already a friend of hers, and Alex made it clear he would not attend without Fiona, Tina agreed.

Fiona was accustomed to being pursued by mature suitors who were transfixed by her beauty and glamor. At Tina's St. Moritz dinner party, Fiona was uncomfortable at first with the attention that Alex lavished on her. Although she found him immature and rather crude, she was aware that he was totally entranced by her, and somehow she resisted the urge to laugh him off.

After the dinner party, Fiona, Alex, and some of the other guests went on to the discotheque of the Palace Hotel, where Fiona danced with Alex and other men. One of her dancing partners complained to Fiona that she was spending much more time with Alexander than was appropriate, and charged that she "would not have given him a second look if his father had not been the super-wealthy Aristotle Onassis." Fiona, enraged at the unjust allegation that she was obsessed with money, delivered a right uppercut that nearly floored her astonished partner. Then she stormed out of the disco in tears, with Alexander running to catch up with her.

Fiona expected that to be the end of the relationship, but Alex was not to be denied. He wooed her as though they were high school students who had just met at the senior prom. She protested at first, but Alex's ardor overcame her resistance, and before she knew it, she was involved in an affair that to her was as embarrassing as it was surprising.

Through the winter and spring of 1967, Fiona accommodated Alex's passion for her, always expecting that it would be a brief affair, nothing more than a lark. She says that she did not find him especially good-looking, but was impressed with the strength and solemnity of his face, accentuated by his faintly olive skin and the heavy horn-rimmed glasses with dark lenses like those worn by his father. Although she enjoyed the novelty of being with Alex, the affair did not fit in with her self-image or her future plans. Despite her maverick ways, she was very conventional when it came to marriage and raising children. She felt certain then that she could never marry Alex, for their age difference would make such a union appear ridiculous in the eyes of her own children and the social circle in which her life was set. She kept telling Alex that it had been fun, but that they ought to end it quickly. Alex would not hear of it.

Fiona was strong enough to have her way, but when it came time to make the final break, she went along for another night, another week, another month. Before they knew it, a year had gone by, and the deepening affair was taking over both of their lives.

Although Fiona has often described her role in the affair as a combination of lover, friend, and substitute parent, she has never fully explained why it went on for over five years. In addition to the physical attractions on both sides, perhaps the over-achieving Fiona found the Onassis legend a challenge that she needed to stand up to when it was thrust at her. The punch she threw at the St. Moritz disco on the night of their first date tells us that the feisty Fiona was sensitive about avoiding the image of selling her charms to high bidders. Blessed with brains and courage as well as beauty, and knowing that if she stuck with Alex she would ultimately be pitted against Aristotle Onassis himself, she may well have decided to fight this battle for her own vindication—and perhaps even for womankind. Bear in mind that Ari openly boasted that Greek husbands beat their wives as of right, and that he never refuted Tina's charges that he attempted to abort the birth of the unwanted Christina by punching his pregnant wife in the stomach.

The testing of Fiona's resolve was not long in coming. The affair embarrassed Alex's mother Tina in the eyes of her St. Moritz society friends, and she was determined to end it. Failing to turn Alex's head by reasoning with him about the sixteen-year age gap, she took to fabricating stories designed to shame Alex into dropping Fiona. "Everybody knows she's nothing but a high-priced whore," Tina told Alex, claiming that she knew a very reliable man in London who said he had paid Fiona £50 for a night's revelry when Fiona was only seventeen. Tina never was able to come up with the name of the reliable man. Alex and Fiona were amused by these crude attempts to break them up. Since Alex really didn't care what Tina thought, and since she had no financial control over him, his mother's efforts to end the affair came to naught.

Fiona and Alex knew that Ari would not be that easy to deal with. But as long as there was no imminent danger of them marrying, Ari was content to let the affair carry on, thinking it would play itself out harmlessly. As we have seen, Ari had urged Alex to have affairs with older women, notably Odile Rubirosa.

During their long-running affair, Fiona and Alex did not live together. Fiona insisted on maintaining her home with her children at Morges, near Lausanne in Switzerland. Alex lived and worked in Monte Carlo. They spent almost every weekend together, most often at the London apartment which Fiona rented. Alex did visit her at Morges, but for the sake of Fiona's children they carried out the pretense that he was merely a family friend. They tried to avoid being seen together in public, and there are few photos of them together. While the adults closest to Fiona and Alex were aware they were discreet lovers, and gossip columnists mentioned them as an item from time to time, few knew the extent of their commitment to each other.

Alex was always wary about letting Ari know how deeply he cared for Fiona, lest he trigger a repeat of the Christina-Bolker marriage fiasco. When Ari perceived that the relationship was getting more serious, he tried to talk Alex into dropping it. But he never unleashed Johnny Meyer to trash Fiona because it did not appear that Alex was going to marry her. Fiona for her part always said they would not marry, and apparently whatever wiretapping Ari employed on Alex did not yield any discussions of marriage plans.

When asked if there was ever a chance they would marry, Fiona replied that the pressure of carrying on the clandestine relationship in the face of Ari's repression made it impossible to seriously consider marriage. If they had later made a go of living together for some years, they might have thought about marriage, but it was simply out of the question during the early 1970s.

Ari had another important reason for avoiding overt sabotage of his son's romance. In October 1968, when Ari and Jackie Kennedy decided to marry, he was concerned about how Alex and Christina would react. He did not disclose his plans to the children until five days before the wedding, knowing that they would automatically oppose it because they still hoped that their mother Tina would remarry him. When rumors of an imminent wedding to Jackie began to appear in the press, Ari summoned his children to an urgent meeting at the Athens villa of his sister Artemis, where Jackie was also staying.

Ari brought Alex and Christina into the library of Artemis's villa, and broke the news as casually as possible. Both children exploded with rage, Christina screaming and smashing vases while Alex turned on his heel and jumped into his Ferrari, driving it at breakneck speed through the darkened streets of Athens to vent his frustration.

With both children refusing to attend the wedding, Ari dispatched emissaries to reason with them. He used his sister Artemis to change Christina's mind, and sent business associates to work on Alex. When that approach failed to shake Alex, Ari had Artemis call Fiona and enlist her support for the wedding. Actually Alex was not as strongly opposed to the marriage as was Christina, since at age twenty he was mature enough to realize that an Ari-Tina remarriage was not likely. But Alex fell in with Christina's emotional condemnation of Jackie as a fortune hunter, stating publicly, "It's a perfect match. My father likes names and Jackie likes money."

Alex realized that for once he had Ari over a barrel, in a situation that did not lend itself to threats of Johnny Meyer's dirty tricks. Alex resolved to exact a price for reluctantly attending the wedding: Ari would have to refrain from criticizing his relationship with Fiona. Ari quickly agreed, and the Skorpios wedding was attended by a tearful Christina and a silently contemptuous Alexander.

Alex continued to play the Jackie card close to his vest, studiously avoiding contact with Jackie and withholding any sign of affection for her, in the hope that this would prevent any move by Ari to come between him and Fiona. While Ari had agreed to leave them alone, Alex was mindful that any such promise by Ari was of questionable value, especially one that had been obtained under duress.

As Ari settled into the marriage with Jackie, he remained uneasy about Alex, for he sensed that his son was struggling to become independent and that Fiona was propping up his backbone. It especially bothered Ari that Fiona did not seem to be afraid of him. He was determined to break up the affair, but his overt efforts took a more subtle approach than the Johnny Meyer tactics. Early in 1970 he bought and presented to Alex a luxurious villa at Lagonissi, a fashionable seaside resort near Athens. Suddenly Alex was a property owner. He could hardly wait to celebrate with Fiona.

Fiona saw Ari's handwriting on the wall. When Alex gave Fiona the great news, she announced that she would rent a house nearby so they could spend the summer together in Greece. Alex was dumbfounded; why would she need to rent a house when she could live in his luxurious villa? "My dear friend," she explained, "I wouldn't put a foot inside that house. Your father is not buying that place just for you. He's also buying it for your mistress. He wants to prove that everybody can be bought!"

It was clear to Fiona that if she moved into the villa, she would become just another Onassis possession, "to be manipulated, brutalized, and treated on any level and on any terms he chooses." She was not about to hand Ari the opportunity to spread the story that she had been bought and was living off the Onassis money. Alex saw the light and rejected the gift of the villa.

Ari was not accustomed to people turning down expensive gifts, especially his dependent son. No doubt he detected Fiona's influence in the rejection, but he still refrained from any direct action to crush the affair.

For once Ari was kept in the dark. Three years after Alex turned down the villa gift, he and Fiona decided it was time for Alex to gain his independence from Ari. They knew they had to go about this task very carefully. Their escape plan bore the unmistakable marks of Fiona's strong will and clear thinking.

Chapter Eight

Breaking Away from Ari

WHEN ALEXANDER ONASSIS BEGAN THE AFFAIR WITH FIONA Thyssen in 1967, he was an eighteen-year-old high school dropout with no professional qualifications, dependent on his father for work, money, and self-esteem. Fiona quickly perceived that all this would have to change if Alex was to have a life of his own, and that education was the key to his liberation. Despite Alex's Paris prep school flunkout, Ari could easily have arranged for private tutoring to overcome that failure and put Alex back on the path toward a university degree. She was convinced that Ari did not really want Alex to complete his education, since that might enable Alex to break away and become independent. She felt that Ari had seized upon the wild weekend partying of the unsupervised sixteen-year-old Alex as a pretext to pull him out of school and keep him under Ari's thumb in the dreaded Monte Carlo office chamber. As Fiona describes it:

> *Ari didn't want to have a son who was going to threaten him on any level. He was jealous of Alexander's attractiveness and charm. His reactions to Alexander's success were not the normal reactions of a father toward his son. He did everything to humiliate him, to belittle him. Look how he impeded him from school on the flimsiest pretext! He simply didn't want Alexander to be cleverer or wiser or better educated than he was.*

During their first few years together, Fiona was not fully committed to making Alex's life over, for she was ambivalent about continuing the affair herself, and in any event Alex was not ready for such a traumatic breakaway. Patiently she sought to build up Alex's self-esteem toward the day when he would be strong enough to defy Ari's stultifying domination. Fortunately, there was a vehicle available for this purpose: Olympic Aviation, the air-taxi subsidiary of Greece's Onassis-owned national airline, Olympic Airways. (To avoid confusion, we'll call Olympic Airways "the airline" and Olympic Aviation "the air-taxi service.")

The air-taxi service consisted of a half-dozen small planes and helicopters, used mainly for charter flights between Athens airport and the outlying Greek islands in the Aegean and Ionian seas. For the most part the island residents had no direct access to air transport. They first had to travel by boat to an island large enough to support an airport. Alex saw this as an opportunity to provide a lifeline for these isolated people, and in the process to demonstrate his own flying skills and business acumen. Since the air-taxi service was then a money-losing operation and did not involve jet-age skills, its employees were paid at a lower rate than those working for the airline. Therefore the most ambitious Olympic employees preferred to work for the airline, providing Alex a chance to make the air-taxi service his own baby.

Alex began flying lessons in 1968, his second year with Fiona. At Ari's direction, he was instructed at first by Captain Paul Ioannidis, the legendary Greek fighter pilot who won the King's Medal for Gallantry and then became the chief pilot and director-general of Olympic Airways. Alex received further instruction from the brothers George and Dimitris Kouris, who served as Ari's personal pilots. Alex had always loved aviation, and now he saw in the air-taxi service the chance of a lifetime to enjoy himself and prove his worth. When Fiona put Alex up to asking Ari for the job of running the air-taxi service, Ari went along. He saw the air-taxi revenues as too miniscule to be concerned about. He was content to let Alex play with these little planes, thinking that his son would soon tire of it and come back begging to learn the shipping business at Ari's feet.

Alex was to surprise Ari and everyone else with the job he did at the air-taxi service. He treated the employees with respect and soon won their confidence and admiration. He became a folk hero of the islands, often answering distress calls to transport the sick and the elderly to medical care on the mainland, sometimes in weather that was considered unsafe for normal flight operations. In one incident, a grateful father gave Alex a tip for flying his ailing son from a small island to the safety of an Athens hospital. Alex didn't have the heart to tell the father he had just tipped the son of the richest man in Greece, so he simply managed to slip the tip money back into the man's pocket.

In February 1971, Alex received an emergency call from the island of Santorini, where a man had suffered serious injuries in a motorcycle crash and was near death. The doctor said that the victim could not survive more than a few hours unless he was flown to Athens for hospital treatment. The weather was wretched and all small aircraft were grounded, but Alex took off in high winds, picked up the injured victim, and got him back to Athens in time to save his life. Only two weeks later, Alex returned to Santorini in marginal weather to save the life of another accident victim. His most publicized rescue flight was made with his friend and flying instructor, Dimitris Kouris, to an outer island where the daughter of the Soviet ambassador to Greece lay close to death. They got the little girl to an Athens hospital in time to save her life.

Apart from these mercy missions, Alex's operation provided scheduled air service to the islands, using small landplanes for those islands large enough to rate airports, and Piaggio amphibians for those which could handle only seaplanes. He extended the service to islands that had never seen an airplane. He took good care of his customers, whether they could pay or not, and went out of his way to treat his personnel fairly.

By the early 1970s, Alex had Olympic Aviation running well and actually earning a profit. In that sense it was doing better than the airline, although Ari claimed that he ran Greece's national airline as a hobby and a public service which he did not expect to be profitable. But the labor relations and customer satisfaction were much better at Alex's little air-taxi service than at the airline, to say nothing of the highly favorable public relations impact of the island mercy flights. Sitting in his beloved Athens office which was filled with pictures and models of airplanes, some hanging from the ceiling, Alex was on a collision course with Ari's ego. He and Fiona knew that Ari would not allow Alex's independent success to last indefinitely, but they enjoyed it while it continued. They both realized that the air-taxi operation was bolstering Alex's self-esteem and building muscle where it would be needed for the eventual break with Ari.

As was his style, Aristotle ran the airline as though it were his personal property rather than a government-granted monopoly of Greek air services. Alex's Olympic Aviation air-taxi service was technically a separate corporation, but Ari blurred the two entities together when it suited his purposes. This practice was followed with Ari's personal airplanes, expensive corporate jets which were at his beck and call around the clock. All of these aircraft were hangared, serviced, and maintained at the airline's Athens airport facilities, even though the Greek Colonels' government provided subsidies to the airline.

This was true of the Learjet model 25 B executive jet, license SX-AS0, which was registered to the airline, Olympic Airways S.A., but was used to transport members of the Onassis family. On February 18, 1972, Ari's personal pilots, George and Dimitris Kouris, flew the Learjet from Athens to Nice, France, to pick up Alexander, who had spent a few days in Monte Carlo.

Just after dark that evening, the Learjet flown by the Kouris brothers was on its final approach to the Nice Airport when it crashed into the sea four nautical miles short of the runway. Rescue boats were dispatched immediately but the plane sank quickly in water that was three hundred feet deep. Some debris of the airplane was recovered, but the plane itself was not brought up. The bodies of the Kouris brothers were not found. The French Ministry of Transport report on the accident found that the flight was entirely normal, with a normal descent to an altitude of 3,500 feet, where it was cleared for final approach. The report noted:

This instruction was confirmed by the plane. No further message was received from the SX-ASO and witnesses reported seeing the plane hit the water at a low angle...comparable with that of a normal landing...about four nautical miles from the start of the runway whilst on the correct approach, having previously flown over the town of Antibes at a much lower height than other planes prior to landing.

There were no difficulties with weather, communications, or the plane itself which might explain the crash. The French investigators recited the findings in similar accidents that occurred during night approaches over water, in which the plane was last seen in a normal landing attitude. They concluded that the probable cause of the Nice Learjet accident was "a classic optical illusion" created by "the total absence of light on the Baie des Anges before a well lit town on a significant slope" which could have resulted in the pilots misjudging their actual height above the water.

Waiting at the Nice airport for the Learjet that never arrived, Alex was shocked and uncomprehending when he was told that the plane apparently had crashed. Two dear friends, who had helped to teach him flying, were killed while flying the empty plane from Athens to pick him up. He felt deep guilt as well as remorse. He threw himself into the search along the coastline for the bodies and the debris, but became even more frustrated when nothing further was found.

Although the French government accident report concluded there had probably been an optical illusion, this type of pilot error finding was inconclusive, leaving an aura of uncertainty and suspicion. Alex could not accept this, and with his father's support he launched a private investigation of the crash. After all, it was Ari's personal plane, and if it had been sabotaged, Ari would have been the most likely target. Fiona flew to Nice to support Alex, and the two of them spent more than a week searching the coastline in vain for the pilots' bodies and further clues to the cause.

The third Kouris brother, Grigoris, was convinced that a bomb had exploded aboard the plane. He urged Alex to join with him to search in the water for pieces of wreckage which could confirm such an explosion. Alex agreed, and sought the help of the renowned French underwater diver Jacques Cousteau. Then suddenly Ari pulled the plug. All Olympic Airways personnel were taken off the investigation, and Alex was ordered to drop it immediately. When an Olympic safety official asked Ari why he terminated the investigation, he replied, "Do not ask any further questions. This matter is closed."

Ari never disclosed why he shut down the investigation, but those close to him, especially Alex, were aware that Ari had become frightened. This was entirely out of keeping with Ari's extreme machismo. Alex speculated that someone must have told Ari that either he or Alex had been the intended victim of the Learjet crash.

This was Alex's first experience with a plane crash that took the lives of people close to him, and he remained inconsolable about the deaths of the Kouris brothers. Months after the crash, he was still expressing feelings of guilt, saying that his friends George and Dimitris would still be alive if he had not decided to return from Monte Carlo at that time.

Later in 1972, when Alex had recovered sufficiently to speak logically about the Learjet crash, he thought of it in the context of his own air safety philosophy. He believed that there was rarely a single reason for a crash, especially when it involved experienced pilots and well-maintained equipment. Usually it was a combination of circumstances, a lot of little things building up into a bigger problem. Any number of little things could go wrong during a night approach at Nice, one of Europe's most difficult airports, and they could combine to cause a fatal problem.

Alex had methodically built a reputation for being a thoughtful, safety-conscious pilot—just the opposite of his reckless operation of sports cars and speedboats. This was partly due to his respect for the more serious risks of reckless flying. Even his weather-defying rescue flights to the islands were carefully planned and sometimes included one of the Kouris brothers. But an even stronger drive was his compelling desire to be accepted as an equal by the professional Olympic pilots. To accomplish this he had to overcome the stigma of being the boss tycoon's young playboy son. This burden required him to act maturely and responsibly in all matters of air safety.

The Learjet crash created a double vacancy in Aristotle Onassis's pilot staff. The Kouris brothers had flown Ari in the Piaggio amphibian which was sometimes stationed aboard the yacht *Christina*, as well as in landplanes like the Learjet. A new Learjet was ordered to replace the one lost at Nice, and new pilots were engaged to fly it, but they were not qualified for seaplanes. This left open the job of flying Ari in the Piaggio, used mainly for short flights to and from Skorpios, which had no airport but had a harbor that could accommodate seaplanes.

The Piaggio was actually operated by Olympic Aviation, the air-taxi subsidiary, since it was often piloted by Alex in flights between Athens and the Greek islands. When Ari requisitioned it for a flight between Athens and Skorpios or a cruise aboard the *Christina*, Ari's personal amphibian pilot would take over.

Alex was convinced that a helicopter would be much more appropriate than the Piaggio aboard the *Christina*. He had been urging Ari to replace the Piaggio with a helicopter for many months, and now that the Learjet crash made it necessary to find a substitute for the Kouris brothers, he renewed this plea. Ari again refused to consider Alex's advice, and ordered his staff to recruit another Piaggio pilot from the ranks of Olympic Airlines captains. They found the perfect man in Donald "Mac" McGregor, a veteran Boeing 707 jet captain who also had extensive flying boat and amphibian experience. Since Mac was nearing the retirement age of sixty for airline pilots, he would have to make a change to smaller aircraft if he wanted to keep flying professionally. Reluctantly, Alex spent the first week of May 1972 checking Mac out in the Piaggio, and Mac then replaced the Kouris brothers as Ari's personal Piaggio pilot.

Alex met his father for dinner in Paris on January 4, 1973. At Fiona's urging, Alex had just had his nose reduced in size, and his new appearance seemed to startle Ari. As usual, Ari dominated the conversation, recounting at length his newly-reached decision to divorce Jackie after less than five years of marriage. This bombshell disclosure seemed to bring Ari and Alex closer together, and the delighted Alex decided to take advantage of this new rapport to press home his long-running plea that the Piaggio be replaced by a helicopter. By that time Mac McGregor had been grounded for medical reasons, making it necessary to find another pilot for the Piaggio, which was undergoing an extensive overhaul at the Olympic Airways maintenance hangar in Athens.

To Alex's amazement, Ari did not shrug off the helicopter idea. Yes, it was time to replace the Piaggio with a helicopter. But Ari wanted to use the Piaggio one more time, for a *Christina* cruise to Florida and the Caribbean which he had arranged for February, just a few weeks away. Ari would agree to take the Piaggio on board the *Christina* and drop it off in Miami to be sold there. If Alex would see to it that the Piaggio overhaul was completed in time for the cruise, and would recruit another Piaggio pilot to replace the ailing McGregor, Ari would agree to switch to a helicopter after the February cruise.

Alex happily agreed to these steps. Right after dinner he phoned Fiona from Paris to impart the double dose of good news: the reviled Jackie would soon be history, and his father actually listened to what he had been saying for months about the Piaggio. He wondered whether his new nose had turned the trick he had been trying so long to pull off.

January 1973 was shaping up to be the most fateful month in Alex's life. During 1972, he and Fiona had one of their periodic breakups, but as usual they found after a few weeks apart that they could not do without each other. After a passionate reunion, they threw themselves even more devotedly into the five-year-old love affair.

Over the years, Fiona had encouraged Alex to talk things out with Ari in the hope of arranging an amicable parting which would leave the father-son relationship in place. She thought there was a chance that despite Ari's monumental ego, eventually love for his son would open his eyes to Alex's need for independence. She hoped that Ari would see the light and agree to let Alex resume his education and pursue a career on his own, with his father's blessing. After all, Ari always boasted of being a self-made man. Surely he would not deny his son the chance to prove himself.

Alex never had any faith in this seemingly reasonable approach because he knew that when it came to control of his children, Ari would not permit even the slightest hint of reason to intrude. Nevertheless, to humor Fiona, Alex tried to talk to his father about independence. Each time he brought up the subject, the predictable result was that Ari simply shouted Alex down, or demonstrated his revulsion by shrieking epithets at Alex. The levelheaded

Fiona found this hard to believe at first, until she noticed the look of horror on Alex's face whenever he spoke on the phone to Ari in her presence. To convince her that it was hopeless, Alex began to tape-record his phone conversations with Ari.

The tapes consisted almost entirely of Ari speaking—or rather shrieking—in near-monologue. When Alex mentioned anything relating to independence, Ari would be apt to burst into irrelevant song, just to demonstrate that his son was out of line to even open up such questions. He would render "Singin' in the Rain" in his rich baritone. At the end of this performance, if Alex dared to reopen the forbidden subject, Ari would begin another song, or simply scream his profanity-laden reproach for five minutes nonstop. These tapes convinced Fiona that Ari would never permit any reasonable discussion of independence for Alex. Indeed, she perceived that Ari was mentally deranged to the extent that he deliberately tried to keep his son in a state of destructive emotional distress. She finally understood why Alex had made an art form out of being in a different city than his father whenever possible.

Then the question became, what could they do to break these chains? Alex had no professional qualifications other than as a pilot, and even these were limited by his poor eyesight which denied him access to an Airline Transport license. He knew something about the shipping business, but if he sought an independent job against Ari's wishes, he would surely be turned down by Ari's maritime friends and enemies alike.

With the 1972 Christmas season coming up, Fiona was convinced that the time had come for the definitive break with Ari. She saw signs that Alex's success with the air-taxi service was making Ari jealous. She felt it was only a matter of time before Ari ordered Alex to leave Olympic Aviation and return to Olympic

Maritime, where he would always be a novice, a glorified go-fer, instead of a more successful aviation executive than his father.

Her basic plan was to make a preemptive strike. Alex would respectfully inform his father that he was resigning from the Onassis business empire to resume his education, moving to Switzerland for that purpose. He would acquire the credits needed to complete his aborted preparatory education; study hard in pursuit of a respectable university degree; and then try his luck in the business world on his own, preferably in aviation. To make it harder for Ari to reverse this decision, Alex would take off for Switzerland without notice to anyone, and would inform Ari from there that he intended to pursue this new life plan.

For her part, Fiona, left financially secure by the Thyssen divorce settlement, was prepared to pay Alex's tuition and living expenses while he completed his education. She had bought a house in the storybook Swiss Alpine village of Morges on Lake Geneva (Audrey Hepburn was a neighbor), where they would finally live together. A whole floor of their dream house was set aside for Alex's tutoring. The timetable for the break would be determined by the readiness of the house at Morges. The renovations were scheduled to be completed by the end of January 1973. That would give Alex a good six months to qualify for university courses starting in September 1973. He had looked into the entrance requirements at the nearby University of Geneva, as well as the tutoring and pre-university cram courses he needed to complete.

In retrospect, given Ari's known propensity for using his massive wealth to run roughshod over his children's hopes when they did not mesh with his own desires, this was a very courageous (if not foolhardy) plan. Fiona and Alex were only too familiar with what had happened when Christina married a successful Los

Angeles businessman and went to live in the United States. Her surprise elopement with Joe Bolker did not involve anything as speculative as trying to hold Ari off for four years while Alex studied for a university degree. Yet the Bolker marriage was quickly destroyed by Ari and his faithful hatchetman Johnny Meyer.

In attempting this high-risk breakaway, perhaps Fiona and Alex were not motivated solely by their love for each other, strong as that love was. Both of them had been driven to loathing Aristotle Onassis as the monster who constantly threatened their self-respect and their freedom to enjoy life together. Both of them must have felt some desire to defeat Ari, or at least show him up. For the spunky Fiona, who was not easily pushed around by anyone, there was an element of gamesmanship: could she defy the ultimate macho devil and take away his greatest treasure? For Alex, there was the realization that Fiona Campbell Thyssen was more beautiful, more independent—indeed, more wealthy—than Ari's trophy wife, Jackie Kennedy.

Fiona and Alex spent the early January weekends together as usual, either in Switzerland or at Fiona's London flat. They could hardly contain their excitement as Fiona reported on the progress of the Morges renovation and Alex told her how he was whittling away the remaining tasks he had to perform in Athens before the breakaway. They planned their very last clandestine weekend tryst for January 20-21 in Morges, at the house Fiona had rented pending the readiness of the one being renovated. Alex was making arrangements to get the new Piaggio pilot, an American, to Athens on Monday January 22. Alex would perform the checkout flight that afternoon and then leave the American pilot to train for another week with Mac McGregor, who would fly as his passenger and provide orientation around the yacht *Christina*, Skorpios, and other places where the Piaggio was used. Thus the

Piaggio checkout flight would be Alex's last job under Ari's control, and on Monday evening he would hop an evening flight to Heathrow, where Fiona, who had to attend her brother Richard's London wedding, would be waiting for him.

That last January weekend at Morges turned out to be the most delightful of all the times they spent together. They had enjoyed many idyllic meetings during the preceding five years, high in the Swiss Alps and on the picturesque Greek islands. But those were furtive trysts, time stolen from the outside world that was mobilized against their being together. At Morges in January, their future plans were settled for the first time. They feasted on the bright prospect of celebrating their happiness openly at last.

Fiona remembers the last Sunday, January 21, as different from all of the many Sundays they had spent together. They had never been this happy, and their love was strengthened by having settled their minds on the definitive plan which was within a few days of launching. Although they customarily ate lunch alone on these Sundays before Alex returned to work, this time he said to Fiona, "I would like to see Chessie and Lorne [Fiona's children]. Can we all have lunch together?"

After lunch they all played Foosball, a table soccer game in which the players kicked the ball by flipping wooden levers that worked the legs of tiny soccer players. The teams were Fiona and her fifteen-year-old daughter Chessie against Alex and Fiona's son Lorne, aged ten. This group activity was unusual, for Fiona normally took great pains to isolate her children from the love affair. This day, they all seemed to sense and adopt Alex's feeling that they were becoming a family. As Alex prepared to depart, he said to Fiona, "It's as if I've never known the children before." Chessie gave him a big hug and said to him, "It's such a shame.

We don't see you nearly enough. Next weekend, we'll play the return match and beat the socks off you!"

An Olympic Airways car arrived at Fiona's house to drive Alex to Geneva airport, from where he would fly to Athens. They stood in the rain as Alex held Fiona close and kissed her goodbye. She gave him what he always wanted as a parting gift: a box of Dairy Milk Tray chocolates, which Alex loved because all the various fillings were pictured on a chart inside the lid, so that he could go right for his favorites. Alex climbed into the car, but before the door was shut he rushed out and ran up the steps of the house to embrace Fiona again. Fiona recalled, "It was raining hard, and he hated the rain because it messed up his hair. He was quite vain, and for him to come back up those steps to give me this tremendous hug—it was all part of the strange mood of that Sunday."

The following morning, Monday January 22, Alex phoned Fiona from his downtown Athens office and they talked for over an hour. Even though he had just spent the weekend with her and was to rejoin her in London that evening, he seemed unwilling to end the conversation. He questioned Fiona about details of the house renovations at Morges, and went on about their plans for his education. He recounted details of how he had wrapped up all his duties in Athens, pending the Piaggio check flight which he would complete that afternoon. Fiona sensed that Alex was prolonging the conversation just to be with her.

Finally he ended the call to Fiona in high spirits. Then it was time to drive to the airport, where the American pilot Don McCusker, the grounded pilot Mac McGregor, and Ari's Piaggio amphibian awaited.

Chapter Nine

The Unfortunate Child

Athens International Airport
Monday, January 22, 1973

It was close to 3 p.m. when Alexander arrived at the airport. Waiting for him there was the American pilot, Don McCusker, who had flown in from New York on Olympic Airways that morning. Alexander immediately directed McCusker and the retiring Piaggio pilot, Mac McGregor, to board the Piaggio with him. Alexander knew that McCusker was overqualified for the job of piloting the little Piaggio, since he had over eight thousand hours of flying time on dozens of advanced military and civilian aircraft types. While he had not flown a Piaggio, he had hundreds of hours in similar small amphibians like the Grumann Widgeon. After acquainting McCusker with the cockpit layout and the takeoff procedures, Alexander took the right seat (where the instructor or check pilot normally sat) and directed McCusker to the left seat, with Mac McGregor sitting in the back seat.

Because McCusker was such an experienced pilot, Alexander decided that he would talk him through the takeoff, with McCusker flying the plane. It was equipped with dual controls, so that Alexander could take over in the unlikely event that McCusker had trouble with the takeoff. Once airborne, Alexander planned to direct McCusker to fly to the nearby islands of Aegina and Poros, where the American pilot would execute enough water landings and takeoffs to demonstrate his fitness for the job.

Alexander figured this routine checkout would take no more than two hours, leaving plenty of time to get back to the Athens airport and catch the evening flight to London where he would be joining Fiona. He explained that after the checkout was completed, the American pilot and Mac McGregor would work together for several more days of orientation. Although McGregor was grounded as a pilot by his medical problem, he could fly as McCusker's passenger and make certain that the new pilot became familiar with the specific uses of the Piaggio in Ari's service.

Alexander handled radio communications with the control tower, arranging for a clearance to taxi to Runway 33, which was then being used for takeoffs. Under Alexander's directions, McCusker taxied the Piaggio to Runway 33. Before receiving takeoff clearance from the tower, the Piaggio had to park at the edge of Runway 33 to await the takeoff of an Air France Boeing 727. There Alexander completed the pre-takeoff check of the engines and instructed McCusker to lower the wing flaps to the 20-degree takeoff position.

After the Air France jet took off, Alexander heard the words he had been anxiously awaiting: "Olympic Aviation SX BDC, you are cleared for takeoff on Runway 33." Alexander acknowledged the clearance and then instructed McCusker to taxi onto the runway to begin the takeoff. It was 3:19 P.M., and the weather was clear and sunny. At last Alexander's waiting was over, and he would soon be with Fiona again—this time, for good.

McCusker taxied the Piaggio onto the takeoff runway and turned it to a heading of 330 degrees, aligning it with the northwesterly direction of the runway. As the plane came to a stop, Alexander talked McCusker through the final pre-takeoff checklist from memory, telling him to switch on the booster pumps so that the engines would deliver full power. Then Alexander signaled to McCusker that he should go ahead with the takeoff. McCusker pushed both throttle levers forward and began the takeoff run.

The engines quickly attained full power, and when the airspeed indicator reached the takeoff speed of 100 miles per hour, McCusker pulled back slowly on the control wheel. The Piaggio lifted smoothly into the air in a normal takeoff. Almost immediately the nose veered to the right, and within two seconds the plane banked sharply to the right, the right wing dropping down at a 45-degree angle. Instinctively McCusker kicked left rudder and turned the control wheel to the left, to bring up the right wing and counteract the right turn. But this only sharpened the bank to the right, and in another few seconds, the plane, having never reached 100 feet altitude, flew into the ground.

The first contact with the runway was made by the right wing tip float, a small pontoon suspended from the bottom of the wing tip which helped to keep the wings level on water. Then the right wingtip itself struck the runway. Continuing its turn to the right, the plane spun off the runway and then it cartwheeled in a circle for nearly 500 feet, smashing the nose, the cockpit, the tail section, and both wings before coming to an abrupt stop. It was 3:20 P.M. in Athens. The disastrous flight—including the uncontrolled cartwheeling on the ground—had lasted less than 15 seconds.

The airport tower personnel watched in horrified disbelief as the crash unfolded under their noses. Quickly they activated the emergency alarms and rescue procedures. First to reach the wrecked Piaggio were U.S. Air Force emergency vehicles stationed at the airport to serve American military aircraft operating under NATO command. Fortunately there was no fire. The Americans found the three occupants unconscious and bleeding profusely. With the help of airport rescue workers, they were able to get the pilots into ambulances quickly and they were rushed to hospitals.

Mac McGregor was the only one to regain consciousness at the crash scene. He awoke to find a uniformed American airman cutting away the legs of his trousers, and was startled when the airman said, "Sorry to do this, Mac." Only later did he learn that American servicemen called everybody "Mac." He was taken by ambulance to the Red Cross Hospital in Athens. Alexander Onassis and Don McCusker were taken to Kat Hospital, in the Athens suburb of Kifissia.

At the Red Cross Hospital, Mac McGregor's injuries were diagnosed as a compression fracture of spinal vertebrae, cerebral concussion, and leg bruises. While these were serious injuries for a man of fifty-nine, Mac had a strong constitution and the attending doctor soon pronounced him out of danger.

At the Kat Hospital, a team which included some of Greece's leading physicians was quickly assembled to deal with this emergency. McCusker's injuries were found to be serious but not life-threatening. His head, neck, ribs, and back had been thrown against the interior of the plane as it struck the ground. There were multiple fractures but none that could not be treated. He regained consciousness in the hospital, and was put on intravenous fluids.

The diagnosis of the third patient painted a darker picture. From the moment Alexander was wheeled into the Kat Hospital it was clear to the treating doctors that his condition was desperate. Sitting in the right seat, he had borne the brunt of the descending right turn which flew the plane into the ground at close to 100 mph and crumpled the right side of the cockpit. Alexander's right temple had been crushed to pulp. Some of those who saw him at the crash scene and in the hospital emergency room said his head injuries were so severe that he could be identified only by the "AO" monogram on his bloodstained pocket handkerchief.

Alexander was rushed into the operating room, where the doctors performed three hours of surgery to remove blood clots and relieve the pressure on his brain. At no time did he show any hopeful signs. He was placed in an oxygen tent and connected to a life-support system which kept him alive, but the doctors agreed that he had no chance of recovery.

At Olympic Airways headquarters, the first to receive the grim news was the president, Ari's cousin and close friend Costas Konialidis. When he recovered from the initial shock he picked up the phone to call Ari, who was in New York. As he dialed Ari's New York number, Costas shuddered at the task of telling Ari what had happened, but hoped he would get through before the word came to Ari from radio or TV or—even worse—from prying reporters. Ari came right on the line and Costas managed to break the devastating news, expecting an explosion. But Ari barely breathed a word. It was as if he had lost the ability to speak.

Tina was dressing for a dinner party at the Palace Hotel in St. Moritz when Costas's call reached her. She could not believe that her son's life was hanging by a thread. Finally, after questioning the report several times, she told Costas that she would leave for Athens immediately.

Costas was unable to reach Christina in Brazil or Fiona in London, as a result of which both got the news from the radio. Christina was on a shopping tour of Rio de Janeiro, riding in a hired car. The driver had the car radio tuned to a Portuguese station, and Christina thought she heard her brother's name mentioned in a news story. Since her Portuguese was weak, she asked the driver to interpret the newscast. He said, "There's been a plane crash in Athens. Alexander Onassis was seriously hurt." Christina aborted the shopping tour and rushed back to her hotel, where she found several phone messages awaiting her. She phoned back her Aunt Artemis in Athens, who told her that Alexander's head had been crushed and he was not expected to live.

Fiona was dressing for her brother's wedding party in London when her mother told her she had heard on BBC radio that Alexander had been injured in an Athens accident. Her efforts to get details on the phone did not succeed, but she knew that she had to fly to Athens immediately. She had always been concerned that Alex would crack up a speeding car, and they had agreed that if it ever happened she would get to his side and be there for him at the hospital.

They all converged on Athens as quickly as they could arrange transportation. Tina's new husband, Stavros Niarchos, Ari's long-time rival, had his own jet which whisked him and Tina to Athens that night. Christina, near collapse from the devastating news, turned to her Brazilian friends for help, and finally had to settle for a regular airline flight that would not get her to Athens until late Tuesday afternoon, the day after the crash. By the time Fiona got the news, the last scheduled airline flight from London to

Athens had departed. She spent hours on the phone in a frantic effort to charter a plane. She finally succeeded in getting an executive jet to fly in from Switzerland to pick her up. It got her into Athens at 6 A.M. on Tuesday.

Ari was not so incapacitated by the shocking news as to lose his sense of command. He managed to organize an international airlift that included an Olympic Airways Boeing 707 which carried him, Jackie, and a leading Boston neurosurgeon from New York's Kennedy Airport; another chartered jet that flew a cardiac specialist from Texas; and a chartered British Airways jet which carried one passenger—the noted British neurosurgeon Alan Richardson—from London to Athens. Ari was not going to give up his son's life without a fight.

By the time Ari and Jackie arrived at the Kat Hospital at 7 A.M. on Tuesday, there was a large crowd blocking the entrance. Jackie got out of the car and tried to make her way through the crowd, but Ari could not move, so she went back into the car and sat down beside him. They sat in the car until the police finally cleared the way for the car to drive to the hospital entrance. As they got out of the car to enter the hospital, they were joined by Tina and Stavros Niarchos. At that moment all the bitterness of the messy divorce and the years of business conflict was washed away, as the four of them embraced in grief.

When Ari, Jackie, Tina, and Stavros made their way to Alexander's room, they found Fiona at his bedside. She had arrived shortly before the others, and the nurses had given her a white robe which made her look taller and paler than usual. Her eyes were locked on Alexander's face as she held his hand, and she did not seem to notice anyone else in the room. Years later she said, "I just sat there thinking that I'll be able to get through to him, that there must be a part of his brain left there. I held his hand and tried to let him know I was there, even though I had to face the fact that there was no way he was going to come back from wherever he'd gone to."

Even when Ari and Tina moved to the bedside to touch their unconscious son, Fiona barely stirred. Her lips moving in silent prayer, she stood her ground and clung to Alexander's hand. Ari, who had never acknowledged Fiona as his son's sweetheart during the five-year romance, did not dare to question her right to be at Alexander's side now.

Despite the fact that Alexander never showed any sign of life and that the doctors told her he never would, Fiona maintained her vigil at his side for nearly twelve hours, from the time she arrived to the moment when Alexander was taken off life support. Although the room was frequently filled with doctors and grieving relatives, she paid no attention to anyone but Alexander. She felt that she was alone with him at last. Occasionally she moved her hand to touch his face, which was bandaged except for his nose and eyes. Later she was to recall, "He was so proud of his new nose, and I immediately thought: Thank God his nose is all right."

Ari spoke at length with each of the doctors in attendance. His hopes were finally dashed when the English neurosurgeon Alan Richardson confirmed the findings of the Greek and American surgeons: Alexander had suffered irrecoverable brain damage. Technically the findings were general contusion and edema of the brain matter; the right temporal lobe had been reduced to pulp; and the right frontal fossa was severely fractured. He was in a very deep coma, unable to breathe without life-support machines. They could keep his heart beating for another three or four days, but he was already brain-dead. There was absolutely no hope of recovery. Dr. Richardson agreed with all the other surgeons: Alexander should be removed from life support and allowed to die.

Still Ari fought against accepting this unanimous verdict. He remembered there was a sacred icon on one of the Greek islands which, according to legend, had miraculous healing powers. Ari ordered it flown to the hospital immediately, but in the grief and confusion of the day, the icon could not be produced quickly, and finally Ari was forced to face the fact that his son was gone. At 1 P.M., he told the doctors to keep Alexander alive long enough for Christina to have a final visit, after which he would give the order to terminate life support. Then he left the hospital and did not return.

In the meantime, Ari, concerned about the disfigurement of Alexander's face, had sent his private Learjet from Athens to Geneva to pick up Dr. Popen, a leading plastic surgeon. He ordered Dr. Popen, "You must fix his face. You must make him look like Alexander again so that I can remember his face as it was." The unconscious Alexander was moved back to the operating room, where the Swiss surgeon skillfully repaired much of the damage done in the Piaggio crash.

Christina arrived at the hospital at 6 P.M., supported by her aunts, Ari's three sisters. She sobbed and screamed hysterically, calling out Alexander's name and begging him to wake up and speak to her. Finally after twenty-five minutes she said goodbye to her brother. Dr. Richardson then phoned Ari to report that Christina had completed her visit, and asked permission to terminate the life support.

Ari then asked, "Doctor, if I give you all my ships, all my property, all my planes, and all the money I have, would there be any hope to save my boy?"

When the doctor said, "I'm afraid not, Mr. Onassis," Ari replied, "Then leave him be in peace."

At 6:55 P.M., the doctors switched off the machines that had been keeping Alexander alive.

Fiona remembered that Alexander had kept his residential suite at the Athens Hilton, since he wished to avoid any sign of a permanent break that might cause Ari to throw roadblocks in the way of his departure. She went to the hotel and got the manager to open Alexander's room, looking for letters or any other mementos that she might want to keep. There she found the box of Dairy Milk Tray chocolates she had given him on Sunday when they parted at Morges. She opened the box and found that three were missing. She knew exactly which ones they would be: the mallows, Alexander's favorite centers. This little vignette, bringing back one of the tender moments of their life together, broke down her resolve to keep up a brave front. The mournful scene at the hospital was not yet real to her, but the chocolates in the empty hotel suite were more than she could bear.

Ari walked the rain-spattered streets of Athens alone much of the night, looking for the church in which he had prayed the night he learned of the death of his grandmother Gethsemane, who had raised him after his mother died when he was six. Finally he found the church and prayed for Alexander before the same altar at which he had mourned Gethsemane half a century ago.

Now there was the funeral to deal with. Treating it almost like a business deal, Ari vacillated between several options. First he promised Fiona that Alexander would be buried in Athens so that she could readily visit the grave. Then he wanted to change the final resting place to Skorpios, where he would have Alexander to himself. Then he shifted to a third plan: he would have Alexander's body deep-frozen and stored in a cryonic-care facility until medical science was able to rebuild the shattered brain. He ordered Johnny Meyer to call the Life Extension Society in Washington D.C., which offered such cryonic services. Here Professor Yiannis Georgakis, Ari's respected friend and mentor in philosophy, intervened and dared to tell Ari that he had no right to impede the journey of Alexander's soul. In this instance, lacking the arrogance that normally characterized his negotiations on both business and personal matters, the grief-stricken Ari gave way and dropped the cryonic plan.

Finally he decided to have two funeral services. First would be a widely-attended memorial service at Saint Lazare Greek Orthodox Church in downtown Athens, to be held on the Wednesday. No public announcement would be made as to the place of burial. Secretly—as secretly as possible—Ari planned the burial for his private island of Skorpios on the Saturday.

As rain poured down on Athens, the church service was attended by celebrities and dignitaries from all over the world. Senator Ted Kennedy was there, along with Jackie and her two children, Caroline and John F. Kennedy Jr. By this time Fiona was near collapse and needed the physical support of two friends to make it through the four-hour service.

After the service, the casket was moved to the tiny Chapel of St. Lazarus in the Athens First Cemetery, where it could be viewed by the thousands who wished to pay their respects. The Athens newspapers reported that more than ten thousand mourners filed past the casket in the St. Lazarus Chapel on Thursday and Friday. They included the premier of Greece and the King's Marshall, who delivered a wreath on behalf of King Constantine of Greece, exiled in Rome. Condolence messages were received from Queen Elizabeth, President Richard Nixon, Vice-President Spiro Agnew, French President Georges Pompidou, and German Chancellor Willy Brandt. (Other front-page stories that day included President Nixon's announcement of a cease-fire in the Vietnam War and the closing of the U. S. Embassy in Athens to mourn the death of former president Lyndon B. Johnson.)

Ari struggled to maintain his composure during the church services. Since the moment when the world learned of the Piaggio crash, the press had been literally occupying the Olympic offices and other places where Ari might appear, intent on getting his reaction to the death of his son. For many years Ari had been cultivating the media, giving them the juicy stories he knew would make them look good with their editors and at the same time would continue to build his legend. Now he wished they would leave him in peace, but he knew they could not let up until he made a statement. He decided to get it over with by holding a press conference right after the church service on Wednesday. It took place at the hall of the Olympic Airways Administrative Council.

The English-language *Athens Daily Post* reported Ari's speech:

> *I wish to thank you, all of you, for your sympathy and feelings shown for the loss of my son. I also thank the officials and unofficials, those I know and those whom I don't know, who have shown such a touching interest for this unfortunate child.*
>
> *The Trumpet of God has called him near Him. The thread of his life ended here.*
>
> *He loved the air, and no power was able to stop him from his weakness. I tried several times to draw his attention toward the sea. But his love of the air prevailed. In a period of four years, he was a superb pilot. I have never known such a pilot who gave attention to every detail concerning piloting. And he continuously improved himself. From a plane pilot he became a helicopter pilot and later a pilot of amphibious planes, in one of which he was destined to meet his death.*
>
> *We all admired him for his love and successes in the air. The amphibious plane in which he met his death was a good*

plane. It was of Italian manufacture, with American engines. I made use of it for 25 years on my yacht, have used it in all the seas of the world, and we never had an accident.

Donald McCusker is an experienced pilot with great experience and thousands of flight hours. He sat at the pilot's place and this was the fateful mistake. The unfortunate child, Alexandros, due to the many qualifications of the American pilot, told him to sit at the pilot's place, and to make the take-off. And Alexandros sat next to him, on the right. If this did not happen, he would probably be alive today.

Perhaps my son wanted to make me a pleasant surprise by engaging McCusker for my private plane. However, my son's fatal error was to allow McCusker to pilot the plane on the first test flight, whereas he should have piloted it himself for two or three times, to enable McCusker to get some experience on this type of plane, and afterwards hand over the controls.

My son probably had confidence in McCusker, who is a first class pilot on amphibious planes with thousands of flying hours but has no experience of this particular type of plane. It was also an error on McCusker's part to accept piloting the plane on the first trial flight.

Alexandros should have taken the pilot's place himself at the takeoff time, and later hand over the piloting to the American. This was the fateful mistake.

This amphibious plane was not used to carry passengers. It was used for personal needs only. And the American pilot was getting ready, because he was to come with me on the yacht, so that he may be at our disposal when the fateful plane was to be used by us. If the unfortunate child were at the pilot's place, things might have been different.

In deference to Ari's obvious grief, the swarm of journalists did not question any of his statements. They asked only when and where the burial would take place. In a broken voice, Ari replied that it was not yet decided. That ended the press conference.

To Jackie Kennedy Onassis, the Piaggio crash was the latest in a seemingly endless chain of air disasters that struck the Kennedy family. Joseph P. Kennedy Jr., who was being groomed for the presidency by his father, the ambassador to Britain, was blown to bits during a wartime volunteer bombing mission that went terribly wrong. In 1948, Kathleen "Kit" Kennedy Hartington, beloved sister of JFK, was killed in a French private plane crash. In a 1964 political campaign flight, Ted Kennedy suffered a broken back and barely escaped with his life despite the death of his aide and the pilot. Bobby Kennedy's wife, Ethel, lost her parents and her brother in two separate plane crashes.

While it might be stretching a point to call all these victims "Kennedys," the warning signs were clear enough to Jackie. When her stepson Alexander was killed in Athens, her sixteen-year-old daughter Caroline was attending Concord Academy in Massachusetts and had been taking private flying lessons at nearby Hanscomb Airport. Jackie ordered Caroline to quit the flying lessons immediately (which she did) and also made the twelve-year-old JFK Junior promise that he would never become a pilot—a promise which unfortunately he was not to keep.

Jackie stood by Ari and did her best to help him cope with the death of Alexander. She was an expert at standing up to grief and was even able to ignore the bad press she received for keeping a fixed smile on her face during funerals. As we have seen, Ari had taken an interest in Jackie's children, and now she hoped to strengthen that relationship, reasoning that the loss of Alexander might make Ari look upon JFK Junior as something more than a stepson. But in the immediate wake of the Piaggio crash, nothing could bring peace to Ari or help him to deal rationally with the tragedy.

Perhaps Ari's only comfort was that he managed to apply his business negotiating tactics to the burial of his son. First he planned to place the coffin inside the tiny chapel of Panayitsa ("Little Virgin") on Skorpios. Even though this was a private chapel which he had built on his private island, he needed the permission of the Greek Orthodox Church. This was refused because burial inside a church was limited to saints. To Ari this was a mere technicality, easily dealt with. The coffin would be buried right next to the outside wall of the church, and after the ceremony was over and the clergymen had departed, he would simply extend the chapel to include the coffin.

On that cold and overcast Saturday, six pallbearers carried Alexander's casket. All were crew members of the yacht *Christina* who had been his close friends. Most of them were sobbing as they made their way into the little chapel. Ari, supported by Jackie and Christina, barely made it through the service without collapsing. Fiona, a friend propping up each arm, stood apart from the family and said her final goodbye to her young lover.

After Alexander was buried, Ari tried to immerse himself in the details of his far-flung business empire, but had difficulty concentrating on anything other than the loss of his son.

Jackie decided that the best tonic was a long cruise on the *Christina*. To liven it up, she persuaded Pierre Salinger, President Kennedy's former press secretary, to come along. Pierre, who never ran out of interesting conversation, seemed just the right man to bring Ari out of his funk.

Chapter Ten

Ari's Rule and the Greek Colonels' Junta

BEFORE DEPARTING ON THE CRUISE WHICH JACKIE HOPED would rejuvenate him, Ari tied up a few loose ends left in the wake of the Piaggio crash. He was aware that the plane's overhaul at the Olympic Airways maintenance base had been completed just before the fatal flight, and that the Greek police who had the duty of investigating the accident had delegated the technical work to the Greek Air Force, which alone had the required facilities and personnel. Olympic officials began to receive feedback from the Air Force investigators which indicated that there might have been something radically wrong with the plane itself when it came out of overhaul, and they passed this along to Ari, noting that the aborted McCusker checkout had been the first flight after the overhaul.

This disquieting information set off alarm bells in Ari's mind, because he was well aware that he had pressured the reluctant

Alexander to push the Piaggio through the complicated overhaul in time for its last cruise on the *Christina* and that if the plane itself had malfunctioned, the blame might be attributed to Olympic Airways, i.e., to Ari himself.

Ari's instinctive reaction was to fall back on his Rule: there was no right or wrong, and because of his ability to manipulate the corrupt government of the Greek Colonels, it was possible for him to avoid the blame by placing it on the shoulders of the American pilot Don McCusker, who was being treated for his injuries at the Kat Hospital in the Athens suburb of Kifissia. He put Johnny Meyer to work spreading the rumor that McCusker was a C.I.A. agent assigned to murder Alex as a way of striking a blow at Ari, a long-time foe of the C.I.A. (Fiona Thyssen vividly recalls that when she met Ari in Athens the day after the crash, the first thing he said to her was, "I think Alexander was murdered. This was sabotage!") Ari knew that Alexander had taped many of their phone conversations, some of which included discussions of the Piaggio, so he ordered Johnny Meyer to find and destroy all those tapes. He followed up by engineering a secret court order which prohibited McCusker from leaving the country until the Greek government's accident investigation was completed. And he took the necessary steps to keep the results of that investigation secret in case it did not put the blame where he wanted it: on Don McCusker.

The day after the accident, Don's wife Helena had flown over from Ohio to be with him, leaving their six school-age children in the care of her parents. When she arrived in Athens with Don's sister, Pat Coffield, she was determined to make certain that Don was receiving adequate medical care, hoping to bring him back to Ohio in a week or two to complete his recovery in an American hospital. She had no idea she was walking into a classic Onassis power play in which she and her husband would become hostages to Ari's Rule.

The Greek physician in charge of intensive care at the Kat Hospital told Helena that Don had suffered fractures of the neck vertebrae, jaw, and pelvis; broken ribs; a severe concussion; and many bruises, but that he was expected to make a full recovery. Don was coherent as he told Helena and Pat how happy he was to see them. They had difficulty understanding him because his fractured jaw restricted his ability to open his mouth. He grasped Helena's hand, and she was reassured by the strength of his grip. He said, "My face must look terrible. I don't know what happened or who was with me in the plane." They told him not to worry about that but just to concentrate on getting well.

On the third day after the crash, Helena visited Don for about twenty minutes and found him very frustrated. He said he would like to get to an American hospital, but was told he couldn't be moved yet. When Helena asked him casually what he remembered, he replied that he had no recollection of getting into the airplane or anything that happened after that. "I heard that Alexander Onassis died," he said. "What did he die from?" Helena replied that it was from head injuries. "Too bad," said Don. "It's a shame. He seemed like such a nice kid."

When Helena and Pat returned to their hotel, they bought the two English-language newspapers, the *Athens Daily Post* and the *Athens News*. They were troubled by the accounts of the previous day's press conference, in which Onassis appeared to be blaming Don for the crash.

The next morning Helena's brother, Herbert A. Mehlhorn, phoned her from his office in Massachusetts. He tried to avoid frightening Helena, but told her he had read disturbing reports in the Boston newspapers about Onassis blaming Don. He suggested that Helena get a Greek lawyer to protect Don, and gave her some advice on how to go about it. She was grateful for Herb's concern and respected his advice, but decided that she had her hands full at the moment trying to deal with the aftermath of Don's injuries. She told Herb that a government investigation was under way, and that surely Mac McGregor (the third man aboard the Piaggio) would recall what happened and clear Don of blame. Herb wasn't so confident of this and repeated the advice to get the best available lawyer as quickly as possible.

Don received a visit from Captain Paul Ioannidis, the Director General of Olympic Airways, whom the hospital personnel treated as a celebrity. He impressed Helena as being genuinely concerned about comforting Don and expediting his recovery. At the hotel that evening, Helena found a dozen red roses and a lovely box of candy, with a card from Captain Ioannidis on which he had written, "With sincere wishes for a speedy recovery to your husband." To the beleaguered Helena it was like finding an oasis in the desert.

On the first Sunday afternoon after the crash, Helena and Pat met with Mac McGregor and his wife Peggy in Mac's Red Cross Hospital room. Mac was very sore from bruises but was making a good recovery. He said that Alexander had planned to have Don fly the Piaggio just long enough to show that he was able to handle it. Since Alexander was only available on the Monday, and Mac's license had lapsed due to a medical problem, the plan was for Alexander to lease the plane to Don after the checkout flight. Then Mac could legally fly as Don's passenger, while he talked Don through several more days of familiarization with the plane and the Onassis regimen so that Don would be ready to take over as the Piaggio pilot in time for the *Christina's* February cruise.

Mac said that the takeoff had been normal, but as soon as they were airborne the right wing dipped. As the dipping to the right quickly became more extreme, Mac remembered yelling, "We're going to crash!" He did not say who was at the controls, and Helena did not ask. She regarded this meeting with the McGregors as an icebreaker, and did not want to presume upon their hospitality to press her own concerns about Onassis's attempt to blame Don.

During the second week, Helena found that Don's condition had regressed. On Friday February 2, Don was still in and out of the picture mentally. He thought he was in a railroad car, then a garage, which he said was very noisy. That day Athens police officers came to question Don. He was unable to recollect anything about the accident. The police officers were cordial and thanked Don for his assistance. They told Helena that they had Don's jacket and his passport. It did not occur to Helena that they were holding the passport because Ari had obtained a secret order detaining Don in Greece indefinitely.

On Thursday February 8 the surgeons wired Don's jaws shut to promote proper healing, which required him to take his meals through a straw for 30 days. They treated his neck vertebrae and pelvis fractures by putting him in traction for 30 days.

After a long day at the hospital, Helena found a message at the hotel from Katherine Barry, a staff employee of the American Embassy, suggesting that Helena should get a lawyer. Then came a call from John Rigos, UPI's Athens correspondent. He said that he heard Don was to be charged with involuntary manslaughter and that the charges would appear in the morning paper. This shocking news rendered Helena almost speechless. Rigos said he would call her again the next day after he learned how the Greek newspapers were treating the charges.

The next morning, February 13, Helena read in the *Athens News*, under the headline ONASSIS PILOT:

> *Pilot Donald McCusker, 49, of Ohio, was remanded in custody yesterday pending his trial for manslaughter through negligence.*
>
> *McCusker was piloting the plane which crashed on takeoff, killing Alexandros Onassis.*

Later John Rigos told Helena that the picture was not as bleak as it appeared from the news articles. Don was not actually to be taken into custody at that point. The Greek criminal procedure was to publish the charges as a preliminary step, in order to open a formal court investigation which would lead to a decision on whether or not to prosecute. Rigos echoed the advice that Helena was receiving from everyone: you're up against Aristotle Onassis, so get a lawyer *now*.

Apart from her preoccupation with Don's health and her limited experience with lawyers, Helena was inhibited from hiring a lawyer by the family's meager finances. Don had served as a Navy fighter pilot during World War II, and then worked as a test pilot for major aircraft manufacturers like Martin Marietta and North American Rockwell. Before defense cutbacks forced him and other test pilots to be laid off in 1971, Don was earning more than $30,000 per year, today's equivalent of a six-figure income. In 1972 he tried his hand at real estate sales, but the market for homes in the suburbs of Columbus, Ohio, was barely strong enough to provide a living for a natural-born salesman, which Don was not. His entire income for 1972 was barely $2,000, a precarious situation for the father of six children ranging in age from six to sixteen.

Helena sent a cable to her brother Herb requesting him to wire her $1,000 which she might need to hire a lawyer. Then at the hospital she asked the attending physician whether she should tell Don about the charges and the need to hire a lawyer. The doctor advised against it, because it might depress Don severely.

That evening Rob Nelson, Don's oldest friend, phoned Helena from Maine. He had been in close touch with Helena by phone ever since the accident, and now that he had read about the manslaughter charges in the American newspapers, he felt he should fly over and help Don and Helena cope with this crisis. He told Helena that he would be there by the weekend, prepared to help her find a good lawyer and to provide financial assistance if needed. This gave Helena's flagging energy and spirit a huge lift, and enabled Don's sister Pat to return to her family in Pennsylvania.

Rob Nelson's plane landed at Athens on the evening of February 17, and he made straight for the hospital. The sight of good old Robbie instantly boosted the morale of both McCuskers. He had been Don McCusker's closest friend since both were five-year-old boys in South Portland, Maine. Knowing that the McCuskers could not cope with the financial drains of their predicament, he raised a fund which reached over $20,000 by the time he flew to Athens, contributing $5,000 himself even though that sum was equal to a large chunk of the profits of his modest Portland florist shop in a good year. As he prepared to meet Helena and Don in Athens, he knew that apart from lending moral support, his main job was to help Helena to get the best Greek lawyer they could find, one who could fight off the manslaughter charges and leave Don free to return to Ohio once he was well enough to leave the hospital.

Rob had steeled himself for his first glimpse of Don, and was pleasantly surprised that he didn't look too bad considering what he had been through. Rob's immediate concern was the cleanliness of the hospital. Despite the assurances of all the doctors that this was the best hospital in Greece, Rob's experience as a volunteer worker in a Maine hospital (where his wife Rowe was chief physical therapist) told him that this was not what he would call a clean hospital.

Helena told Rob that the job of helping Don cope with the aftermath of his injuries was consuming all her time and strength, and she did not have the energy or experience to find a suitable lawyer. Rob had asked his own lawyer in Maine whether it would make sense to retain an American lawyer. He was told that only a Greek lawyer could help Don at that point. So Rob's primary mission was clear: identify a suitable Greek lawyer; take Helena to meet the lawyer; help her to decide whether to hire the lawyer; and arrange to pay the lawyer's fees from the fund he had raised.

Rob began by meeting with Charles S. ("Stu") Kennedy Jr., Chief of the Consular Section at the heavily guarded American Embassy in Athens. By that time Rob had learned that the ambassador and his staff dealt with matters of official U.S. government business and policy, while the consular officers handled problems of American citizens visiting or doing business in the foreign country. Stu Kennedy was the man to speak to, and he told Rob that Don was in a very sticky situation. Don was in the process of being charged with manslaughter, and his passport was being held by the Greek police, so that he could not leave the country. "All that the United States government can do for Mr. McCusker officially at this point is to make certain he is afforded proper legal protection under the Greek system of justice," said Kennedy.

Rob asked, "What about all the aid we gave to Greece under the Marshall Plan? On the way over here I saw a beautiful statue of Harry Truman, and I heard he was made an honorary citizen of Greece for helping so much in their time of need. Doesn't that give you some clout in helping an innocent American citizen out of a legal trap here?"

"I'm afraid not, Mr. Nelson. The Greeks have rather short memories when it comes to the help we gave them in recovering from the German occupation and the effects of their own civil war in the 1940s."

"Aren't we still subsidizing them today?"

"Yes, we are furnishing very substantial military and economic assistance, but we're accused of doing that solely to use Greece as a strategic military base in the Cold War against the Soviets. There are lots of conflicting political viewpoints in this country, and we're not all that popular here right now. We even have serious security problems. One of our Navy jeeps was firebombed, and two people were killed by a bomb planted in the embassy parking lot. We also found an incendiary device in one of the embassy bathrooms!"

Kennedy told Rob that the State Department in Washington had forwarded to the embassy a cluster of queries from senators and congressmen, seeking assurances that the government would do everything possible to get the manslaughter charges dropped and enable Don to rejoin his family in Ohio. Kennedy said that he and the ambassador, Henry J. Tasca, had answered these queries personally, and that both of them were dedicated to doing everything possible to get Don out of this mess. Rob was impressed with Kennedy's grasp of the case, but he was frustrated by the vague promises of "doing everything possible." Rob's hardheaded New England logic told him that this was meaningless in view of Kennedy's flat statement that Don was really at the mercy of the Greek judicial system, which obviously could be manipulated by that staunch friend of the Greek military dictatorship, Aristotle Onassis.

The only tangible help that Rob got from his meeting with Stu Kennedy was a list of five Greek lawyers to whom the embassy had directed other Americans with local legal problems in the past. Rob started phoning them from the embassy. On the first call, after describing Don McCusker's predicament, he was put on hold by the secretary, who came back a few minutes later to tell Rob that the lawyer regretted he could not handle the case. The same thing happened on the next two calls, and that was enough to convince Rob that he was wasting his time by blindly searching for a Greek lawyer who would dare to challenge the Onassis power. A World War II Navy veteran himself, Rob asked Stu Kennedy for the address of the U.S. Naval Headquarters. Surely the Navy would not give one of its wartime fliers the runaround.

At the Navy's office in a nearby high-rise building, Rob was quickly ushered into the office of a Lieutenant Wylie. Rob was encouraged when Wylie showed some familiarity with the case. He told Wylie of his lack of progress through the embassy, and asked whether the Navy might have its own staff lawyer who could help Don. Wylie took some notes and then asked Rob to wait while he consulted his superiors.

Lieutenant Wylie returned to the room after thirty minutes. With some embarrassment he said, "I'm very sorry, Mr. Nelson, but there is nothing we can do to help Mr. McCusker at this time."

"You mean to say you can't lift a finger to help a fellow Naval officer get a lawyer to fight these outrageous charges?"

"I only mean to say that the Navy is not permitted to get involved in the Greek court system over an accident that did not involve a Naval aircraft," replied Lieutenant Wylie. He went on to explain that the Navy's position in Greece was precarious, since they were right in the middle of trying to implement "homeporting" of significant units of the 6th Fleet in Greece—using Greece as the home port for American aircraft carriers and missile ships involved in NATO defense deployment. Since some of these ships carried nuclear weapons, they automatically made Greece a target for Soviet first-strike nuclear missiles the moment the Cold War turned hot. There was fierce opposition to this homeporting policy among nearly all sectors of Greek opinion, and so the more than ten thousand U.S. Naval personnel in Greece were unwelcome guests who felt like they were walking on eggs.

Rob Nelson shuddered at the prospect of having to report to Helena that he was batting zero in the lawyer department. Helena had told Rob that the Roman Catholic Bishop of Athens had come to the hospital to comfort her and had offered to help in any way he could. Surely the diocese had used local lawyers who could be trusted to do their best for Don? Rob thought it was a long shot, but given the disastrous results of his visits to the embassy and to Navy headquarters, it was certainly worth a try. He went to the office of the Roman Catholic Diocese, where he was given the names of the brothers Nicholas and George Foundedakis, who were the lawyers for the diocese. Nicholas agreed to meet with Helena and Rob that evening, but suggested that the meeting be at his home instead of at the law office. Rob wasn't sure whether the home meeting was simply an evening convenience or was based on the lawyer's desire to avoid public notice that he was willing to consider representing the pilot blamed for the death of Aristotle Onassis's son.

Nicholas Foundedakis turned out to be the first good news of the day. His English was passable and he appeared to have a good grasp of the law and procedure in Greek manslaughter cases. Most importantly, he showed no hesitancy in taking on Don's defense. He said he would have to check with the magistrate in charge of the case, but expressed the opinion that what the press called a charge of manslaughter was probably not an official indictment. He thought it more likely that it was a preliminary order calling on a magistrate judge to investigate the accident and decide whether formal criminal charges should be filed against Don. He assured them that this was a routine procedure in all fatal accidents that occurred in Greece. He was, of course, fully aware of the Onassis power, but he believed that as Don's lawyer he would get access to the government investigation report, and if it showed that Don was not at fault, he would not be successfully prosecuted. That was a pretty big "if," especially since Onassis had the clout to manipulate the government investigators. But at least it was a ray of hope.

Helena and Rob nodded at each other and decided to retain Nicholas Foundedakis, henceforth to be known simply as "Nick." They were pleased that his initial fee of 30,000 drachmas was less than 1,000 U.S. dollars, but he warned that if Aristotle Onassis persisted in blaming Don, there would be heavier expenses ahead. He said he would get back to Helena and Rob as soon as he was able to speak to the magistrate.

The next day, Nick phoned Helena to confirm that no formal charges had actually been filed against Don. As Nick expected, a magistrate named Papadakis had been ordered to investigate the accident and decide whether any charges should be filed. Nick had arranged a meeting with the magistrate for the following Monday, February 26. He wanted Helena and Rob to attend, and would send a car to pick them up at the hotel.

Helena was encouraged by this morsel of positive news, and now that she had some grasp of the legal procedures, she felt it was time to let Don know what was going on. When he awoke from his morning nap she told him about the magistrate's proceedings and the hiring of lawyer Nick to represent him. Don took the news calmly and seemed happy that Helena and Rob had a favorable impression of lawyer Nick. He trusted their instincts in such matters. Helena felt greatly relieved after disclosing to Don the burden she had been carrying alone. It seemed a little less threatening now that they were facing it together.

The next day, lawyer Nick drove Helena and Rob to his office, where they reviewed the history of how Don came to be aboard the Piaggio. Helena showed Nick a family photograph complete with the six young children. Nick said he would hold on to it for the moment. Then he, Helena, and Rob walked the short distance to Magistrate Papadakis's office. Nick introduced Helena and Rob, and then carried on a conversation with the magistrate in Greek. At one point he showed the family photograph to the magistrate.

As they walked back to Nick's office, he summarized what he had learned: the magistrate expected to complete his investigation in about a month; it would be handled like any other case, and the involvement of Onassis would not make any difference. Nick said he was well satisfied with the magistrate's attitude. He thought it was important to show that Don had a clean record on both character and flying ability. He asked Helena and Rob to get him documents showing that Don had no criminal record and that he was highly regarded both as a professional pilot and a law-abiding citizen.

The next day, it was time for Rob to return to Maine. He was far from an expert on legal affairs, but he believed that he had accomplished his primary goal of finding a competent Greek lawyer who appeared to be willing and able to stand up to Onassis and fight for Don's rights. As he said goodbye to his oldest friends, he still had uneasy feelings about Don's predicament, but he hoped for the best. Whenever he needed a shot of optimism, Rob thought back to his wartime Navy Service.

Rob Nelson had been hard of hearing since birth. At first blush, his assignment to sonar duty would appear to be a typical bureaucratic snafu, since his mission was to detect the underwater sounds made by submarine propellers. But the Navy had discovered that people with Rob's form of hearing disability often had superior pitch discrimination, the vital skill in sonar detection. Whenever his destroyer shipmates determined they were in submarine-endangered waters, they would send for "the deaf guy," Rob Nelson, to put on the sonar earphones. Rob would turn up the volume to the point where the next man on duty nearly had his ears blown out, but somehow Rob would sense the submarines that others had missed.

This time he hoped he had sensed a way through the legal minefield that Aristotle Onassis had sown in Don's path.

———————————

Near the end of Don's first month of hospitalization, one of the attending doctors beckoned Helena into the hospital corridor and handed her a blue envelope bearing a Swiss postmark. He told her that he had been instructed not to give her the letter even though it was addressed to "Mr. Donald McCuskie." He said that if she ever told anyone that he had given her the letter, he would deny it. Then he left her to read the letter.

As she opened the envelope, Helena formed the impression that it had been opened and then resealed by someone else. The handwritten six-page letter was from Fiona Thyssen, and it was dated January 29, 1973—seven days after the fatal crash, and three weeks prior to the time when the doctor surreptitiously delivered it to her. Tears formed in Helena's eyes as she read Fiona's neat handwriting. The letter said in part:

By the time you read this letter, you will be aware of the final tragedy. It will be an emotional letter, but unless you know the background, my words of comfort will mean nothing to you.

Alexander and I were deeply in love....

Of all the people who were near him at his death, mine was the deepest and most personal love, as apart from being his lover, I was also a mother, friend, companion, and anything else that a forty year old woman would be for a younger man. We had an uncanny awareness and understanding of each other's minds, and it is on this basis that I write to you....

As a passionate pilot himself, he had immense sympathy and understanding of the pressures pilots undergo during flight, and of the possibilities for misjudgment because of unfamiliarity or what ever other reason. He was the most meticulously fair person in the world and would never pass a judgment on anyone until knowing the facts, and even then would not condemn him. He believed that one mistake rarely caused an accident, but rather many small ones....

Finally, whether it was a human or a pilot error, a mechanical failure or what, he is tragically dead, and nothing will make him mine again.

I know he would not wish you to suffer any more than you have done...

I do not write this with casual sympathy, but because I know his mind as no one else did.

You at least have the disagreeable distraction of physical suffering, while I have nothing but an emotional and psychic wound which can never heal. The intensity of the love we had for each other frightened us both, and despite exterior pressures it grew daily. Our last few weeks together have been the happiest of our entire relationship...

Let my understanding of Alexander's thoughts be a comfort to you. He would, under all circumstances, share the responsibility with you.

I send you my sincerest wishes for a successful and speedy recovery, both physical and mental...

Kindest wishes,

Fiona Thyssen

This remarkably thoughtful and well-intentioned letter was comforting to Don and Helena. But as Don reread it in later days, he was appalled by the realization that Fiona had swallowed the Onassis media hype which blamed Don for the crash, even though none of the vital facts had been disclosed by the investigators who held exclusive possession of the Piaggio's wreckage and documentary history. It was repugnant to Don that he should share any blame for the accident in the absence of the investigation reports. But in the reply letter which Helena wrote to Fiona with Don's approval, she thanked Fiona warmly and did not mention responsibility for the crash.

Don and Helena had struggled with the question of whether it was appropriate to write condolence letters to Alexander's parents. They had received conflicting advice from those whom they asked. But the inspiration of Fiona's letter impelled them to write to Ari and Tina. Ari did not reply, but Tina wrote to Helena from her St. Moritz villa:

Thank you for your kind words of sympathy for Alexander. These things are in God's hands so we can only believe and pray.

I saw your husband in the hospital and he was in a coma also. I hope he is all right now.

Yours Sincerely and Sadly,

Tina Niarchos

After Rob Nelson's departure on March 1, Helena and Don were left alone again, but now they had Nick the lawyer to carry on the legal fight. During the first week of March, they heard nothing new from Nick. They spent their time trying to speed Don's recovery. Mac McGregor, the third occupant of the Piaggio, was a frequent visitor at the hospital, with his wife Peggy. Stu Kennedy, the General Counsul at the embassy, also visited, with his wife Ellen.

When Helena arrived in Athens two days after the January 22 crash, she was overwhelmed by the burden of Don's injuries and hospital care. She had no reason then to believe that Don would be charged with a crime or that his passport would be confiscated to prevent his departure from Greece. But these possibilities quickly occurred to Helena's brother, Dr. Herbert A. Mehlhorn, especially after the widely publicized press conference of January 24 at which Onassis began to place blame on Don.

It didn't require a rocket scientist to discern that Don was potentially in big trouble. But, fortunately for Don and Helena, Herb Mehlhorn *was* a rocket scientist. Moreover, as an executive of Raytheon Company's Missile Systems Division he was in everyday contact with government agencies, particularly the Washington establishment. He held sensitive positions in several important missile programs, and he knew how to cut through the bureaucratic red tape and energize the government officials who held the levers of power.

Herb lost no time in pressing the necessary buttons. First he spoke to David Hudson, head of Special Consular Services at the State Department in Washington, who would bear direct responsibility for protecting Don's legal rights. Hudson immediately agreed to do everything possible to protect Don, but Herb knew that to assure effective assistance he would have to get senators and other important Washington figures to pound away at the State Department and make certain that Ambassador Tasca and his Athens embassy staff were constantly kept aware that Washington was watching the case.

Herb's office and home was in Massachusetts, whose senators were the Democrat Ted Kennedy and the Republican Edward Brooke. Both of them agreed to register their official interest in Don's case with the State Department. Ted Kennedy followed through even though he was in an uncomfortable position because Jackie Kennedy was the wife of Aristotle Onassis. Because of that conflict, and also because the Republican Nixon administration was in power, it was decided that Senator Brooke would take the laboring oar. He assured Herb that he would require State to report to him at least once a week on the status of the case, and that his staff would keep Herb up to date on these reports.

Senator Brooke spoke to George T. Churchill, Country Director for Greece (i.e., head of the State Department's "Greek desk"), who sent this diplomatic wire to Ambassador Tasca on January 26, 1973:

SUBJECT: CRASH OF ONASSIS AIRCRAFT
   ON BEHALF OF HIS CONSITUENT HERBERT
MEHLHORN, BROTHER-IN-LAW OF DONALD
MCCUSKER, SENATOR BROOKE REQUESTS
EMBASSY MAINTAIN CLOSE CONTACT WITH
MCCUSKER AND WIFE, REPORTEDLY ALSO IN
ATHENS. SENATOR BROOKE ALSO REQUESTS
EMBASSY FOLLOW INVESTIGATION OF CRASH
CAREFULLY, WITH MCCUSKER'S INTERESTS IN
MIND.

This carefully drafted message was a clear signal to Ambassador Tasca and his staff that a constituent of an important senator was in danger, and that the senator was looking to the ambassador (a Nixon appointee) to prevent the Greek government from mistreating him. Note that the subject of the message was "CRASH OF ONASSIS AIRCRAFT" even though the Piaggio was owned and operated by Olympic, not Onassis. This mention of Onassis reflected the approach that Herb Mehlhorn took in his Washington campaign. As he summarized it in a letter he wrote to Helena on January 29, even before the specter of manslaughter charges appeared:

The point I made with these senators is that you and Don are powerless to establish the facts, conceivably at the mercy of adversaries who find great favor in Greece, and with little support from home. I have said firmly that I want my government to lend you all possible support whether it is usual or not. I think you will get it.

At no time did any official of the State Department, either in Washington or in Greece, express any doubt that Aristotle Onassis was the adversary "who found great favor in Greece." In fact, as we shall see, all the diplomats, military attachés, and lawyers who were familiar with the case, as well as the highest officials of Olympic Airways, were fully aware that Ari was using his influence with the corrupt Greek government to publicly blame Don, to prosecute him, and detain him in Greece indefinitely.

Herb Mehlhorn resolved to keep this Washington pressure focused relentlessly on the Athens embassy. His x-ray vision of the governmental hierarchy told him that as long as Senator Brooke's staff required a weekly report from George Churchill at the Greek desk, Churchill in turn would maintain the pressure on the

Athens embassy to convince the Greek authorities that the United States would not accept the trashing of Don McCusker's legal rights by Onassis. To Herb, the key factors were accountability to Washington and staying power to enforce that accountability. He was satisfied that he could achieve this so long as Senator Brooke continued to receive weekly reports from George Churchill.

Among those who registered their official interest and concern with the State Department were Senator Hugh Scott of Pennsylvania, where Don's sister Pat resided; Senator Robert Taft Jr. and Representative Samuel L. Devine of Ohio, where Helena and Don lived; and Representative Peter Kyros of Maine, who was contacted by Herb and Helena's father, Herbert E. Mehlhorn, a lifelong resident of Maine.

Don and Helena were cheered when they received a package from Helena's father containing more than a dozen glowing testimonials to Don's flying ability, including two from famous pilots with whom Don had flown: the test pilot Scott Crossfield, first to fly at Mach 2 (twice the speed of sound), and the astronaut Jack Swigert, who piloted the Apollo 13 command module safely back to earth after a catastrophic inflight explosion. These letters were turned over to lawyer Nick for filing with the investigating magistrate.

If Magistrate Papadakis had read these letters, he would have learned that Don McCusker's flying career was a page out of the All-American saga that Tom Wolfe depicted so skillfully in his book *The Right Stuff.* Don did not attempt to become an astronaut because the initial program was limited to military pilots. By the time it was opened to civilians, he was over the age limit. But he graduated from the Navy Test Pilot School at Patuxent River, Maryland, where John Glenn and many of the other early astronauts also trained. And he flew side by side with the legendary pioneer test pilots like Chuck Yeager at Edwards Air Force Base in the California desert. Indeed, he went a step beyond *The Right Stuff* by testing experimental aircraft that were being developed for use by astronauts in the space program.

In 1964, after the Martin aircraft were phased out of production, Don joined North American Rockwell at Edwards Air Force Base. He was assigned to test the Rogallo Wing, a newly designed para-glider recovery system for space vehicles. Due to controllability problems, the previous test pilot had suffered injuries which knocked him out of the program. Flying a Gemini-type spacecraft, Don and his fellow test pilot Jack Swigert were charged with demonstrating "pilot capability to land the para-glider in a pre-designated area and to make navigational fixes during spacecraft recovery." Struggling to control a spacecraft that had disabled his predecessor, Don made a hard landing in the targeted area of the dry lakebed and was hospitalized with fractured back vertebrae. He quickly checked himself out of the hospital and returned to complete the test program in a heavy back brace, piloting eight of the thirteen test flights. For this feat, Don and Jack Swigert were jointly awarded the 1966 Octave Chanute Award by the American Institute of Aeronautics and Astronautics. The citation read:

> *For outstanding contributions and accomplishments to the aerospace objectives through demonstration of the Rogallo Wing as a feasible concept to withstand the rigors of space travel, re-entry and deployment, and capable of achieving a safe and reliable land landing system for returning space vehicles and astronauts.*

All in all, Don's flying records showed more than eight thousand hours of piloting virtually every type of aircraft, without any accidents other than the hard landing of the experimental space-craft during the trial-and-error process of developing a safe land-ing technique for the astronauts.

On March 17, Don was cleared to leave the hospital. Peggy and Mac McGregor picked them up at the hospital and drove them to the hotel, where they held a dual celebration: St. Patrick's Day and deliverance from the Kat Hospital. After nearly two months in Greece, it was time for Helena to book her return flight to Ohio, which she set for March 30.

On March 26 Don and Helena met with U.S. Air Force Colonel Jim French, the air attaché at the American embassy. He told them that he had spoken to Greek Air Force officers who were involved in the Piaggio investigation but had not been able to learn anything about it. He regarded this as very unusual since he had a good working rapport with those officers. They were being exceptionally secretive, and every time he raised the ques-tion they changed the subject. There was no doubt in his mind that they were clamming up because of the Onassis influence.

On March 28, Don and Helena had their first meeting with Tryfon J. Koutalidis, director of Olympic Airways' legal depart-ment, at the airline's headquarters. Koutalidis explained that since Don was not an Olympic employee, he had been listed as a pas-senger and was issued a ticket which provided for payment of up to $18,000 (in U.S. dollars) as compensation for injuries and expenses. He felt certain that the entire $18,000 would be paid to Don by the insurance company, and that if this did not cover all the expenses, he was sure that Olympic Airways would make up the difference. He said that this decision to pay the additional expenses would be up to Paul Ioannidis, Director General of Olympic, who had visited Don and Helena frequently and had pledged his personal support to Don. They left this meeting with positive feelings about compensation. They did not permit themselves to speculate about whether Aristotle Onassis would revoke the promises made by Olympic lawyer Koutalidis and the courtly fellow pilot, Captain Ioannidis.

Helena said her grateful goodbyes to all those who had helped her and Don in their time of need, especially the McGregors and Father Paul Buhayiar, the local Roman Catholic parish priest who had worked tirelessly to comfort them. On March 30, Don rode out to the airport with her in an Olympic car, and he masked the pain as they embraced like the carefree Maine college kids who had met on a blind date more than twenty years earlier.

On his own in Athens, Don devoted his full time to trying to clear his name and get home to his family. Unknown to him, he had two strong allies in Olympic Airways' top management: Chairman Yanni Georgakis and Director General Paul Ioannidis.

Professor Yanni Georgakis, retired from his post as chairman of Criminal Law and Sociology at the University of Athens, was a witty intellectual whose company Ari enjoyed immensely, both in business meetings and in long drinking bouts at *bouzoukias* (Greek nightclubs). Their relationship went far beyond the business of Olympic Airways, where Ari had installed Yanni as chairman. They debated philosophy and religion regularly, and Ari frequently sought Yanni's advice on personal matters, including the marriage to Jackie Kennedy, Alexander's school problems, and the religious ceremonies marking Alexander's death. It was generally agreed that Ari respected Yanni above all his other advisors and friends.

Captain Paul Ioannidis was a sort of Greek Eddie Rickenbacker—a war-hero Greek Air Force pilot who became a leading airline executive when Ari took over Olympic Airways. Ioannidis had served as King Paul's personal pilot, and he flew the whole royal family to exile in Rome when the Colonels took over Greece in 1967. Ari had great respect for Paul's integrity and his knowledge of aviation.

Both Georgakis and Ioannidis learned soon after the Piaggio crash that the investigators had found serious problems with the overhaul conducted at Olympic's maintenance base, and that the government report would probably blame Olympic and exonerate Don McCusker. Both of them tried to get this message across to Ari, but they found that Ari had a closed mind on the subject. Ari *knew* that McCusker was to blame, and he did not wish to hear any evidence to the contrary.

It is impossible to learn how strongly Georgakis and Ioannidis felt about the injustice of blaming, detaining, and prosecuting McCusker. It was to their credit that they even dared to broach the subject to Ari, knowing the measures he was taking to put the blame on McCusker and the C.I.A. It is known that they were deeply concerned about the side effects of Ari's campaign: it was hurting Olympic's public image and its ticket sales. Passengers could hardly be blamed for seeking other means of travel when the owner was publicly trumpeting that Olympic's safety was being undermined by the C.I.A. Ari was even pushing the prosecutors to indict half a dozen Olympic mechanics along with McCusker. Moreover, Ari's offer of a $1 million reward for evidence of the McCusker-C.I.A. conspiracy was producing a steady stream of crackpot informants, and Ari insisted that all of their hare-brained theories be investigated by Olympic's hard-pressed staff. But despite the sympathy of Georgakis and Ioannidis for McCusker's plight, they were not able to help him clear his name or escape his detention.

Don sought help from other sympathetic people at the U.S. Embassy and lawyer Nick, but they all told him that nothing could be accomplished until the Greek Air Force report was available. The latest estimate was that it would be completed around the middle of April. While waiting impatiently for it, he ran into another problem: he began to feel nauseous and weak in the knees. On April 9, he went back to the Kat Hospital for a checkup. The doctors there found he had contracted hepatitis, which others told him was probably caused by a blood transfusion or "something not clean at the Kat Hospital." He was sent to the General Clinic of Athens, where his recovery from hepatitis would require confinement for the next six weeks.

Chapter Eleven

Suppressing the Greek Air Force Report

LIEUTENANT A.P.D. KAKOULI OF THE GREEK POLICE WAS ordered to determine the cause of the Piaggio accident, but neither the police nor the Civil Aviation Authority had the facilities or personnel to conduct a full-scale technical investigation. Only the Greek Air Force had this capability. Therefore, Lt. Kakouli appointed a five-member commission to conduct the technical investigation and compile a report. Four of the commission members were Greek Air Force officers and the fifth was a sergeant-major. For these reasons, the investigating commission's report became known as the Greek Air Force Report. It begins with the listing of the names and ranks of the commission members, who officially opened the investigation on January 25, 1973, three days after the accident. (The full text of the report, which has never been published before, is translated in the Appendix.)

In Section III, *Sequence of Events,* the report laid out the basic facts that were available without detailed investigation. In paragraph #1, it noted that Alexander Onassis was scheduled as the pilot for the flight, which was to make a number of water landings and takeoffs in the area of Poros Isle before returning to the airport. The pilot (Alexander) submitted the flight schedule which listed two foreigners, McGregor and McCusker, as passengers (#2). Alexander, "the pilot in command," sat in the right seat, with Don McCusker in the left seat, and Mac McGregor in a rear passenger seat (#3). Thus the report found that Alexander was in command of the Piaggio, with Don McCusker legally and factually in the position of a passenger who was under the direction and control of Alexander, even when Don was actually doing the flying.

Immediately after the plane left the ground, it suddenly turned to the right, causing the right wing to strike the runway surface, and the plane crashed between the runway and the taxiway at 15:20 (3:20 P.M.) Athens time (#5).

In Section IV, *Investigation,* the report laid out the details of the commission's factual findings in 46 numbered paragraphs.

In paragraph #15 of *Investigation,* it noted that the lever controlling the wing flaps was in the "up" position, as were the wing flaps themselves, whereas they should have been extended in the "down" position for takeoff. The reason for this discrepancy was explained later in the report, as we shall see.

The conversations between Alexander and the control tower were taped pursuant to routine procedure, and the tapes enabled the commission to verify that Alexander was the one handling the radio contacts throughout the flight (#22).

Then came the first of several bombshells. In paragraph 26c, the commission reported:

The aileron control system and all its parts were in good con-
dition. But the tests showed that its last position was the
opposite of the correct one. The commission and the specialized
technicians made this observation; they came to the conclusion
that the reason for this was the fact that the control cables were
connected wrongly in a reverse manner.

An aileron is a small hinged panel at the trailing edge of each
wing, which moves up or down in response to the pilot's movement of controls. The two ailerons enable the pilot to bank the
wings in the direction he wishes to turn the plane—a left bank for
a left turn, a right bank for a right turn. The pilot has a control
wheel that resembles a small automobile steering wheel. To make
a left turn, the pilot would turn the control wheel to the left, also
pushing the left rudder pedal with his left foot to turn the nose to
the left in coordination with the left bank. In response to the pilot
turning the control wheel to the left, the aileron on the left wing
moves upward, and the aileron on the right wing moves down-
ward, which lowers the left wing and puts the plane into a bank
to the left. (*Figure 8* is a diagram of the aileron control system
taken from the Piaggio Maintenance Manual.)

What the commission reported here is that the aileron controls were hooked up in reverse, so that when the pilot turned the
control wheel to the left, the ailerons would actually turn the plane
the opposite way, to the right! This was tantamount to rigging an
auto's steering wheel so that when the driver turned it to the left,
the car would turn to the right. I recall having a toy auto in my
childhood which worked that way, but in the adult world it is a
prescription for disaster.

Without further comment at this point, the commission
leaves the reader in suspense as to how this reversal of controls
occurred, and what role it played in the crash. The report returned

to routine recitals of the purpose and conduct of the flight, noting that Alexander held a "B" class (commercial) pilot's license and was authorized to "examine pilots to qualify them to fly" the Piaggio (#28a). Based on the statement of Mac McGregor, all the pre-flight checks were done by Alexander while he was simultaneously explaining these procedures to Don McCusker (#31a) who taxied the plane from the parking area to the beginning of the runway (#31b) where the final runup and testing of the engines was performed by Alexander (#31c).

Then the report moved to the airworthiness history of the Piaggio during the months when it was being overhauled in the Olympic Airways shop at the Athens Airport. A Certificate of Airworthiness ("C of A") is good for one year, and without it no plane can be operated legally. The previous C of A had expired on November 29, 1972, while the Piaggio was in the Olympic shop for overhaul (#35). The Piaggio had been flown for a total of 1081 hours since new (#36). On November 15, 1972, Olympic's mechanics removed the ailerons and the aileron control systems "since they had exceeded the estimated life period" of five years (#38b). Ten days later, on November 25, 1972, new ailerons and aileron control systems were installed (#38c).

On November 29, Olympic applied to the Civil Aviation Authority (C.A.A.) for renewal of the C of A, representing that the Piaggio was "fit for safe flight under the responsibility of Olympic Airways" (#39). The C.A.A. notified Olympic that it had appointed two of its staff aeronautical engineers as airworthiness inspectors to process the application for renewal of the C of A (#40). Then on December 4, Olympic applied for a special license to conduct the test flight required for renewal of the C of A (#41). The C.A.A. approved the special license for the required test flight on December 14 (#42).

On January 18, 1973, one of the C.A.A. engineers who had been appointed as airworthiness inspector submitted a written inspection report which certified that the Piaggio was "fit for flight," and on the basis of his report, the C of A was renewed on January 18 for one year (#43). Then came the second bombshell:

44. Please note here that the test flight requested by Olympic Airways was not carried out.

Thus the commission found that Olympic created the paperwork for renewing the Certificate of Airworthiness, and thereby represented to the Civil Aviation Authority that the plane had been inspected and test-flown and was once again airworthy, but Olympic never actually made the detailed inspection and test flight required to renew the certificate. This meant that the fatal flight of January 22 with Alexander, Don, and Mac aboard became the "test flight," since it was the first flight after replacement of the aileron controls and the other overhaul work. Nevertheless, despite the omission of these crucial steps, the Certificate of Airworthiness was renewed for a full year.

The report did not delve into details of how such mind-boggling events as reversal of aileron controls and C of A renewal without the required test flight got by the Olympic and government inspectors without being detected. It went on to Section V, *Analysis,* where in 27 numbered paragraphs the Greek Air Force officers applied their aviation expertise to the factual findings they had made.

The report noted that the wind velocity was 8 knots (nautical miles per hour, equal to 9.2 statute miles per hour) from 240 degrees, which meant it was blowing from the left side of the Piaggio and would therefore cause the plane to drift to the right (paragraph #9 of *Analysis*). Mac McGregor's statement confirmed that the takeoff was executed by Don McCusker, "sitting in the left seat, under the supervision of Alexander Onassis" (#12).

The report then described the takeoff, the Piaggio becoming airborne at the normal liftoff speed of 100 miles per hour; the banking to the right, which caused the right-hand wing tip float to contact the runway; and the increasing right bank, which carried the plane off to the right of the runway (#13). It then explained why the pilot (Don McCusker at this point) would probably have retracted the wing flaps: the plane's response to his control movements would cause him to presume "that the continuous and intense bank to the right was due to a disparate position of the flaps" (#14). By this they meant that it was reasonable for Don to assume that his inability to pull the right wing out of its bank was caused by uneven extension of the left and right wing flaps, which are designed to extend evenly on both sides but sometimes do not, resulting in impairment of the pilot's ability to control the direction of flight. The remedy for uneven extension of the wing flaps was to retract them.

Then the commission explained exactly how the reversed aileron controls caused the plane to crash, noting that "the functioning of the ailerons was the opposite of the correct function, due to the reverse connection of the aileron control cables" (#18) which explains the Piaggio's continuous right turn after takeoff (#19). With the wind coming from the pilot's left and blowing the plane to the right, the pilot's efforts to turn it back to the left turned it the wrong way, "even further to the right," thus causing the crash to the right of the runway (#22). As the bank to the right increased, the pilot's instinctive reaction would be to turn the control wheel all the way to the left, thereby (unintentionally) making it impossible to maintain control (#23).

Thus we see that the reversed rigging of the aileron controls turned the Piaggio into a deathtrap. It was as if someone had assembled a rifle so that the bullets fired backwards into the head of the shooter.

The commission returned briefly to Olympic's atrocious maintenance and overhaul performance, stating that they considered it appropriate "to note the quality of the maintenance work carried out by the personnel of Olympic Airways" (#20). After reciting the bungling of the aileron control replacement and creation of the false paperwork which led to renewal of the C of A without the required inspections and test flight, the commission, in a masterpiece of understatement, found that "in the execution of maintenance on the aircraft in question, the necessary attention and care due to such work was not duly paid" (#20).

The report noted that an Air France Boeing 727 had taken off from the same runway about two minutes ahead of the Piaggio, measuring the time gap with the assistance of the control tower tape recordings (#10). There have been cases in which pilots of light planes have lost control by flying into the "wake turbulence" created by the preceding takeoff of a heavier plane, but the commission ruled out that possibility, noting that wake turbulence only comes into play from the point at which the heavier plane leaves the ground. Since the Boeing 727 used much of the runway before lifting off, the Piaggio never reached the point on the runway where it could possibly have been affected by wake turbulence (#24).

The commission then considered pilot error, normally the favorite cause of aircraft accident investigators:

> 27. The commission believes it is its obligation at this point to refer to the actions of the pilot of the aircraft in the takeoff phase. The actions taken by him were the appropriate and required actions assuming that the ailerons were properly connected, and not connected in reverse as was the case here. However, as the fact of the reverse connection of the ailerons

was not known to the pilot, and because the aircraft was fly-
ing at low ground speed in the takeoff phase, it was not possi-
ble for him to react otherwise.

The term "pilot of the aircraft in the takeoff phase" unmistak-
ably refers to Don McCusker, who was piloting the Piaggio at the
time of the actual takeoff, and distinguishes him from the pilot in
command/checkout pilot, Alexander. This finding cleared Don
completely of any fault or responsibility.

The report closed with Section VI, *Conclusions*:

1. The accident was not the result of poor technique or mistake
of the pilot of the aircraft at the time of the accident.

2. The main cause of the accident was the mistakes of the
maintenance personnel of Olympic Airways which consisted of:
   a) The reversed connection of the ailerons during the work
     for the replacement of the controls of the aircraft, and
   b) The inadequate inspection by the inspector of Olympic
     Airways of the work which had been carried out on the
     aircraft.

3. Contributory causes of the accident are believed to be the
following:
   a) The faulty operational check of the aircraft by the author-
     ized official of the Civil Aeronautics Authority for the
     renewal of the Certificate of Airworthiness.
   b) The omission by the pilot to use the checklist and as a result
     the omission by the pilot to carry out the required check of
     the ailerons before takeoff, which resulted in the failure to
     notice the reverse connection and operation of the ailerons.

The last contributory cause (omission by the pilot to use the checklist and to check the ailerons before takeoff) refers to Alexander, who was the pilot in command and was held to be responsible for the pre-takeoff checks. Therefore, even this very limited criticism of pilot performance did not relate to Don McCusker.

The Piaggio, like other small planes, did not carry any "black boxes" which could help investigators to determine the cause. The investigating commission of Greek Air Force officers appointed by the police had sole access to the wreckage, the documentary evidence, and the witnesses. Therefore, their report was the definitive conclusion on the cause.

Considering that the commission consisted of military officers who were serving a military dictatorship government; that Aristotle Onassis had strong influence with that corrupt government; and that Olympic Airways, owned by Onassis, had a state-granted monopoly of air transportation, the report was a remarkably forthright document. In no uncertain terms, it completely cleared Don McCusker, who had been publicly branded as the culprit by Onassis, and it laid heavy blame on Olympic itself; on the Greek government inspectors who approved a deathtrap as airworthy; and to a lesser extent on Alexander Onasssis.

A report of this kind is of great value to the aviation community, for it furnishes the basis for avoiding similar accidents in the future. Without such publication, a cloud hangs over the type of aircraft and equipment involved: was there some manufacturing or design defect that might cause others to be injured or killed? Normally such reports are distributed to the media and are filed with aviation safety organizations. But this one was never published or distributed until now. While Ari was not able to write the report the way he wanted it to read, he did get it suppressed so that he could continue to blame, detain, and prosecute Don McCusker for the death of his son.

Neither Don nor lawyer Nick saw the report until June 5, more than six weeks after it was issued. On that day they received it in the original Greek, and a staff interpreter at the U.S. Embassy made a rough translation into English. By that time there was another Greek document awaiting Don's attention, and it too was translated by the embassy staff. It read as follows:

The Prosecutor of the Athens Magistrates,
In the Name of the Law,
To Donald F. McCusker, of Ohio, U.S.A.:

You are charged with the following crimes committed in one act through your negligence on January 22, 1973:

The manslaughter of Alexander Onassis and the infliction of bodily injuries to the Canadian citizen Donald Benjamin McGregor.

You were joint commander with the above Alexander Onassis and you occupied the left forward seat in aircraft SX-BDC Piaggio 136 of Olympic Airways. In that capacity you undertook to pilot the aircraft and taxied it to the beginning of the runway, and thereafter you attempted to perform the take-off operation. However, you lacked the care and attention which you should have exerted because of your profession as an aircraft commander; and as such:

1. Prior to takeoff you should have checked with the appropriate devices and with your eyes the proper operation of the ailerons, but you omitted to do so because you failed to obtain the indispensable checkoff list. Thus, you did not perceive that because of the reverse connection of the cables which start at the base of the controls and through pulleys transmit movement to the wings, the ailerons were moving in a direction contrary to what you wished, i.e., when the controls were turned to the left the aircraft moved to the right.

2. After taxiing it to the runway and running it up to a speed of 100 miles per hour, the aircraft you had undertaken to pilot rose from No. 33 runway, but while it should have turned to the left, because of the reverse connection of the ailerons it started leaning to the right. Whereupon, instead of eliminating this leaning of the aircraft by using the control wheel with the simultaneous assistance of the left rudder pedal and by gaining altitude, you raised the flaps, acting contrary to what was indicated at the time. This resulted in further loss of stability and climbing ability of the aircraft.

3. While at about 15:21 Athens time, a Boeing 727 aircraft of Air France had taken off from runway No. 33, and you knew that because of the vortices and air turbulence caused by its wingtips, taxiing and takeoff should be avoided for the first 3 to 5 minute period during which the maintenance of control of the ailerons becomes problematic, you requested permission from the Control Tower to take off after only one minute and fifty seconds. Because of all the above factors, i.e., the reverse connection of the ailerons and the effects of the air turbulence caused by the wingtips of the Air France B-727 aircraft, the aircraft piloted by you started leaning to the right and, because of the raising of the flaps, it suffered further loss of stability and climbing ability; its right float came into contact with the runway, and thereafter its right wing also came into contact with the runway together with the right wheel, which was skidding. This made the aircraft lift off the ground and deviate from the right side of the runway. It then caused a descent of the aircraft, which made a circular orbit of approximately 300 degrees

*and, because of its speed, the nose of the aircraft hit the ground
and the cabin was smashed, with the result that Alexander
Onassis suffered the following injuries:*

    *an extensive hematoma over the whole extent of the vault
        of the skull;*

    a general contusion of the brain matter;

    *a severe oedema of the brain while the right temple lobe of
        the brain was reduced to pulp;*

    a depressed fracture of the right frontal fossa;

    a very extensive hemorrhage of the sub-arachnoid,

    *as the result of and only as the result of which injuries, his
        death occurred on January 23, 1973. The co-passenger,
        McGregor, suffered the following:*

    a contusive wound of the bregmatic region;

    *a contusive wound of the inner surface of the arch of the
        right foot;*

    *a fracture of the left transversal apophysis of the first lum-
        bar vertebra;*

    abrasions of the face, legs, arms, and hips.

    ***You failed to foresee these results, in violation of Articles
26, paragraph 1b, 28, 94, 302, 314 footnote (a) and 315
paragraph 1, footnote (b) of the Penal Code.***

    What do you have to say in your defense?

    Reply by June 9, 1973.

Anyone reading this indictment would have to assume that
the government investigation report did not exist, for it was not
mentioned in the indictment even though the investigation had
been conducted under police orders for the very purpose of determining whether any crime had been committed. Indeed, the

charges in the indictment were directly refuted by the police-ordered report.

The indictment charged Don with being "joint commander," a nonexistent position. There could have been only one "pilot in command," just as there is only one captain of a ship. The government investigation report named Alexander Onassis as the pilot in command. Indeed, the authors of the indictment slipped up by calling Mac McGregor "the co-passenger," meaning there was more than one passenger. The second passenger could only have been Don McCusker, and both of them were actually issued passenger tickets. (It was probably not a coincidence that Don's passenger ticket was confiscated by the Greek police after the crash.) Since Alexander did not have an instructor's rating, for insurance purposes he had to list the other two occupants as passengers rather than students. His plan was to treat Don as a potential charterer, whose flying proficiency Alexander could legally determine by a check flight. During the check flight, Don would legally be a passenger, and after Alexander was satisfied about Don's proficiency, he would charter the Piaggio to Don, who would then carry McGregor as a passenger during another week of familiarization flights after Alexander joined Fiona in London.

Had the indictment mentioned the purpose of the flight, which was for Alexander, the pilot in command, to determine Don's proficiency in the Piaggio, it would have been even more ludicrous to label Don "joint commander." The drafters carefully avoided any mention of the purpose.

Paragraph 1 of the indictment charged Don with failing to obtain and use the "indispensable" before-takeoff checklist, which allegedly would have caused Don to observe that the aileron controls were reversed. As we have seen, the government report found that "all relevant flight checks were done by Alexandros Onassis," the pilot in command. It would have been the height of brass for Don to upstage his potential employer, Alexander, by telling him how to conduct the pre-flight checks.

It is true that Alexander did not bring the before-takeoff checklist with him, but according to Mac McGregor, Alexander went through its simple steps from memory. Even if he had produced and read from the checklist, the item relating to checking of flight controls (which includes the ailerons) directs the pilot to check only their "full and free movement," which would not have disclosed the reversed cable problem.

Don was not told that this was to be the Piaggio's first flight after its overhaul. Alexander knew it had just come out of overhaul, and it was up to him to ascertain from the Olympic maintenance people or from the aircraft logbook whether the required post-overhaul test flight had been accomplished. In fact, as the investigation report found, the overhaul records and the logbook had been falsified by Olympic to show that there had been both a post-overhaul inspection and a test flight when in fact none was performed. Had there been a proper post-overhaul inspection and test flight, the control cable reversal would have been obvious, and the crash that killed Alexander would not have occurred. But this indictment sought to hold Don responsible for a falsified logbook written in Greek, as to which his pilot in command, Alexander, had full responsibility for checking.

Paragraph 2 accused Don of improperly raising the wing flaps. As we saw in their report, the government investigators explained that when the plane kept banking to the right after Don turned his control to the left, it was reasonable for him to assume that this was caused by an uneven extension of the flaps. As a test pilot, Don was trained to take the precaution of raising the flaps if he was unable to turn the plane in the desired direction, and he had actually done that during an emergency years earlier. Don's amnesia had wiped out his memory of what he actually did, but the Greek government investigators spoke for him by ruling out his handling of the flaps as a cause of the crash. This did not prevent the corrupt officials of the Colonels' Junta from simply pretending the report did not exist, so that they could charge him with manslaughter based on the precautionary raising of the flaps.

The same was true of the indictment's third count, based on the proximity of the Piaggio to the Air France Boeing 727 taking off ahead of it. The investigation report ruled this out as a potential cause, because the Piaggio never entered the area where there could have been "wake turbulence" from the Air France plane. The report found that the Piaggio took off over two minutes after the Air France plane, more than enough to comply with the legal safety margin.

The key to this false indictment was the invention of the term "joint commander," by which Ari's accomplices sought to saddle Don with criminal responsibility for all the mistakes made by Alexander (the sole pilot in command) and the Olympic mechanics who falsified the maintenance records.

Don worked with Nick the lawyer to draft a written response to these charges, spelling out in detail how each one of them was refuted by the report of the commission appointed by the police to investigate the accident. At the same time, U.S. Ambassador to Greece Albert J. Tasca sent a diplomatic cable to Secretary of State William Rogers (soon to be succeeded by Henry Kissinger):

Date: 6 June 1973
From: AMEMBASSY ATHENS
To: SECSTATE WASHDC
Subject: DONALD MCCUSKER

1. McCusker charged with manslaughter and having caused bodily injuries by negligence. Subject scheduled to appear before examining magistrate June 9, 1973, to make his defense statement.

2. According to technical report findings, accident caused by a defect in takeoff control system for which Olympic Airways technicians are blamed. McCusker charged with having neglected to check on such control system prior to takeoff.

3. Embassy in continuous consultations and contact with subject and his lawyers. Further developments will be reported immediately. Senators Taft and Scott interested.
TASCA.

On June 9, Nick the lawyer and Don appeared before Magistrate Papadakis to answer the indictment. Nick presented a long written defense and also argued orally that since there was no evidence to support the indictment, it should be dismissed without waiting for a trial. He was interrupted frequently by the magistrate, especially when he tried to read the portions of the government investigation report that completely refuted the indictment. The magistrate was especially annoyed when Nick read the conclusions of the report that the actions taken by Don "were the appropriate and required actions" and that the "accident was not the result of poor technique or mistake" on Don's part. When Nick tried to raise the subject of Onassis's corrupting influence, the magistrate cut him off and threatened to hold him in contempt if he mentioned

Ari's name again. The brief hearing ended with the magistrate taking no official action on Nick's application to dismiss the indictment. This meant that it would remain in place until the case was called for trial, the time of which, as everyone knew, would depend upon the wishes of Aristotle Onassis.

This left Don stranded in Greece without his passport, unable to get home to his family, and—if he ever got home—facing the grim prospect of seeking a flying job with a manslaughter indictment hanging over his head, accused of the highly-publicized killing of Aristotole Onassis's son. Nick the lawyer felt that he could win an acquittal if the case came to trial, but he was pessimistic about the chances of bringing it on for trial in view of Ari's ability to manipulate the corrupt government. It appeared to suit Ari's purposes to keep the indictment pending indefinitely while he sought evidence to support it by dangling the million-dollar reward offer and using Johnny Meyer's media hype to convict Don in the minds of the public. By busying himself with the campaign to place the blame on Don, Ari was avoiding the need to face up to his own role in the disaster.

When Don complained to Nick about the unjust handling of the case, the lawyer told him that the magistrate's hands were tied—if he dared to dismiss the indictment or reveal that he knew it was a travesty, Ari would see to it that he was removed from office, if not worse. Nick said that he had done everything he could to get rid of the indictment, but now Don's only hope was to bring the influence of the United States government directly into play. Nick didn't know exactly how that could be done, but he was aware that it would require all the prestige and leverage of Ambassador Tasca.

Tasca had been meeting with officials of the Greek government, seeking a quiet way out of the impasse because his main responsibility at the moment was to avoid any diplomatic problem which might imperil the vital NATO naval base. The Greek officials with whom he discussed the case were aware that the McCusker indictment was being manipulated by Onassis. Several of them told Tasca that if anyone could reason with Ari, it was Professor Yanni Georgakis, chairman of Olympic Airways. Tasca met with Georgakis and was pleased to find that the professor was convinced that McCusker was innocent, and was unhappy with both the criminal charges and Ari's ongoing $1 million reward campaign. By that time, in addition to the charges against Don, Ari had managed to procure manslaughter indictments against five Olympic Airways mechanics who had worked on the Piaggio.

Ambassador Tasca did his best to convince Georgakis that it was in everyone's best interests for him to get Ari to quietly drop the McCusker indictment. The professor replied that he and Paul Ioannidis had been trying to do so for months, but that Ari was obsessed with his charge that Don and the C.I.A. had conspired to murder Alexander. When they brought up the government report which had exonerated Don, Ari told them it couldn't be trusted because it was produced by the corrupt government which was a tool of the C.I.A. Just recently they had managed to open a small wedge by convincing Ari that he should get a private report from an independent investigator who was not under C.I.A. influence. They had found a suitable investigator and had engaged him to produce an independent report for Ari.

Ambassador Tasca arranged another meeting with the professor, and applied maximum pressure by stating that his bosses in Washington had run out of patience with the mistreatment of an innocent American pilot, and were on the verge of ordering the embassy to file an official protest. Armed with the threat of disclosures that would embarrass Ari and Olympic Airways,

Georgakis and Ioannidis went back to Ari and finally arranged a compromise which would enable McCusker to return to Ohio. Tasca listened to the proposal and replied that it sounded as if it might solve the problem for the moment, but he could not speak for McCusker. He suggested that Professor Georgakis meet with McCusker at the embassy to explain the proposal. Georgakis agreed, and the meeting was set for June 25 in the office of Stu Kennedy, chief of the Consular Section.

At the embassy meeting, Don McCusker found Yanni Georgakis to be charming, animated, and ingratiating, much like the popular description of Aristotle Onassis. Yanni made it clear that he had read the Greek Air Force report and fully agreed that Don was a totally innocent victim rather than a perpetrator. He said there was no chance that Don would be convicted, but for "special reasons," it was impossible to get the charges dismissed right now. He said that Don had to appreciate the devastating effect that Alexander's death had on Ari. "Despite his great success in business, he often thinks with his heart rather than his head," said Yanni. "Even though five months have now passed since the accident, he has made no real progress in adapting to it."

When Don asked how falsely charging him with manslaughter would help Ari get over his grief, Yanni replied, "I can't explain it logically, except that he seems to feel that as long as the indictment is pending, he is holding on to a remnant of Alexander's life— somehow he is keeping faith with Alexander. We've tried to talk him out of it. Believe me, all of us at Olympic, the executives and technical people, even the lawyers, have told him there is no merit in this prosecution. But he is too emotional to accept advice right now. I hope his thoughts will mellow as time goes by, but at the moment there is only one step we can accomplish for you. It is a most important step which I hope will satisfy you for the moment."

"And what is that step?" asked Don.

"I believe that if your lawyer makes a formal application for your release on bail pending trial of the manslaughter charges, the court will grant it. Then, armed with the court's order releasing you on bail, you could go to the police and retrieve your passport. That would leave you free to return to the United States on the next flight. Of course, Olympic would provide you with a first-class ticket for your return flight to Ohio. And nobody would raise any objection to your leaving Greece."

Don started to question Yanni about details, but Stu Kennedy interrupted and asked Yanni,"What would be the amount of the bail?"

"This is all very unofficial, of course, off the record as you Americans say. I believe that bail of 120,000 drachmas would be considered appropriate."

There was an awkward silence as Don calculated that 120,000 drachmas converted to about $4,000 in U.S. money, a sum that was beyond his cash resources. Then Yanni continued, "Ah, I believe Olympic Airways would be willing to lend you that sum, say for one year, without interest ."

"I see," said Don. "And what happens to the manslaughter charges?"

"As I said, all of us at Olympic feel that they are without merit, and will never be brought to trial, but for the moment, it is not possible to get them dismissed. No doubt the trial date will be put off for some considerable time, say, something like twelve months or so. By that time, perhaps the air will have cleared sufficiently so that all those interested will agree that the charges should be dismissed."

"And if the air isn't cleared by then?" asked Don.

"Well, then, the chances are that the trial date will be postponed again."

Don thought this over for a few moments, and then said to Yanni, "I can see that the bail arrangement will get me home, which is my immediate objective, and—don't get me wrong, I do appreciate your efforts and your offer to lend me the bail money. But you can see where that leaves me. I still have the cloud of manslaughter charges over me, while I go out and try to get another flying job to support my family."

"I appreciate that, Captain McCusker," replied Yanni. "What I have described is perhaps not a perfect, complete solution, but it is the best that can be achieved at this time. Believe me, it was not easy to convince Mr. Onassis to agree to the bail arrangement. It would simply not be possible to get him to agree to anything beyond that at this time. And without his agreement, the court would not even grant you release on bail."

Don then asked Yanni whether Olympic was prepared to compensate him for his injuries and loss of earnings, as the company's lawyer had promised him. Yanni said he was aware of the discussions and hoped that Don would be compensated eventually, but that no settlement or payment was possible while the indictment was still pending.

Don thanked Yanni for his help, and said he would have to think over the bail proposal. After Yanni departed, Don resumed the discussion with Stu Kennedy, who seemed disappointed that Don had not jumped at Yanni's proposal. "Sure, Don," he said, "it would be just great if you could walk out of Greece with the charges dismissed and a big compensation check from Olympic in your pocket. But it just isn't possible for Yanni to move Onassis that far so quickly. Yanni has really stuck his neck out, risking the loss of his close relationship with Onassis because he happens to be a decent guy and he also wants this thing to go away quietly for Olympic's sake. But when he says that the bail deal is as far as he can push Onassis right now, we've got to take his word for it. At least you'll be out of here safely. If you stick around and try to fight this battle from Athens, you might find yourself in even deeper trouble."

"How can I be in any worse trouble than now?"

"Well, you know that Onassis is offering a million-dollar reward to anyone who produces evidence of a plot to murder Alexander. We also happen to know that he is obsessed with the idea that the C.I.A. has been after him for years, and he's hired private investigators to come up with a C.I.A. connection. With all that money he's tossing around, he's bound to come up with some kind of cock and bull story that you were working for the C.I.A."

"That's ridiculous. I've never been involved with the C.I.A., and after all, I was on the plane myself!"

"Sure it's ridiculous, but that won't help you if some phony investigator or informer sells Ari the story he wants to hear. And I can assure you that the slightest mention of any C.I.A. involvement would be highly distressing to Ambassador Tasca and the State Department in Washington. Practically every day here we have to fight off charges that the C.I.A. engineered the Colonels' coup and is actually running Greece through the puppet government of the Colonels."

When Don nodded impatiently to indicate that he'd heard the C.I.A. puppet story before, Kennedy launched into a further explanation of just how shaky the American position in Greece was. He told Don that with a Democratic Congress fighting President Nixon on foreign policy, both houses kept attaching riders to the foreign aid appropriations, trying to condition the aid to Greece on the fulfillment of the Colonels' promises to hold democratic elections and cease the repression of civil rights. President

Nixon had the final say, and managed to outmaneuver Congress so far, but each year Ambassador Tasca was required to face Congressional grilling and do a song-and-dance act about the Colonels' nonexistent democratization program. Kennedy made it clear that Don had picked the wrong country in which to get himself into a jam that required the embassy to rescue him. Finally he said pointedly, "I'm speaking for the ambassador now when I tell you that this is the best deal you're going to get, and that you'd better grab it while it's still available."

Don was disappointed that the embassy could produce no more than the bail deal, and he resented the pressure applied by Stu Kennedy, which he saw as serving the embassy's convenience rather than the basic rights of an innocent U.S. citizen. But when he discussed the proposal with Helena on the phone that evening, they agreed that as long as Don was being held hostage in Greece, he lacked the leverage to clear his name or collect compensation. They decided that bail was the best they could achieve, and at least that would reunite Don with his family and open the way for rebuilding his career and his life.

The next day, June 26, Don informed Stu Kennedy that he would accept the bail deal. Stu was delighted, and said he would phone Yanni to start the wheels moving. Stu told Don to meet with Nick the lawyer to get the bail application filed in court as quickly as possible.

Don had assumed that he would be on his way back to Ohio within a day or two after agreeing to the bail deal, but the process of getting a court order for his release on bail, plus the posting of the $4,000 in bail money and the retrieval of his passport from the Greek police, was to keep Don in Athens for another agonizing sixteen days. At one point he appeared to hit a snag in getting the promised $4,000 loan from Olympic Airways, whereupon Mac

McGregor offered to lend Don the money—a munificent gesture considering the strapped financial condition of the two grounded pilots.

Finally, on the morning of July 12, everything fell into place. Don picked up the $4,000 check at the Olympic office, then rushed by taxi to Nick's office so that the lawyer could deposit it in court and pick up the order for Don's release, which Don exchanged for his passport at the police station near the airport. At noon he was sitting in the first class cabin of Olympic flight 411, glancing furtively out the window, half expecting to see a police car speed across the tarmac to drag him off the plane in handcuffs at the last minute. He did not begin to relax until the Boeing 707 cleared the ground and pointed its nose toward New York.

Now in the skies over the Atlantic, 172 days after flying into Athens Airport to be checked out in Ari's Piaggio, Don contemplated the results of his miscarried Greek adventure. He had gone there for an audition after being without a flying job for nearly a year, the longest such stretch in his career, but at least he had a spotless flying record when he arrived in Athens. Now he was still without a flying job, weakened by the residual effects of hepatitis, uncertain even of passing the F.A.A. flight physical. Plus, he was under indictment for killing the son of Aristotle Onassis by reckless flying, and mired under a pile of debt. He fought off these chilling prospects by picturing Helena and the six children who would be waiting at Port Columbus to give him a hero's welcome.

Then his thoughts turned to the job for which he had auditioned with Alexander. What would it have been like to work for Ari? He reviewed the events in Greece as he knew them. There were many details about the Piaggio, the yacht *Christina*, and the actual terms of his proposed employment that he had never learned. What he did know about the Piaggio story somehow did not seem to add up. Had he really gone through a job audition—or was it some kind of intrigue?

If Don McCusker had known more about the saga of Aristotle Onassis, he would have been aware that it was a life story deliberately filled with intrigue, deception, and fraud. Since Don was a trusting soul, it did not occur to him then that Ari had planned to hire him to unwittingly become part of an ongoing fraud designed to maintain the pretense of Ari's invincibility.

Chapter Twelve

The Myth of Ari's Sea-Going Piaggio

ANY SEAPLANE, FLYING BOAT, OR AMPHIBIAN PILOT WILL TELL you that it would be suicidal to operate a Piaggio in the open sea. Planes of that size are not built to withstand waves of more than two feet in height, and the ocean waves are much higher than that even in moderate seas. Indeed, the commercial airlines that operate amphibians much larger and hardier than the Piaggio restrict landings and takeoffs to sheltered harbors with waves no higher than 2.5 feet. Therefore, Ari's statement at the press conference following Alexander's death that he used the Piaggio safely "in all the seas of the world" was pure fantasy. He used the Piaggio to sail the seas of the world lashed to the deck of *Christina*, for no pilot in his right mind would permit the plane to be lifted overboard into the open sea. The mere presence of the Piaggio on the deck, coupled with Ari's talent for hype, was sufficient to create the false impression that (as he told journalists and biographers) he was "able to leave a yacht party in mid-Mediterranean, fly to London for a meeting, and be back in time for dinner with his guests."

Because this fraud is crucial in fixing responsibility for the killing of Alexander Onassis, it is necessary for us to consider it in some detail.

Limitations on Wave Heights

The ability of an airplane hull to withstand the destructive force of ocean waves is proportional to the weight of the airplane. According to charts developed by David B. Thurston, a leading seaplane designer and consultant to the U.S. Navy, airplanes the size of the Piaggio, which has a maximum gross weight of 6,603 pounds, cannot be safely operated in wave heights of more than two feet. In *Design for Flying*, Thurston writes:

> *There is a great tendency to expect too much of any hull, or to underestimate wave height, with equally unfortunate results in either case.... Since waves have been known to break over the flight deck of aircraft carriers, the use of amphibians and seaplanes for open ocean operation will be restricted to large displacement hulls and acceptable surface conditions.*

Professor of Aviation Dale De Remer, in his widely used manual *Seaplane Operations*, adopts David Thurston's calculations and adds the warning that because it is not easy to determine the height of waves from above, pilots should double their visual estimates of wave height.

In addition to wave height, a limiting factor is the space between the waves. In his book *Notes of a Seaplane Instructor*, veteran pilot Burke Mees points out that waves are less dangerous if spaced close together, as they often are in small bodies of water such as lakes. But he warns:

> *However, if they are spaced far apart (as only happens in large bodies of water) you will go from the top of one wave into the trough of the next, which creates the effect that you might expect from landing a wheelplane [landplane] on a street with large speed bumps.*

Thus the widely-spaced ocean waves pose two grave threats to amphibians, especially small ones like the Piaggio. There is the basic hazard of sinking because of sea water entering the plane through punctures in the hull, and the added danger of the "speed bumps" flipping the plane over on its side or back, in which position it would be highly vulnerable to structural damage and sinking.

Mediterranean and Atlantic wave heights

Ari planned to cruise the *Christina* from Athens to Miami in February 1973. For that purpose the Piaggio overhaul was to be completed and the new pilot, Don McCusker, was to be checked out and hired in January. Therefore, let us focus on the wave heights along the route which the *Christina* would have taken during that cruise, in the Mediterranean Sea and the Atlantic Ocean.

There are two types of ocean wave systems: wind waves and swells, the swells being the residue of prior wind systems. But these technicalities do not concern us, for both wind waves and swells pose serious threats to the safety of seaplanes. Therefore, we will use "waves" to cover both wind waves and swells.

James Clarke's *Atlantic Pilot Atlas* contains detailed monthly charts for all areas of the Mediterranean and the Atlantic, showing historical winds, currents, and wave heights. For any route from Greece to Florida in February, the charts show the predominance of "moderate" winds and wave heights in both the Mediterranean and the Atlantic. According to the World Meteorological Organization, moderate waves are six to twelve feet high. The charts also show that waves higher than twelve feet will be encountered over as much as 30 percent of the route.

Not surprisingly, maritime history demonstrates that the expected wave heights along the *Christina's* route would have been anywhere from three to six times as high as the safe two-foot level. Therefore, there would have been practically no safe position for an open-sea takeoff or landing in the Piaggio.

Lindbergh and the airline flying boats

In 1933, Charles A. Lindbergh made a five-month flying survey of potential trans-Atlantic routes for Pan American Airways. With his wife Anne on board as radio operator, Lindy flew a Lockheed Sirius seaplane which had a maximum gross weight of 7,099 pounds, slightly heavier than the Piaggio. In his *Autobiography of Values,* Lindy recounts that he had to stick to sheltered harbors for takeoffs and landings because the ocean waves were too high for his "relatively small seaplane."

Lindbergh played a vital role in the planning of Pan Am's pioneering transoceanic services. In the 1930s, there were few airports capable of handling large transport planes, and so transoceanic flights began with flying boats (which differed from amphibians only in that they did not have landing wheels). Lindy accepted the necessity of using flying boats at that stage, but only because of the lack of airports. He did not believe that the flying boat afforded any substantial safety advantage because of its ability to make emergency landings in the open sea. He conducted a long-running debate with André Priester, Pan Am's resident engineering chief, on the issue of whether any of the flying boats—even the heaviest and strongest—could actually survive in the ocean. Priester argued that since a flying boat had a slightly better chance of keeping afloat on the ocean until rescuers arrived, this was important psychologically to the crew and the passengers. Lindy countered that "safety lay in airworthiness rather than seaworthiness" and that flying boat "hulls could not be designed with sufficient strength for landing [on the ocean] no matter how heavy the metal put in them." In other words, if you build flying boats light enough to fly, their hulls will be too fragile to operate even in moderate seas.

The leading airline historian Ronald E.G. Davies, Curator of Air Transport at the National Air and Space Museum in Washington D.C., wrote in his history of Pan Am that the flying boat "stood an outside chance of remaining afloat until help arrived." Retired Pan Am pilot Thomas G. Foxworth put it more colorfully:

> ...to offer the idea of a seaworthy hull between one's bottom and the implacable sea seemed a reasonable way to attract the timid to embark on ambitious transoceanic aerial journeys. Of course, it all was myth. The "flying ocean liners" in reality imparted a false sense of security to their cosseted clientele.

Dramatic proof of the inability of even the largest flying boats to survive the destructive forces of moderate seas came on January 21, 1939. The *Cavalier*, operated by Imperial Airways (predecessor of British Airways), was a four-engine flying boat of the Short S-23 Empire class, with a maximum gross weight of 30,500 pounds, well over four times as heavy as the Piaggio. It departed the New York flying boat base at Port Washington for a scheduled flight to Bermuda carrying eight passengers and a crew of five.

Halfway through the flight, a radio message from the *Cavalier* informed the Port Washington base that it was experiencing carburetor icing troubles and might have to make a forced landing in the Atlantic. The final radio log entries tell the chilling story:

> *12:59—All engines failing through ice. Altitude 1,500 feet. Forced landing in a few minutes.*
> *1:07—Still up. Have two motors going. Trying to get others started.*
> *1:08—Have just sent distress signal on 500 kilocycles.*
> *1:11—Landing now.*
> *1:12—Landed O.K. Switches off. Stand by.*
> *1:13—Sinking.*

Captain M.R. Alderson, having regained power in two of his four engines, made what he considered a well-controlled landing ("landed O.K.") in the Gulf Stream about 350 miles east of Norfolk, Virginia. He and the other crew members were shocked when it became apparent in less than a minute that the hull had been punctured and the sea water that was pouring in would soon sink them. The sea conditions were described by the navigator, Neil Richardson:

> *There was quite a ground swell but the water was not choppy. Fortunately it was also quite warm.*

One of the passengers suffered fatal injuries when he stood up during the landing. On the captain's orders, the other twelve occupants made their way out into the sea with life preservers just before the plane sank. They managed to tie their life preservers together and formed a "common raft" by holding on to each other.

Heroically, those who survived kept their limbs linked for more than ten hours, singing and keeping each other's spirits up even after darkness descended. When one of the passengers showed signs of weakening, other passengers or crew members would swim over to help. The captain and a steward, Robert Spence, exhausted themselves in these supporting efforts. After nearly seven hours, the steward slipped away and drowned. The oldest passenger, J. Gordon Noakes of New York, aged sixty-two, had suffered head injuries and apparently died in the water when his sixty-year-old wife could no longer support him. Captain Alderson passed out but was supported by the others in the human raft.

Finally a Standard Oil tanker passed nearby, and two of the crew members detached themselves from the common raft so they could swim close enough to the tanker to be heard. The ten survivors were picked up by the tanker's lifeboats.

Of the six surviving passengers, four were women over forty; one was a twenty-four-year-old woman; and one was a young man whose arm had been broken in a recent skiing accident. One of the surviving passengers, forty-three-year-old Mrs. Edna Watson of Bermuda, described the sea conditions:

> *For about an hour and a half after the plane disappeared the ocean was not very rough. The waves were only little ones, but every once in a while a bigger one came along and bounced us.*

Captain Frank Spurr, skipper of the tanker *Esso Baytown*, said the survivors were fortunate that it was a "windless, quiet night" which enabled his crew to hear their cries and come to their rescue.

The *Cavalier* rescue was a remarkable story of courage and unselfishness, which *Life* magazine called "one of the great air dramas of our time." But for those who hoped that large commercial flying boats could make safe landings in moderate seas, it was the moment of truth. Pan American, at that time the world's largest operator of flying boats, never ordered another one after the *Cavalier* went down. In its investigation report, the British Air Ministry found that there was "a moderate sea" with wave heights between three and ten feet, but concluded that even those conditions "were too severe to make a good landing possible." Had the sea conditions been any worse than moderate, it is unlikely that the survivors could have held their makeshift common raft together with their intertwined arms and legs for ten hours.

The zenith of the flying boat was reached in the 1939-1945 period of World War II, when Pan Am operated the Boeing B-314 Clipper, the largest airplane of its day, which afforded luxury that would never again be achieved in an airliner, not even in the jet age. A four-engine flying boat, it was built to carry seventy-four passengers and a crew of eight. Its interior arrangements, with sleeping berths, private compartments, and gourmet dining rooms, resembled a combination of the Orient Express and a suite at the Ritz. Its wing was so large that it contained a walkway which permitted crew members to examine all four engines in flight if repairs were necessary. With a maximum gross weight of 82,500 pounds, it was more than twelve times as heavy as the Piaggio.

Pan Am began the first scheduled trans-Atlantic service in June 1939, using the B-314. The route was over the South Atlantic from New York to Lisbon, with required refueling stops at Bermuda and Horta in the Azores. Horta was chosen because there was no alternative, it being the only convenient port between Europe and North America suitable for refueling and servicing flying boats.

Horta was to create great difficulties for Pan Am. Because its harbor was too narrow to accommodate the huge B-314s, landings and takeoffs had to be made just outside the breakwater.

Even that close to the sheltered harbor, the ocean swells often caused moderate wave heights of six to twelve feet. After two of their early landings at Horta resulted in serious hull damage, Pan Am fixed the maximum wave-height limit for all B-314 operations: three feet.

If the waves were any higher than three feet, Pan Am considered it a "No-Go" item, and the great flying boats would have to sit at Horta until the waves diminished. This wreaked havoc with Pan Am's trans-Atlantic schedules, especially in winter, when the waves just outside Horta's harbor would often stay above three feet for days on end. In one famous incident, three of the Atlantic Division's five B-314s—the *Yankee, Atlantic,* and *Dixie Clippers*—were stranded together in Horta for eleven days. Another time when a *Clipper* flight was delayed at Horta for more than a week, the passengers fought off their boredom by publishing their own newspaper, the *Horta Swell.*

The Horta delays were no laughing matter to Pan Am, since the B-314s regularly carried such wartime priority passengers as General Eisenhower, Harry Hopkins, and President Roosevelt himself. Yet the world's most experienced over-water airline would not dare to attempt takeoffs or landings in waves above three feet, even in the largest and safest flying boat airliner ever operated.

During World War II, many heroic open-sea rescues of downed American fliers were made by flying boats, especially the Consolidated Catalina, known to the Navy as the PBY, to the Army Air Forces as the OA-10, and to grateful rescued airmen as "Dumbo." The Catalina was designed for combat conditions, manned by crews trained for rescue work. Even so, their open-sea landings and takeoffs almost invariably resulted in structural hull damage, often requiring the frantic efforts of ten crew members to bail out sea water that was pouring in through sprung plates. The Official Air Force History of World War II reported that during one critical period in 1944, "half the Catalinas sent on rescue missions cracked up on landing, leaving two planes in trouble instead of one." For this reason, the flying boats were limited to search missions whenever possible, leaving the rescue pickups to a surface vessel or (as in the case of the president-to-be George H.W. Bush) a submarine. Those Catalina crews that managed to complete open-sea rescues often received decorations, as high as the Medal of Honor.

After World War II, when large airports were built all over the world and reliable long-range landplanes became available, the reality of Lindbergh's airworthiness dislodged Priester's illusion of seaworthiness, and the flying boats—romantic as they were—disappeared from the world's major air routes. They have lingered on in the form of the Grumann G-73 Mallard, a twin-engine amphibian used for scheduled air services to and from sheltered harbors in South Florida, the Bahamas, and the Virgin Islands. The Mallard, which can carry ten passengers, has a maximum gross weight of 12,750 pounds, nearly double that of the Piaggio. The F.A.A.-approved Airplane Flight Manual for the Mallard, issued by Grumann, includes this provision:

Section I — Operating Limitations
Note: Compliance with the operating limitations noted in SECTION I is required by law....

8. WAVE HEIGHT. The airplane may be landed or taken off from the water with waves 2½ ft. high.

Interviews with the F.A.A. officials who regulate Mallard operations in South Florida confirm that the 2.5 foot limitation is treated as an absolute bar to landings and takeoffs in higher waves.

The Piaggio literature

The Airplane Flight Manual issued by Piaggio for its P 136 L-2 contains no mention of wave height limitations. Piaggio and other manufacturers of small seaplanes concluded that it would be inappropriate to mention any "safe" wave height in their flight manuals, lest pilots be misled into attempting landings or takeoffs in dangerous open-sea conditions. As we have seen, it is very difficult to estimate wave heights accurately, and there are other hazards such as wave-spacing which add to the dangers.

In its sales brochure, Piaggio makes it clear that open-sea operations are not within the wildest stretch of the imagination. The brochure, translated from Italian to English, explains that the "pusher" arrangement, with the propellers pushing the plane from behind the wing, positions the engines and propellers closer to the water than the conventional "tractor" design, thus exposing them to more water spray. This provides an additional reason for Piaggio pilots to avoid waves. The brochure goes on to point out that this is not a serious disadvantage because the Piaggio was not designed for any conceivable open-sea operation:

> On a small-size aircraft, pusher propellers showed the drawback of being more exposed to spray in the tail-down trim in water, but this disadvantage, not very serious in an aircraft with no pretence to operate on the open sea at the limit of possibilities, was largely compensated by the compact and sharp architecture due to the "gull-wing/pusher propeller" solution.

On the back page of the Piaggio brochure is a color photo of SX-BDC, the plane in which Alexander Onassis was later killed. It bears this caption:

The P.136 L that Aristotle Onassis kept aboard his yacht as a "tender" was used also for air-taxi service; its generous avionics fit is shown by its numerous antennas.

The maritime dictionary *An A-to-Z of Sailing Terms* defines "tender" as:

Originally a small vessel attached temporarily to a larger ship for general harbour duties such as collection of mail, etc. It is now the term used for the dinghy kept on the deck of a yacht, or other pleasure vessel, or hung from davits at the stern, and is used for going ashore when the vessel is at anchor or lying to a mooring.

Thus the very plane that Ari touted as being capable of flying him from mid-ocean to any place he wished to go is described by the manufacturer as a harbor dinghy.

Alexander's Paris Dinner with Ari, January 4, 1973

We have seen that Alex was elated when, during the Paris dinner, Ari appeared to agree to replace the Piaggio aboard the *Christina* with a helicopter.

Our knowledge of the Paris dinner conversation comes in second-hand fragments from those to whom Alex spoke about it: Fiona Thyssen and Alex's business associates at Olympic Aviation. Since both participants are dead, we can only guess at what was actually said. But the circumstances surrounding Ari's promise, and what he did to perform it, point inexorably to the conclusion that he was lying to his son, which he often did when it suited his purposes. We have seen from Ari's life history, going back to his Argentine tobacco days in the 1920s, that lying came more naturally to him than telling the truth, whether in business or personal affairs. Fiona Thyssen confirms that both she and Alex expected Ari to lie about anything that was important to Alex. It was part of Ari's game of showing Alex who was boss and crushing his son's initiative.

Why would Ari lie to Alexander about replacing the Piaggio?

If Ari needed a special reason for following his lifetime practice of lying to his son, there were several at hand. At the Paris dinner he told Alex that he was embarking on the collaboration with Roy Cohn and Johnny Meyer to divorce Jackie as cheaply as possible. For that project he would need Alex's support, since there were lies to be told and corroborated about "the widow" (as Alex and Christina called her) in order to terminate the marriage at the lowest cost to Ari. Therefore, Ari may have used his ostensible consent to the helicopter as a tradeoff for Alex's assistance in the divorce.

There was also Johnny Meyer's surveillance and wiretapping of Alex, which remained active because Ari was determined to avoid an encore of the intelligence failure that permitted Christina to marry Joe Bolker without Ari's knowledge. While Alex and Fiona did not discuss marriage on the phone, it is likely that their conversations and movements as reported by Johnny Meyer indicated to Ari that Fiona's determination to liberate Alex from his father's domination was entering a more activist phase. Thus it was a time for Ari to soothe his son's feelings and make it appear that along with his change of marital status, he was having a change of heart—a change so radical as to cause him to consider his son's suggestions on matters within Alex's expertise. Arbitrarily rejecting the oft-suggested helicopter switch again would have been more likely to bolster any breakaway plans that Alex and Fiona might be hatching.

Perhaps Ari had simply tired of listening to Alex's arguments for switching to a helicopter. Whatever his reasons for lying about this, it is clear that he could not have intended to replace the Piaggio at any time in the immediate future. Otherwise, why did he insist that the Piaggio be carried on board *Christina* during his upcoming February cruise, complete with a newly-hired American amphibian pilot?

The proposed sale in Miami

All the accounts of the Paris dinner agree that while Ari appeared to consent to replacing the Piaggio with a helicopter, his avowed plan was to put the Piaggio aboard the *Christina* for the February cruise to Miami, and then leave the plane there to be sold. This assumes that it made sense to sell the Piaggio in the U.S.A. rather than in Europe. But as with many of Ari's lies, the opposite is true.

To begin with, Ari had purchased the Piaggio new in 1967 for $69,000, and its 1973 market value either in Europe or the U.S.A. was only in the five-figure bracket, no more than chicken feed in Ari's financial picture. Apart from that, the plane was actually worth more in Europe than in America.

The Piaggio P 136 was originally produced in 1949 for the Italian Air Force, which bought a total of 23. In 1954 Piaggio began producing it for civilian purchasers, most of them Europeans. A handful were sold in the United States, including one to Francis J. Trecker, a Milwaukee machine-tool manufacturer. Trecker liked his plane so much that in 1956 he formed Royal Aircraft Corporation, to market the P 136 in the United States. Under agreement with Piaggio, he imported disassembled aircraft and assembled them in Milwaukee, installing American-made instruments, accessories, radios, and avionics in place of the European brands used at the Piaggio factory. This made maintenance and operation of the American P 136, known as the Trecker Royal Super Gull, much easier for American owners.

By the time of Ari's February 1973 cruise, the American market for Piaggios was served entirely by the Trecker plant in Milwaukee. There was an ample supply of Trecker Royal Super Gulls, complete with American instruments, accessories, radios, and avionics. Therefore, Ari's Italian Piaggio, loaded with foreign and metric-scale equipment, would have been a fish out of water in the American market. Americans with the funds to buy such a plane would have no incentive to pay a comparable price for the European model. There would be no logical reason for Americans to take on operational and maintenance problems that they could avoid with the Trecker Royal Super Gull.

Therefore, it made no economic sense for Ari to try to sell the Piaggio in Miami or any other place in the United States. As a distinctly European aircraft, it was worth much more in the European market. Ari himself had established the Piaggio in Europe as a glamorous luxury plane. Besides using it to transport visiting celebrities and tycoons, he was photographed pursuing his courtship of Maria Callas by Piaggio all over Europe. When Grace Kelly married Prince Rainier, Ari's Piaggio was there, scattering red and white carnations over the Monte Carlo harbor from the air. Other prestigious Piaggio owners were Egypt's King Farouk and Stavros Livanos, father of Ari's first wife Tina. Incidently, both Farouk and Livanos owned large yachts as well as Piaggios, but they operated the plane from sheltered harbors and lakes in Europe instead of carrying it aboard a yacht.

Thus it is undeniable that if Ari really intended to sell the Piaggio, he would have come out far ahead financially by selling it in Europe as a complete ready-to-fly luxury European transport with an impressive European provenance.   When the expense and effort of hiring Don McCusker for a single one-way trip is factored in, the Miami sale story makes even less economic sense. No pilot expense would have been incurred if Ari really planned to sell the Piaggio. Furthermore, offloading the Piaggio at Miami for sale there would have left the *Christina* without an aircraft or a pilot for the remainder of the Caribbean cruise and the voyage home.

The Olympic helicopters and pilots on hand

If Ari had really intended to use a helicopter on the *Christina*, he could have done so immediately, since Alex's Olympic Aviation owned and operated two excellent helicopters: an Alouette II and an Aloutte III, built by the French company Aerospatiale, co-manufacturers of the Concorde. The smaller helicopter, the Alouette II, had seats for only a pilot and two passengers, but the larger Alouette III could carry a pilot and seven passengers, compared to a maximum of four passengers in the Piaggio.

The Alouette III would have been an ideal shipboard helicopter for the *Christina*. Although it was about five feet longer than the Piaggio, it would have been able to land and take off comfortably in the space allocated to the Piaggio at the rear of the boat deck, thus avoiding the ocean wave problems of the amphibian airplane. There were qualified helicopter pilots already on the Olympic Aviation payroll who had often landed the Alouettes on Ari's private helipad at Skorpios and could have served aboard the *Christina*. Therefore, if Ari had not been lying to Alex about switching to a helicopter, the change could have been made in plenty of time for the February cruise, eliminating the need to rush the Piaggio through its overhaul or to audition a new pilot from America. Don McCusker was not qualified to fly helicopters, and the employment ad he answered did not mention helicopters.

Ari's attitude toward helicopters

Ari had often been a passenger in helicopters, especially during the 1950s when helicopters served as the eyes of his whaling fleet, spotting their (mostly illegal) prey for the harpooners. Like others in the oil business, Ari was accustomed to the sight of helicopters flying grease-stained workers to and from offshore drilling platforms and performing other services in support of manual labor. It was natural for him to look upon the helicopter as an aerial truck or utility vehicle rather than a flying limousine like the Piaggio.

He had other good reasons to believe that the noisy helicopters of the 1970s would not project the dashing image of the amphibian that could operate "in all the seas of the world." In addition to being slower than the Piaggio, they had extremely short ranges, on the order of 150 to 250 miles, compared to the 1,000-mile range of the Piaggio. Not even Ari's spellbinding hype could have convinced the media that he would be able to leave *Christina* in mid-Mediterranean, hop to London in his helicopter, and be back on board for dinner.

Little wonder, then, that Ari chose to shun his Alouette helicopters and carry on the Myth of the Sea-Going Piaggio.

The Piaggio as a "deathtrap"

Some second-hand accounts of the Paris dinner claim that Alex told Ari the Piaggio was a "deathtrap," an inherently dangerous and outmoded plane. In fact, it was considered the best-designed and safest small amphibian in the world. The Piaggio company in Genoa produced many successful aircraft going all the way back to the first World War, as well as the popular Vespa scooter. The P 136 L-2 held the key performance records for its class, as well as an excellent safety record, and was adopted by NATO. Alex had flown the Piaggio in bad weather and difficult landing areas. On his last flight he entrusted it to an American pilot who had never flown a Piaggio before. Therefore, if Alex actually called it a deathtrap, he was referring to its use in the open sea, where it certainly would have been a deathtrap. Given Alex's longing to be accepted as a professional by his aviation peers, he was never comfortable with the pretext that the Piaggio could be launched in the open sea. Replacing it with a helicopter would finally erase that fraud, which reflected on Alex's professional integrity.

The Piaggio Ari bought in 1958 had served him until 1972, when it was found to have extensive corrosion and was scrapped. Corrosion is a problem with any seaplane operated in salt water. The only counter-measure is to hose the plane down with fresh water after each flight. The fact that the first Piaggio L-2 developed corrosion after fourteen years of service hardly made it a deathtrap. The second Onassis Piaggio was the last one to come off the Genoa assembly line, delivered new in April 1967. At the time of the fatal crash, it had flown 1,081 hours, a modest total for a commercial aircraft. The extensive 1972 overhaul at the Olympic hangar, in which the plane was completely disassembled, did not reveal any signs of corrosion or other airworthiness problems.

Far from being considered a deathtrap, many Piaggios were flying wealthy celebrities and commercial passengers all over the world in 1973, and some are still flying in 2004, treasured as the classic Ferraris of the amphibians.

Why was Don McCusker to be taken on the cruise?

Ari had a special reason to continue the charade of the ocean-going Piaggio during the February cruise. He expected to be fighting legal battles with Jackie by then, and needed to impress her with his ability to communicate with his lawyers and show up in court quickly. The February cruise in the slow-moving *Christina* was to take three to four weeks, a long time to be unavailable for legal maneuvering.

As we have seen, Ari had already lost Monte Carlo, and shedding Jackie would deprive him of another important trophy. He was also suffering through a losing streak in business, notably the embarrassing 1971 collapse of his huge Omega project which was designed to match Niarchos's Greek oil refinery. At that point in his life, he needed more than ever to maintain the Myth of the Sea-going Piaggio. Don McCusker had commanded many over-ocean flights. Having Don on board in an Olympic Airways uniform would have signaled to the world that Ari was still the master of his fate, even on the high seas.

Would Don actually have flown the Piaggio during the February cruise? Ari had used it occasionally during past cruises to fly around the West Indies when the *Christina* was docked at a sheltered port, but that was not the unique image he was seeking to maintain. Anyone could charter an amphibian in the West Indies to fly from island to island. The real mission of the Piaggio was to stand on the deck of the ocean-going *Christina* as the symbol of Ari's invincibility.

We don't have to guess at Ari's plans for Don McCusker. He told the world in his own words at the Athens press conference held the day after Alex's death:

*And the American pilot was getting ready, because he was to
come with me on the yacht, so that he may be at our disposal
when the fateful plane was to be used by us.*

Ari's statement is inconsistent with carrying the Piaggio to
Miami to be sold. If that had been his intention, it is more likely
that he would have mentioned it at the press conference instead of
giving the impression that Don McCusker was hired to be at Ari's
disposal whenever he wanted to use the plane, especially, as Ari
said at the same press conference, "in all the seas of the world."

The manner in which Don was brought over to Athens for his
audition bespeaks Ari's duplicity. Don had mailed his resumé to a
blind box number in response to an aviation trade paper want ad
for an experienced amphibian pilot. Constantine Adassis of
Olympic Aviation phoned Don from Athens to explain that the
prospective job was to serve as pilot for Aristotle Onassis's
Piaggio, and to ask if Don could fly to Athens immediately at
Olympic's expense to audition for the job. Adassis sidestepped
Don's questions about salary and other employment provisions,
saying those would be discussed in Athens. Don needed the job
badly enough that he was willing to wait for those details. He
brought up these questions again with other Olympic officials
before the Athens check flight, and was told that he would get
that information after he passed the check. If they intended to
offer him the job of sailing to Miami on the *Christina* and then
immediately being made redundant as the Piaggio was off-loaded
to be sold in the U.S.A., they would have had to offer a strong
financial incentive, even to an out-of-work pilot like Don. Indeed,
we do not know how many calls Adassis had to make before he
found a pilot willing to come all the way to Athens without knowing any details of the proposed job.

It seems most likely that neither Alex nor his Olympic colleagues knew exactly what Don's status would be, since it was all up to Ari. If Ari intended to keep the Piaggio aboard the *Christina* and therefore retain McCusker indefinitely, he would not have told Alex or anyone else at that point, for that would have revealed that he was lying to Alex at the Paris dinner. This was typical of Ari's dealings with his employees and properties. He often kept his own close associates in the dark as to what he was actually going to do, until the last minute. He was fond of pulling this trick on Alex, to reaffirm his absolute control. For his part, Alex was more straightforward with his employees, especially the professional pilots whose respect he always craved.

The foregoing evidence, including Ari's own statements, shows clearly that Ari's deceit, his megalomania, his insatiable need for control, and his manipulation of Alexander, trapped his son aboard the fatally misrigged Piaggio which caused his death.

Yet the arrogantly self-centered Aristotle Onassis could have been expected to write off this circumstantial evidence as pure coincidence, without assuming any blame himself.

Let us now examine what he actually said and did in the wake of the Piaggio crash.

Chapter Thirteen

The Guilt Trip to the Final Fall

ALEXANDER'S DEATH IN JANUARY 1973 CAUSED ARI TO PUT his divorce plans on hold, as he turned to Jackie for the solace that she was so expert at providing. The *Christina's* projected voyage to Miami was scrapped in favor of a cruise to the West African port of Dakar and on to the Antilles. As we have seen, Jackie persuaded Pierre Salinger, President Kennedy's former press secretary and a world-class raconteur, to join the party at Dakar.

Pierre did his best to lift Ari's spirits, but the task was too difficult even for his considerable talents. Throughout the two-week cruise, Ari and Pierre spent many hours debating politics, history, and espionage. But Pierre and other passengers could not avoid noticing that Ari was not his ebullient self.

At that point, less than a month after Alex's fatal crash, nobody expected Ari to have fully overcome his grief. But those close to Ari felt that with his zest for life, his egocentric nature, his resiliency, and his many interests, he would soon rebound. While he loved Alex in his own way, he was not the type of father whose whole life was wrapped up in his son. Indeed, he had not really been close to Alex in the conventional way, and most of their time together during the previous ten years had been devoted to verbal sparring matches. He still had Christina, whom he often said had a better head for business than Alex, and was more willing to follow his lead and work toward stepping into his shoes. And he still had the driving need to top his archrival Stavros Niarchos.

When Ari returned from the February cruise, despite the backlog of business details that accumulated during his absence, he threw himself into the task of proving that Don McCusker's misconduct had killed Alexander. When he learned that the Greek Air Force officers investigating the crash had completely exonerated Don and had found that the ailerons were rigged backwards, Ari shifted his sights toward proving that his son had been murdered by a deliberate act of sabotage. He offered a million-dollar reward for evidence that would support this theory, and he hired his own investigators to search for the saboteurs. His principal suspects were the C.I.A. and Stavros Niarchos, possibly working together as they had in 1954 when they jointly exposed Ari's bribery in Saudi Arabia and sabotaged his Jiddah Agreement.

The C.I.A., hated by nearly all Greeks apart from the Colonels, made a perfect scapegoat for Ari's diversionary hype. In fact, Ari began concocting the sabotage pretext long before it became known that the aileron controls had been reversed. As we have seen, on the day after the crash, the first thing he said to Fiona Thyssen was, "I think Alexander was murdered. This was sabotage!" He also ordered Johnny Meyer to find and destroy all the audiotapes Alexander had made of their phone conversations, which might have contained evidence of Ari's false commitment to replace the Piaggio with a helicopter, and the pressure he had put on Alexander to rush the Piaggio through overhaul in time for the *Christina's* planned February cruise.

Ari spent a small fortune investigating Don McCusker, hoping to prove that he was a C.I.A. agent or that he had otherwise played a sinister role in sabotaging the Piaggio. To Ari it was no coincidence that Don took the left seat, for if Don had been aware that the misrigged ailerons would turn the plane to the right, he would have known that the occupant of the right seat would bear the brunt of the impact. Besides, Don fitted Ari's stereotype for all C.I.A. and F.B.I. agents: "hayseeds from Ohio."

As we have seen, the two top officials of Olympic Airways, Chairman Yanni Georgakis and Director General Paul Ioannidis, pleaded with Ari to drop his private investigations and permit Don to leave the country without being prosecuted. Although they risked intruding on Ari's grief, they told him that it would be impossible to prove sabotage, and that prolonging the inquiries would reflect badly on Olympic Airways itself, since the crash involved Olympic's airplane, Olympic's pilot-in-command (Alexander), and Olympic maintenance personnel who had botched the rigging of the ailerons or at the very least had failed in their duty to confirm by inspection that they were properly rigged. Furthermore, Ari's million-dollar reward offer for evidence of sabotage had produced hundreds of false or useless tips, but Ari insisted that each of them be fully investigated. On top of that, the reward offer was causing prospective Olympic passengers to wonder how safe their planes were. But in spite of Ari's great respect for Georgakis and Ioannidis, he turned a deaf ear to their pleas. The sabotage investigations would go on, and Ari would not lift a finger to stop the criminal prosecution which his charges against Don had put into motion.

Ari refused to accept the conclusions of the Greek investigating commission's report, especially since it found that Alex was the pilot-in-command and that Olympic Airways' maintenance personnel had been highly negligent. Ari argued that the investigators were officers of the Greek Air Force, who would be controlled by the Greek military dictatorship which in turn was nothing more than a tool of the C.I.A. Georgakis and Ioannidis finally convinced Ari that Olympic should commission a highly qualified aviation accident investigator to make an independent inquiry and report his findings privately to Olympic. Since Olympic was a good customer of Boeing, they sought the advice of Boeing officials on which investigator they should hire. Their number one choice was Alan B. Hunter, a London-based consulting aeronautical engineer who had conducted confidential investigations for Boeing and other aviation companies.

A call late in June to Hunter's London office revealed that he was on vacation, but Ari had him tracked down and quickly flown to Athens. Hunter agreed to conduct the investigation secretly and to report only to Olympic, so that if his report was not what they hoped for, its contents would never be revealed.

Hunter examined the Piaggio wreckage, studied all the records of the Greek investigation, and questioned the key witnesses. He delivered his comprehensive eighteen-page report to Olympic on July 6, 1973. It agreed with the conclusions of the Greek Air Force report, and went further to explain in detail how the ailerons had come to be rigged backwards and why this was the direct cause of the crash.

Hunter found that Alexander was in fact the pilot-in-command, and that "placing McCusker in the left hand seat for evaluation would not be unusual for this type of exercise in a simple aircraft."

Hunter's conclusion as to the cause of the crash, published here for the first time, exonerates Don McCusker in the same way as had the Greek Air Force report:

> *The accident was caused by an incorrectly routed aileron control system, causing the ailerons to give right bank for a left bank demand at the control wheel and vice versa.*
>
> *The short time and very low altitude available to the pilot/pilots when the fault manifested itself upon the first corrective bank movement was entirely inadequate to permit recognition or the application of corrective measures which would need to be contrary to instructive reaction.*
>
> *The failure of either pilot to view and recognize the correct direction of aileron travel is not so much due to the absence of a check list, but rather represents a general trend today whereby pilots tend to concentrate upon freedom from locks and a full range of travel, since in many modern aircraft the controls cannot in any event be seen from the cockpit. The crew have to rely upon correct assembly and have become understandably accustomed to do so.*
>
> *This was the first flight following a control column change which represents the last servicing work at which incorrect assembly of controls could have occurred.*

The Greek Air Force investigators had examined the control system immediately after the crash, and reported that the aileron control cables "were connected wrongly and in an opposite way." Hunter did not see the wreckage until five months after the crash, by which time the control system had been dismantled by the Greek investigators. Nevertheless, he forestalled any doubt about the ailerons being connected backwards by conducting an experiment with another Piaggio. He began with the established fact that the wind had been coming from the left and would therefore have blown the plane off course to the right unless the pilot turned his wheel to the left immediately after takeoff. Bear in mind that with the aileron controls properly rigged, if a bank to the left were desired, the pilot would turn his control wheel to the left, causing the left aileron to go up and the right aileron to go down; and to bank to the right the pilot would turn his control wheel to the right, which would cause the right aileron to go up and the left aileron to go down. Thus, with the wind blowing from the left and the pilot turning his wheel to the left to counteract this drift, the right aileron would have been found in the down position if the controls were properly rigged *(see Figure 8)*. Hunter reported:

> *The right aileron of another Piaggio was placed both fully "up" and fully "down" for comparison purposes and it was noted that in the lower portion of the wing aileron cut-out, about ½ inch above the undersurface of the wing, a line of small screw heads protruded to face the aileron leading edge. On the accident aircraft a similar situation existed and these had left a clear and precise shock print upon the remnant of aileron leading edge remaining. These were measured and transferred to the other Piaggio and could only be made to align with the screw heads with the aileron in the "up" position. Indeed there is no way in which the top leading edge surface of the aileron could be so marked if the aileron was "down" at impact.*

Thus Hunter's findings, backed up by detailed drawings, showed conclusively that the misrigged aileron controls had driven the plane farther to the right—and into the ground—at the very moment when the pilot was trying desperately to turn it back to the left in order to counteract the wind drift and maintain alignment with the runway.

Hunter went on to pinpoint the site of the rigging error and explain how it probably came about. He described how the control column works the ailerons by a system of chains, cables, and pulleys. Since chains and cables can only be pulled, not pushed, the system required two separate parallel cables, one attached to each end of the control column chain, one causing the ailerons to produce a left bank and the other a right bank. The safety hazard in this system was that if the mechanics installing it *pulled* on the right cable, it would move the right aileron down, and therefore deliver a left bank. If the mechanic had never installed such a control column and did not carefully study the maintenance manual, he might well conclude that the ailerons were supposed to move in the same direction as the pilot's control wheel, and thereby he could fall into the fatal error of rigging the controls backwards. Hunter reported that this "pulling" error is exactly what happened:

> *The method used during assembly for deciding upon the "correct" cable was to pull it and watch the aileron, before making the connection.*
>
> *It only requires an understandable lapse for someone to believe that it is necessary to "make the cable do what the wheel must do" for a reverse connection to be made. A cable cannot be pushed. This sort of situation is conducive to human error.*

Hunter devoted a section of his report to "Discussion of Crossed Controls" in which he pointed out:

There can be no doubt that crossed aileron controls were present on the flight in question....

It is known that correct procedures were not followed in the removal and reassembly, that there was an interval [of ten days] between these two operations, which were conducted by different personnel and there is the added area for potential confusion in the method chosen for selection of the "correct" cable upon reassembly. These are all factors creating an environment in which human error is possible.

Hunter's bland understatement that "correct procedures were not followed in the removal and reassembly" is based upon his interviews with those who did the work. He found that even then, five months after the crash, these mechanics did not understand the control-rigging principles involved and therefore were not capable of installing and rigging the aileron controls properly. Thus even at that late date they probably would have reversed the aileron controls again without expert guidance.

If Hunter's report had been revealed to the public, it would have been embarrassing to Olympic because it showed their mechanics to be unqualified amateurs when it came to overhauling a Piaggio. The overhaul of an aircraft requires disassembly, replacement, and reassembly, an out-of-the-ordinary regimen—almost a remanufacturing of the plane—that occurs only once every four to five years given the utilization rate of the Piaggio. Indeed, the aileron control cables were scheduled to be changed only once every five years, so that this airplane, in its fifth year of service, was undergoing its very first change of controls. Furthermore, the Piaggio maintenance manuals, published in Italian and English versions, were in a language foreign to Greeks. The polite Englishman Alan Hunter was bending over backwards to avoid offending his client when he described this chaotic situation as "an environment in which human error is possible."

The impact of Hunter's report fell heavily on Ari's ego. It was Ari who had insisted that his Olympic Airways mechanics should do the major overhaul of the Piaggio, instead of having it done at the Piaggio factory in Genoa or in a factory-approved repair station whose mechanics frequently assembled and disassembled Piaggios. The Piaggio that crashed was the last one in Olympic's fleet. Olympic had operated two Piaggios until 1972, but the older one was found to be corroded after fourteen years of saltwater operation, and it was scrapped without undergoing any change of controls. Thus the Olympic mechanics who tried to puzzle out the correct rigging of the control cables in the Piaggio that killed Alexander were performing this exercise—historically one of overhaul procedures most likely to produce catastrophic mistakes—for the first time.

In the 1960s and 1970s, it was customary for small airlines like Olympic to contract the overhaul of their passenger planes to larger airlines that had the factory-scale facilities required to perform the demanding tasks involved. When Olympic began jet operations in 1959 with the De Havilland Comet 4B, it contracted much of the maintenance and all of the overhaul work to British European Airways (BEA), which operated a much larger fleet of Comets. When Olympic switched to Boeing 707 and 727 aircraft in 1966, it contracted the overhaul work to Trans-World Airlines (TWA). By the time Ari's Piaggio was sent to the Olympic shop for overhaul in 1972, Olympic was in the process of undertaking some overhaul work on its Boeing airliners. But unlike the Piaggio overhaul, the Olympic mechanics working on the Boeings were closely familiar with the aircraft, were equipped with Greek-language manuals, and had Boeing field engineers on call to visit the shop.

By putting his personal Piaggio through the crowded Olympic overhaul shop at the Athens airport, Ari was using it as though it were a general overhaul depot capable of handling many types of aircraft. In fact, at that very moment the Greek parliament, having recognized that no such general overhaul depot existed in Greece, was in the process of creating a government-subsidized overhaul facility for a wide range of military and commercial aircraft. That government-owned facility, named Hellenic Aerospace Industries, did not come into being until 1975, more than two years after the ill-advised "overhaul" of Ari's Piaggio. It required a government appropriation of $100 million, a sum that dwarfed Ari's total investment in Olympic Airways.

Ari insisted that Olympic mechanics perform all the maintenance on his personal planes, even though their real job was to maintain the airline's passenger fleet. This was part of his financial gamesmanship, for in saddling Olympic with his maintenance costs, he was cheating the Greek government which subsidized the airline services. He was pocketing a personal financial benefit on which he paid no taxes—tax evasion being an article of faith in Ari's operations. He was also exercising control by doing the maintenance in his own house. In this case, control meant that he could put pressure on the mechanics to complete the overhaul in time for the February cruise on the *Christina*, something that he might not have been able to accomplish if he sent the Piaggio to the factory or an approved repair station. Ironically, Ari also believed that he could better control sabotage in his own Olympic shop than in an outside overhaul facility.

We have seen that Ari was a control freak, with an insatiable drive to dominate the people and things closest to him. Here his role models were the two business tycoons he admired most, his friends J. Paul Getty and Howard Hughes. Getty could have served as the poster boy for family disfunction, with his record of cheating his mother out of part of her inheritance; shutting his parents out of all five of his weddings, and refusing to attend any of his sons' weddings; browbeating the four sons who worked in his oil company until they all failed miserably or—in the case of the one son who seemed to be headed for success—committed suicide; and his crowning achievement, at a time when he was considered the richest man in the world, treating his grandson's kidnapping as though it were a business deal, by putting one of his oil executives in charge of prolonging the ransom negotiations for months, until the kidnappers made good their threat to deliver the grandson's ear in the mail.

Robert Maheu, who ran Howard Hughes's Las Vegas properties for thirteen years, wrote in his autobiography that Hughes was obsessed with control. For example, he told of how Hughes ordered him to sign seven beauty contest winners to movie contracts. Hughes had no intention of putting them into movies. He provided each one with a Hollywood apartment, paid them a weekly salary, and kept them under surveillance so that they could not do anything other than wait for a call from Hughes which never came. According to Maheu, Hughes never touched them or even saw them, but he derived great pleasure from controlling their lives.

Alan Hunter's reconstruction of the comic-opera antics in the Olympic maintenance shop could only have deepened Ari's feelings of guilt over causing Alexander's death himself. This was another "but for" in the equation: *but for* Ari's insistence that the Piaggio be overhauled at Olympic in order to facilitate his tax cheating, his need for control, and his cruise timetable, the beginner's mistake of rigging the ailerons backwards could never have occurred, for it is inconceivable that the Piaggio factory technicians would make such a gaffe, and in any event a Piaggio factory pilot would have made the test flight, not Alex.

Turning his back on the incontrovertible facts reported by Alan Hunter, his own skilled investigator, Ari tried to escape public responsibility for his frauds. Always a heavy drinker, he fell into true alcohol abuse as he fought against the truth that was confronting him. Beyond Hunter's exposure of the unfitness of the Olympic mechanics, Ari was aware that if he had not insisted that the Piaggio be carried aboard the *Christina* to support his fraudulent boast of its ability to fly from mid-ocean, there would have been no reason for Alex to be killed in it. If Ari had not reneged on his Paris promise to substitute a helicopter for the Piaggio, there would have been no reason for either Alex or Don McCusker to be trapped aboard the lethal Piaggio on its final flight.

At the press conference on the day of Alex's death, one of Ari's many lies was this:

> *Perhaps my son wanted to make me a pleasant surprise by engaging McCusker for my private plane.*

Thus Ari tried to distance himself publicly from the check flight that resulted in Alex's death. But Ari was fully aware that Mac McGregor had been grounded by his eye ailment and was not even able to apply for renewal of his medical certificate when it expired on November 9, 1972. Therefore, it was anything but a surprise that Alex engaged Don McCusker, or that Alex would have to check out the new pilot, because Ari knew that as of November 9, more than two months before the crash, Alex was Olympic's only Piaggio pilot. Alex was forced to do the McCusker check flight—which was also the maintenance test flight—because Ari insisted that the Piaggio be put back on the *Christina,* complete with a new pilot, for his February cruise. Alex and Ari had to have discussed the need to check out a new pilot during the December Paris dinner, as part of the planning for carrying the Piaggio aboard the *Christina* during the February cruise. And it would not have been a "pleasant surprise" to Ari if Alex had simply hired a new American pilot to replace McGregor for Ari's "private plane" without consulting Ari, a change which Alex had no authority to make on his own.

There were others who could be assigned some blame, technically or legally: the Olympic mechanics who let ten days elapse between the removal of the old aileron cables and the installation of the new cables by a different mechanic, and who struggled in vain with the unfamiliar task of rigging the cables without access to a Greek manual or Piaggio factory expertise; the Greek Civil Aviation Authority and Olympic Airways inspectors who spent several hours going over the Piaggio before it was granted a new (and unwarranted) Certificate of Airworthiness, apparently never bothering to check which way the ailerons moved when the pilot turned the control wheel; and Alexander, who knew that the plane had not been test-flown since the overhaul and should have checked the aileron movement himself on the ground. A flight safety perfectionist might argue that Don McCusker, although completely exonerated by the investigators, should have insisted on checking the aileron movement himself, even though he was reporting to his new boss for a check flight in the boss's airplane and he was not aware that the cables had just been replaced. Perhaps it could even be argued that Mac McGregor, who was also cleared by the investigators, should have checked the aileron movement, even though he had not been told he was to be on the flight and had been recruited at the last minute to ride as a passenger as part of Alex's scheme to shorten the time he would have to devote to the McCusker checkout.

All these people were involved in events leading to the accident, and any of them could have prevented it if they had been able to anticipate the results of their actions and inactions. Yet all of them were trying to do their jobs under pressure of time and unreasonable demands on their skills. There was only one person morally responsible for the killing of Alexander Onassis: Aristotle Onassis himself. Unlike the others, he was cheating at the time of the crash, and it was his cheating about the Piaggio that created the pressures on all the others. It was he who insisted that the Myth of the Sea-Going Piaggio be carried on to satisfy his mania for control. His lifetime of sin caught up with him that day at the Athens airport, and his actions after the death of his son demonstrate clearly that in the end he was crushed by his moral guilt.

As a lawyer, I do not use the word "killing" lightly. I do not suggest that Ari planned or intended to kill his son. Therefore, his actions do not amount to murder or manslaughter in the strict legal sense. I do claim that Ari's arrogance, greed, and lifetime practice of fraud led *directly* to Alexander's death, so that he—and he alone—is morally responsible for killing his son. I say "directly" because his frauds set in motion the chain of events that trapped Alexander in an airplane which could not be flown safely.

That Ari was reacting strangely to the death of his son became apparent even to casual observers during the summer of 1973, six months after the Piaggio crash, when Ari spent an inordinate amount of time on Skorpios, where Alex was buried. In the past Ari had often stayed awake until dawn celebrating at nightclubs. Now on Skorpios he sat up all night beside Alexander's tomb, rocking back and forth on his haunches as he held his head in his hands, sobbing and muttering garbled messages to his departed son for hours at a time. His employees on Skorpios, fearing Ari would catch cold sitting on the damp grass for hours, took to placing a blanket on the grass near Alex's tomb. Sometimes Ari would take along two drinking glasses so that he could pour whisky or ouzo for himself and Alex. He told relatives, guests, and employees on Skorpios that he often heard his son's voice. This bizarre conduct was witnessed by, among others, Ari's daughter Christina and her visiting friend Marina Dodero, who tried in vain to bring Ari out of his stupor. Ari's sister Artemis was deeply concerned about this morbid behavior. When he waved off her protests, she asked the bishop of Lefkada, the nearby large island, to tell Ari that it wasn't right for him to disturb the dead.

The chief of Ari's American operations, Costa Gratsos, who had been one of Ari's closest friends for half a century, observed: "Ari blamed himself. He felt somehow responsible for the crash, for Alexander's death. That destroyed him. He did not really want to live any more." Here Ari was visibly struggling with his own guilt, but the "somehow responsible" tells us that he made this disingenuous confession to Gratsos because he lacked the character to explain how he had actually been responsible for the crash.

Likewise, according to Maria Callas's biographer Arianna Stassinopoulos Huffington, when Ari first visited the opera star after Alexander's death, she was appalled by his changed appearance and demeanor. Maria felt that "it was as if a lifetime of guilt had crystallized around Alexander's death," and that Ari's "grief and rage, unchecked and turned against himself, were destroying him." But again Ari was careful to give a rambling account of his reasons for feeling guilty, one that might fit any bereaved father, without touching on the deceitful manipulations which gave him ample reason to shoulder direct responsibility for the fatal crash.

The noted bandleader Peter Duchin, who was often invited to parties by Ari and Jackie, concluded that "Alexander's death knocked Ari out of the box. It completely changed his personality. He became morose, snapping, nitpicking, critical—just extremely difficult to even be in the same room with. All the spark he had was gone."

Another frequent Onassis guest, New York socialite Helene Gaillet, told of a visit to Skorpios when Ari took her to Alex's tomb: "He talked as if he expected Alexander to join us any minute. He said, 'Alexander is just as living to me as you are. He comes to me often. Unfortunately, until I die, I cannot go to him.' Ari had, for a brief moment, a haunted face, a look of terrible longing. I think Ari started letting go of his life after his son died. He began to lose interest. He began to give up. I had that strong feeling."

The year before Alex's death, Ari had hired Nicholas Papanikolaou, the son of a family friend, to work as a junior executive in his New York office. Nicholas was the same age as Alex. After Alex's death, Ari spent a lot of time talking to young Nicholas when he was in New York. To Nicholas, the change wrought by Alex's death was readily apparent: "The death of his son really broke him."

Ari's macabre brooding cannot be explained by the ordinary pangs of regret suffered by parents who lose a child, such as "I didn't spend enough time with him when he was growing up" or "I wish I hadn't been so harsh in my criticisms." The strong-willed, self-centered Ari was the least likely of fathers to be troubled by such regrets. He had raised Alex exactly in accordance with his own cardinal rule: there are no rules, so if you are Aristotle Onassis—or J. Paul Getty or Howard Hughes—you do whatever you please, and you get away with it. It was the realization that he did not get away with the Piaggio fraud that was destroying Ari.

Ari's desperate need to avoid the truth also explains his persistence in publicly blaming Don McCusker and mythical saboteurs for Alex's death. Skimpy as these lifelines were, if he let go of them he would have been submerged in the black sea of his own guilt. Thus it was imperative that the McCusker manslaughter indictment be kept alive. He ordered his hatchetman Johnny Meyer, "Keep the case open. No matter what you have to do, keep the case against McCusker open. Don't tell me there is no case. If we keep the case open, something may turn up!"

Between trips to Alexander's haunted tomb on Skorpios, Ari busied himself with training Christina to succeed him, enlisting the help of his New York aides as well as outside shipping executives and bankers to provide her with cram courses in all phases of his business operations. He was pleasantly surprised at the positive results: Christina, unlike Alex, wanted to learn how to take Ari's place when the time came, and she was proving herself capable of doing the job.

The tanker business was booming in 1973, but suffered a temporary setback during the third Arab-Israeli war which began that fall, causing Ari to cut back on construction of new tankers. Then he embarked on an ambitious effort to overcome the failure of his Omega oil refinery project. Still determined to trump Niarchos's Greek refinery, this time Ari chose a new location: the Granite State of New Hampshire. Ari was able to gain the support of the governor and the state's leading newspaper, and he appeared in person to answer questions from the press and the public. But in a town meeting held in the gymnasium of the Oyster River High School in Durham, New Hampshire, on March 6, 1974, under the cameras of six television networks, Ari's refinery proposal was turned down by a vote of 1,254 to 144.

Ari was sorely disappointed, but he had another major American project up his sleeve. Later In 1974, his Olympic Tower, a fifty-two-story Fifth Avenue skyscraper overlooking St. Patrick's Cathedral, was formally dedicated. It contained 250 outrageously expensive condominium apartments and nineteen floors of office space. Johnny Meyer planted stories in the American media that Ari and Jackie would soon take up residence there. This helped to spur sales of the apartments, but by that time Ari and Jackie, after the brief reconciliation brought on by Alex's death, had drifted farther apart than ever. By the fall of 1974, both of them were talking seriously to their lawyers about divorce plans.

On September 10, 1974, Tina Livanos Onassis Niarchos was found dead in the Niarchos Paris residence. The attending physician attributed her death to an edema of the lung. Her health had steadily deteriorated under the massive doses of barbiturates and tranquilizers she mixed with alcohol to get herself through life. In a joint statement brought on by Christina's suspicions of foul play, the Niarchos and Onassis families called for an autopsy. The autopsy results confirmed the original findings, with no evidence that anything other than overdosing had contributed to Tina's death. She was forty-five.

Now Christina, who had lost her brother and her mother in less than two years, suffered physical and emotional difficulties. But she soon snapped back (unfortunately, not without resorting to her own pill regimen) and again applied herself to the task of learning how to run the Onassis business empire.

Despite his ongoing aberrant behavior about the death of Alex, Ari carried on with much of his normal business activity, taking in stride the fall of the Colonels' junta which restored parliamentary democracy to Greece in July 1974. There was one exception: he refused to have anything to do with Olympic Airways, leaving his aides to struggle with its diminishing fortunes. By December 1974 its service had deteriorated so badly that the new Greek government took over its management and announced that it would buy Ari out. This brought Ari's attention back to the airline for the first time since Alex's death. At the last minute he tried to thwart the government takeover, but finally had to settle for a $69 million buyout which left him with a net profit of about $35 million after payment of Olympic's debts. It was not a bad return on the $2 million he had invested to buy the airline eighteen years earlier, but Ari considered it an unfair exploitation of the effort he had expended to build it into a respected international carrier.

Despite his brooding over Alex and his excessive drinking, Ari's health had remained remarkably good. He had just turned sixty-seven when Alex was killed, and he carried on with a Jet-Set lifestyle that would have exhausted most forty-year-old men. He continued the lifelong dedication to vigorous swimming which had kept him in good physical shape. Even after marrying Jackie in 1968, he had never ceased his affair with Maria Callas. After Alex's death he increased the time he spent with Maria, mostly in her Paris apartment.

In March 1974, after experiencing loss of energy and difficulty in keeping his eyes open, Ari checked into New York Hospital for tests. There it was determined that he was suffering from myasthenia gravis, a nonfatal disorder that can be controlled by steroid drugs like cortisone. He was under the care of Dr. Isadore Rosenfeld, the renowned New York cardiologist and medical author whom he originally consulted in 1970 because of concerns over heart disease, his father Socrates having died of a heart attack at age fifty-eight.

Dr. Rosenfeld was satisfied that Ari's heart palpitations were not life-threatening, and that the onset of myasthenia gravis in 1974 was not related to any heart problems. As he put it, "You don't catch myasthenia gravis from anything. It's an autoimmune disorder produced by the body itself in later years and often following an overwhelming emotional crisis. That was the case with Onassis after the death of his son. When he developed the first symptoms of this disease, I admitted him to New York Hospital under a pseudonym. They started him on a steroid program and it worked very well, relieving the myasthenia gravis considerably."

Ari managed to undermine this progress by taking the drug Procain, prescribed for him in Greece by a Romanian doctor who claimed that it would keep him young in energy, memory, and sex drive. The myasthenia gravis symptoms returned, stronger than in the earlier episode. When Ari came back to New York and told Dr. Rosenfeld he had been taking Procain, the doctor made him stop that drug immediately, but the damage prevented the cortisone from working as well as it had the first time. The return of myasthenia gravis decreased Ari's energy and caused him difficulty in keeping his eyelids open, but still it was not a life-threatening condition. He continued to take the cortisone, and he dealt with his drooping eyelids by taping them to his eyebrows, covering the tape with the dark glasses that he always wore in public.

Despite the effects of myasthenia gravis, Ari continued pretty much on his customary schedule, running his businesses, training Christina, and staying up most of the night drinking everything in sight at his old stomping grounds, New York's El Morocco and Maxim's in Paris. The Christmas holidays of 1974 found him alone at his villa in Glyfada, near Athens. He contracted a bad case of the flu, and his sister Artemis became concerned when he refused to eat or take his steroid medication. On February 3, 1975, still alone in Greece and having lost nearly forty pounds, Ari suffered severe abdominal pains and collapsed. Artemis frantically phoned Jackie in New York. Jackie immediately arranged to fly to Greece on a chartered plane, bringing along Dr. Rosenfeld.

When Jackie and Dr. Rosenfeld arrived at Glyfada, Christina was at her father's bedside with a gastroenterologist, Professor Jean Caroli, whom she had flown in from Paris. They found that Ari had developed a stone in the common bile duct that leads from the gallbladder to the intestine. Dr. Caroli recommended that Ari be flown to the American Hospital in Paris to have the gallbladder removed. Dr. Rosenfeld was concerned that Ari would be a poor candidate for major surgery because the steroid medication had severely lowered his resistance to infection. Dr. Rosenfeld strongly recommended that he be flown to New York, where a local procedure could be performed to dislodge the stone and leave it to drain outside, thus solving the problem without life-threatening surgery. Although an Olympic Airways 707 was waiting at the Athens airport to fly him to New York, Ari chose to follow Dr. Caroli's advice and he was flown to Paris instead.

Ari's gallbladder was removed at the American Hospital in Paris on February 9, with Jackie, Christina, and Artemis standing by. Also present was Nicholas Papanikolaou, the young New York aide whose company Ari enjoyed because he was Alex's age. The operation was successful, but Ari developed a serious respiratory infection which did not appear to be responding to antibiotics. During the long vigil that followed the surgery, Nicholas did his best to comfort Ari, but reported that Ari showed little will to improve and many times he implored those attending him, "Let me die."

Ari's hospital stay was to last five weeks. Near the end of the third week, after being told that Ari was slowly improving, Jackie announced that she would fly to New York to look after her children, and would commute to Paris thereafter as long as necessary.

Christina remained at her father's side and was given a suite across from his room so that she would not have to leave the hospital.

Also present at the hospital was Johnny Meyer, who kept the media informed of Ari's condition. Johnny reported that he had tried in vain to cheer up his boss. Ari said to him, "Soon I shall be on Skorpios with Alexander." Johnny replied, "You're crazy, Ari. Who ever heard of anybody dying from droopy eyelids?" It was during the Paris hospital stay that Ari again ordered Johnny to keep the manslaughter case against Don McCusker alive. Meyer recalled, "Right until the end, Onassis had this conviction that the C.I.A. had killed his son, and as long as he could keep McCusker on the hook something was sure to come out. He couldn't bear to let it end. He wanted it to go on and on, as if the case against McCusker itself was the only thing keeping Alexander's memory alive."

Jackie returned to Paris early in March to visit Ari at the hospital and pray for him at Notre Dame Cathedral. He did not appear to be improving, but the doctors told Jackie that he might linger on in the same condition for weeks or months. Jackie again flew to New York, explaining that a television program her daughter Caroline helped to produce was to air on March 16, and she was giving a party to celebrate Caroline's success.

On Saturday, March 15, 1975, a day of incessant rain in Paris, Ari's life came to an end at age sixty-nine. Christina was at her father's bedside, but Jackie was in New York, a circumstance for which she was to suffer much public criticism despite her claim that she had not been warned of Ari's deteriorating condition.

The public announcement was made by Dr. Maurice Mercadier, one of Ari's attending physicians. Dr. Mercadier said, "Death was due to bronchial pneumonia, which resisted all antibiotics. Mr. Onassis had been receiving cortisone treatment, which lowered his resistance to infection and made the pneumonia uncontrollable." Thus Dr. Isadore Rosenfeld's worst fears were realized.

Dr. Rosenfeld, who had become Ari's close friend, admirer, dinner companion, and confidant during the five years he treated Ari, believes that Ari knew he would die in Paris, and that he did not really want to live. Dr. Rosenfeld observed, "He really fell apart after his son died. He lost his will to live, in my opinion." As to the gallbladder decision, Dr. Rosenfeld concluded, "I believe that if Onassis had elected to come to New York instead of Paris, and avoided the gallbladder operation, he could have been saved."

Dr. Rosenfeld flew over to Greece and stuck his neck out for his friend Ari by advising against the gallbladder removal in the presence of the French doctor, Jean Caroli, who was a stranger to Ari. Dr. Rosenfeld gave Ari a chance to live by avoiding the major gallbladder surgery. If Ari had wanted to live, he would have had nothing to lose by flying to New York and trying the local procedure recommended by Dr. Rosenfeld. If that failed to solve the problem, he could then have had the gallbladder removed by an eminent surgeon in New York, whom Dr. Rosenfeld had standing by.

Therefore, it is clear that Dr. Rosenfeld is correct in his conclusion—corroborated by Costa Gratsos, Nicholas Papanikolaou, and others close to Ari—that Ari had lost the will to live. He finally chose death in Paris because the chance of life in New York only meant that he would have to go on, day after day, facing his haunting responsibility for the death of Alexander.

Yet, even in the ultimate spiritual crisis of his life, Ari reverted to his habitual deceit, conveying the false impression, which has persisted until now, that he was dying of parental grief rather than homicidal guilt. He falsely portrayed himself as the devoted father who was dying of a broken heart because he could not survive the loss of his son. But internally he could not hold back the tide of guilt over the knowledge that his frauds had trapped Alex in the deadly Piaggio. Most difficult for Ari to bear was the unavoidable realization that Alexander, at the last moment of his life when his brain was being crushed to pulp, knew who had killed him.

To me it is clear that Ari died of guilt rather than grief. Some may conclude that in this situation, it is impossible to distinguish the two, even though there was nothing in Ari's history or personality to indicate that he was unselfish enough to give up his life purely out of grief. Certainly this is a subjective conclusion about which reasonable people may differ. But it is important to note that the question of why Ari lost the will to live is entirely separate from the question of whether he caused Alex's death. As further support for the conclusion that Ari caused Alex's death, I have submitted what I believe is compelling evidence that Ari acknowledged his own guilt. But even if that evidence of guilt acknowledgement is disregarded, the separate evidence demonstrating that Alex was killed by Ari's greed, arrogance, and deceit stands on its own and, I believe, is irrefutable.

It is also clear that the Piaggio crash was the turning point of Ari's life—the event that turned it from dazzling success to excruciating failure.

―――――――――――――

Jackie was mobbed by the media on her arrival at Orly Airport the day after Ari died. She issued a short statement:

Aristotle Onassis rescued me at a moment when my life was engulfed with shadows. He meant a lot to me. He brought me into a world where one could find both happiness and love. We lived through many beautiful experiences together which cannot be forgotten, and for which I will be eternally grateful.

The *New York Times* devoted a full page to Ari's obituary, noting that he was known to both admirers and detractors as "the Golden Greek." Twenty-five years later, on January 1, 2000, the daily newspaper *Lloyd's List*, regarded as the bible of the shipping industry, proclaimed Ari its "Man of the Century." In the thousands of words that *Lloyd's List* devoted to "Onassis and his legacy" in 2000, there was no mention of the frauds we have reviewed here. Instead, the editors quoted an anonymous "close associate" who assured them: "From the beginning, his tactics were rough but they were always legal." Ari and Johnny Meyer would have had a long belly-laugh together if they had known that their fraudulent hype would weather the turn of the century none the worse for wear.

The funeral of Aristotle Onassis took place on Skorpios on March 18, 1975. Among the mourners were Christina, Jackie, John F. Kennedy Jr., and Senator Ted Kennedy. On his deathbed, Ari had ordered that the procedure used for Alexander's burial be applied to his grave. In his final act of gamesmanship, he would be buried just outside the Chapel of the Little Virgin. After the priests departed, Ari's architects would move in to build a chamber around his tomb, so that in death he—like his son Alexander—would forever defy the religious rule against burial inside the walls of the church. It was a posthumous fraud, a trick that Stavros Niarchos could never equal.

After the service, Christina led the mourners down the hill to the bay, where the yacht *Christina* lay at anchor. She invited aboard the funeral party and the island's Onassis employees.

There on the deck of the ship which symbolized all that Ari's life stood for, the red-white-and-blue flag was flying at half mast. It was not the flag of the United States, or France, or Great Britain, or Greece, or any other nation in which Ari had lived his life. It was the flag of Liberia, the symbol of Ari's cheating on taxes, short-changing seamen's wages, and trashing safety regulations. In itself it was one of Ari's most heralded achievements, the flag of convenience, which marked the *Christina* as a "ship of easy virtue" in the sailors' bitter words. It might as well have been the pirate's skull and crossbones. But this message was lost on Christina Onassis, who threw out her arms as she addressed the crew and the Skorpios employees:

This boat and this island are mine. You are all my people now!

Chapter Fourteen

Christina Takes Charge

It was July 12, 1973, when Don McCusker's flight from Athens landed at the Columbus airport. Helena and the six children were there to give him a royal welcome. At first they didn't recognize him, since he'd lost a lot of weight during the hepatitis siege and he'd also grown a mustache.

The initial euphoria of being reunited with his family and breathing the free air of Ohio lifted Don's spirits and carried him through the rest of the summer. He was still too weak from hepatitis to work, but he was able to endure the extensive dental work needed to repair his broken teeth. Since the Olympic Airways in-house lawyer, Tryfon Koutalidis, had promised they would pay all Don's future medical and dental bills for the accident injuries, Don sent the $822 dental bill to Koutalidis. There was no response.

Don's strength was gradually returning, and by late fall he began to send out resumés, still hoping for a flying job. The good news was that he made a fast recovery from his injuries and was able to pass the F.A.A. flight physical which he needed to keep his pilot's license current. The bad news was that there was no apparent interest in hiring a forty-nine-year-old pilot whose last flight had ended in a crash that was a front-page story all over the world, resulting in the manslaughter indictment which was still pending.

The McCuskers managed to get through the rest of 1973 by borrowing from relatives and friends, as well as exhausting the loan reserve of Don's life insurance policies. Their total income for 1973 was exactly $1,073. Helena advertised to do sewing and alterations, and Don took a job stacking bricks. He stayed at it for a few months until it nearly wrecked his health. Then he tried selling—sewing machines, hearing aids—but he was not cut out for sales work. Many of the sales leads he was given were to families that could hardly afford to buy food, and Don did not feel comfortable trying to tap their meager resources for nonessential items.

Swallowing their pride, the McCuskers went on food stamps for over a year. Helena had to do the shopping because Don could not bring himself to present the food stamps at the checkout counter even though he was clearly eligible for the program. Through these disastrous times, Don and Helena managed to raise their children with positive attitudes and values, even though they were in the free school lunch program that was a mark of poverty, and could not afford to buy their class pictures, and never had treats like sugared cereal, soda pop, potato chips, deli meats, store-bought clothing, or the latest music. The older children took on newspaper delivery routes and other part-time jobs that helped the family budget, while Helena made the childrens' clothes. Despite the family's reduced circumstances, all the children did well in their studies and continued to take part in athletics and church activities.

After months of fruitlessly searching for a full-time flying job, Don had to settle for part-time work as a pilot for a small firm at the Columbus airport that installed and repaired aviation electronic equipment. Don would have preferred a steady job as a business pilot, flying executives in their company planes, but that door was shut as long as he was under indictment. The electronics flying was spasmodic, and although Don was happy to get any piloting assignments, his hourly fees added up to less than $7,000 per year during the 1974-1977 period when he did this work.

In September 1974 Helena took a $6-per-hour job as a teacher's aide at the elementary school which the two youngest children attended. This enabled her to be home at the same time as the children. Don kept trying, mostly in vain, to augment his meager flying income with sales commissions, and he also worked as a driving instructor. All told, during the four years following the Athens crash, Don and Helena never were able to reach an annual earnings total of more than $12,000 between them.

Through those dark days, Don clung to the hope of clearing his name in the Greek court and collecting compensation from Olympic Airways for his injuries. His faithful Athens lawyer, Nicholas Foundedakis, kept him informed about the manslaughter case, which was called for trial twice a year, only to be postponed each time for another six months without any disposition. Mac McGregor, who had retired to England in November 1973 after failing his flight physical, did his best to help Don by flying to Athens to be present in court when the case was called for trial. A consular officer from the U.S. Embassy also attended each time as an observer, to reaffirm the interest of the United States in protecting Don's reputation.

Don was deeply grateful to Mac, whom he had met for the first time just a couple of hours before the crash. But it was obvious to Don that the case would never be tried because the Greek Air Force officers appointed by the police to investigate the accident had completely exonerated him. Yet the Onassis influence was strong enough to keep the indictment alive, and the mere fact that it was pending put Don on the equivalent of a pilot's blacklist. Don did not have enough clout to force it to trial, nor did he have the money to fly to Greece or pay the expenses of a trial. Indeed, he could not risk returning to Athens after having been fortunate enough to escape his detention, because there was always a chance that Greek justice would miscarry and land him in prison.

As before, the manslaughter indictment was blocking any chance of collecting compensation from Olympic. Don kept sending letters to Olympic requesting reimbursement of his unpaid expenses and compensation for his injuries and loss of income, but the reply was always that nothing could be paid until the indictment was disposed of. Mac McGregor, who had not been indicted, wrote in July 1974, eighteen months after the accident, that he had finally collected compensation of $15,000 for his injuries, which were not quite as serious as Don's.

Don's hopes rose when he learned on July 24, 1974 that the dictatorship of the Greek Colonels had fallen and Greece was returning to democracy. Surely, thought Don, under a democratic government, Onassis could not continue to block the clearing of Don's name by keeping the fraudulent indictment alive. Here Don underestimated the staying power of Ari's hype as well as the anti-American bitterness that lingered in the wake of the C.I.A.'s intervention in Greek affairs.

From the day of the Colonel's coup in 1967, it was regarded by nearly all thinking Greeks as a C.I.A. operation. Colonel George

Papadopoulos, who became the prime minister of the dictatorship, was trained by the C.I.A and was widely reputed to have been on the C.I.A. payroll since 1952. The defining image of the November 1967 coup was the television picture of the Colonels and their soldiers rumbling through the streets of Athens in American-made tanks. Throughout the seven-year reign of the Colonels, the money and arms needed to sustain their power came largely from the United States, at the behest of the C.I.A. To American policy-makers in the Johnson and Nixon administrations, the Colonels were a necessary evil who had to be supported in order to avoid a Communist takeover of naval bases that were crucial to containment of the global Soviet threat. To Greeks, the Colonels were murderers, torturers, terrorists, and thieves who were unworthy of support no matter what the consequences. The fact that much of Greece had been controlled by Communist forces during the Civil War of 1946-1949 did not legitimize the dictatorship of the Colonels. When they were thrown out, all those who had helped them became targets for retribution.

In *Greece: A Country Study,* a handbook prepared by the Library of Congress for the U.S. Army, the authors report:

> *In 1975, the United States Central Intelligence Agency was still widely held responsible for aiding the junta's accession and supporting its regime. This hostility was partly a backlash against the dependent relationship of postwar Greece to the United States, partly the result of resentment for United States support of the junta.*

When Constantine Karamanlis, a pre-junta prime minister, returned from exile to lead Greece back to democracy in July 1974, he was hailed as the Greek De Gaulle. He stated publicly that Greece was "no longer under American protection" and "no longer depended financially or militarily on the United States." Among the many problems he faced was the tricky task of meting out appropriate punishment to the Colonels and their henchmen without alienating the high-ranking army officers who still had some sympathy for their former leaders. Greece was still too unstable to assure that there would not be another coup if Karamanlis came down too harshly on the Colonels and thereby lost the support of the army. Therefore, in 1974 Karamanlis focused on other major problems, including the weak Greek economy, the need for a new constitution, and the never-ending conflict with Turkey over Cyprus. He put the trials of the Colonels on hold, and it was not until early 1977 that they were completed. In the end, eighteen of the twenty-four junta leaders were convicted, with three (including Colonel Papadopoulus) receiving death sentences which were later commuted to imprisonment for life.

In the interval of more than two years between the return of Karamanlis and the conviction of the Colonels, they were investigated and questioned, and their lawyers maneuvered to defend their interests. It was expected that this process would yield new information on the extent of C.I.A. involvement in the junta. Therefore, given the charges floated by Ari that the C.I.A. had killed his son and that Don McCusker was a C.I.A. agent, the Greek government could not seriously consider dropping Don's manslaughter indictment. There was always a chance that one of the junta leaders on trial for his life would plea-bargain and disclose evidence that supported Ari's sabotage charges. If that evidence implicated Don, the government would look very bad unless the indictment remained active.

Thus the indictment stayed on the books for more than four years, well beyond Ari's death in March 1975. Don thought that

Ari's death might remove the pressure on the Greek prosecutors and open the way for the U.S. Embassy to get the indictment dropped. But even after Ari passed from the scene, the poisonous fraud that he and Johnny Meyer had spread was deadly enough to keep the indictment alive, since the very existence of the manslaughter charges prevented any progress until the Colonels' trials were completed.

Don and his brother-in-law, the rocket scientist Herb Mehlhorn, kept pushing the State Department to get the indictment dismissed, but during the early years of the Karamanlis government, U.S. influence in Greece fell to a very low level. The homeporting agreement for the 6th Fleet, which Ambassador Tasca had worked so hard to achieve, was put on hold while Karamanlis renegotiated its terms during 1975 and 1976. The new 1975 constitution condemned the principle of stationing foreign forces in Greece, and prohibited them unless approved by the Greek parliament. This meant that the American embassy personnel in Athens had to be more careful than ever to avoid antagonizing Greek officials, and it pushed removal of the McCusker indictment down to a very low priority now that Don was safely back in the United States.

Since neither the Greek Air Force report nor the Alan Hunter report was published, the only conclusions about the cause of the Piaggio crash available to the Greek public were those spread by Ari: that it was the result of sabotage, probably engineered by the C.I.A. and its hayseed-from-Ohio agent, U.S. Naval Reserve officer Don McCusker. Given the disastrous image of the C.I.A. in Greece at that time, it is not surprising that many Greeks were ready to believe Ari's charges. What is surprising is the number of well-informed Greeks who are still willing to believe them today.

I learned of that attitude during the research for this book, which included interviews with Greek journalists, university professors, and former government officials and judges who lived through the junta and its aftermath. As a group these people were liberal democrats who were not predisposed to either believe or admire Aristotle Onassis. Yet nearly all of them consider the Piaggio crash an unsolved mystery which might very well have been the result of a C.I.A. sabotage plot. Some of them even feel that the McCusker manslaughter indictment should have been kept alive until the complete history of C.I.A. operations in Greece was disclosed. Perhaps this attitude is partially explained by the observations of C.M. Woodhouse, an English expert on Greece who fell in love with the country when he served there in the British forces resisting the Nazi invasion during World War II. In his 1985 book, *The Rise and Fall of the Greek Colonels*, Woodhouse writes of the legacy left by the Greek Colonels after they had been convicted:

> *Their legacy was almost entirely liquidated, but it left one characteristic relic. The Greek habit of believing that whatever befalls them is always due to foreign intrigue, never to themselves, was still operative. Since 1967, the C.I.A. has been cast in the role of permanent villain. Even after the fall of the junta, no event could be regarded as purely accidental...*

An obvious impediment to serious consideration of the sabotage theory is the fact that the aileron controls could have been switched only during the extensive aircraft overhaul, which would then require a test flight before passengers could be carried. Therefore, neither Ari nor any other passenger could have been the target of sabotage, since the switched ailerons would have done their deadly work on Alexander during the test flight. To the argument that there was no logical reason for the C.I.A. to murder Alex regardless of how dangerous they might have considered Ari to be, the Greeks have an answer: the ancient Balkan tradition of attacking a man by killing his son, thus inflicting greater anguish than by killing the father.

Even if we assume that the C.I.A. was familiar with this tradition, there would have been no reason for the C.I.A. to believe that misrigging the ailerons would have killed Alex. The reversing of controls would have to be accomplished while the plane was disassembled weeks before the crash, after which it was subject to scrutiny by Olympic and government inspectors who would be expected to check the working of the ailerons by manipulating the controls on the ground. Circumventing these crucial safety inspections would have required the C.I.A. to bribe at least half a dozen Olympic and government mechanics and inspectors. The mere effort to pull off such a harebrained scheme would have exposed the C.I.A. to betrayal by one honest man among the small army of conspirator-recruits. Even then Alex himself would have been likely to spot the reversal, for he had a reputation as a careful pilot and the saboteurs could not have known in advance that he would be in a hurry to complete the McCusker checkout so he could join Fiona in London that night.

If the C.I.A. had really been interested in disposing of Alex, it would have been surer and simpler to have him shot during a staged robbery or kidnapping, operations that were much more familiar to C.I.A. agents than the switching of aileron controls. Even if the C.I.A. had been intent upon sabotaging the Piaggio, crossing the aileron controls would have ranked far down the list of choices, both as to likelihood of causing a fatal crash and chance of escaping detection.

The history of Don McCusker's engagement by Olympic belies any C.I.A. involvement, for he got to Athens by answering a blind Olympic advertisement for an amphibian pilot months before the crash. Even if we assume that the C.I.A. could actually recruit an experienced pilot to fly a plane knowing that the ailerons were rigged backwards, that pilot would have to be stupid enough to destroy his career for little or no money. Otherwise Don would not have wound up having to put his family on food stamps when he returned to Ohio, a financial fact Ari's high-priced sleuths would have turned up in their investigation of Don.

Of course, many of these facts are unknown to the Greeks who are willing to entertain the C.I.A. sabotage theory, because the investigation reports were suppressed and the Onassis/Meyer hype show has had the stage to itself until now.

In the 1977 Greek elections, the socialist PASOK party led by Andreas Papandreou gained ground on Karamanlis's New Democracy party, foreshadowing the shift to a socialist government which was to come four years later. This 1977 parliamentary gain strengthened the position of the labor unions and helped to clear the way for Don's vindication, because the five Olympic mechanics who had been indicted along with Don were union members. So it was that on November 7, 1977, when Don had all but given up hope of getting the indictment dismissed, he received a phone call. It was the State Department in Washington. Don was so astounded that he did not catch the name of the person calling, but he did get the message: the manslaughter case against Don and the five Olympic mechanics had been called for trial in Athens that morning, and the court had acquitted all six of them.

In addition to the increased clout of the mechanics' labor union, it is possible that two other factors contributed to Don's acquittal. One was that relations between the United States and Greece were improving in 1977, which gave the American Embassy a little more leverage, certainly enough to insist that if the mechanics were to be acquitted, the same must be done for Don, who was himself a victim of their negligence in misrigging the ailerons. Second, Greece was interested in showing the world that the rule of law was firmly established under the democratic government, since it had been a favorite trick of the Colonels to immediately remove from office any judge or prosecutor who dared to enforce the law in cases where the Colonels did not wish it to be enforced. Don never learned exactly what caused the sudden acquittal in 1977, but he took it as an omen that the McCusker family prospects were looking up at last.

Don received the electrifying State Department call in Brookings, South Dakota. In May 1977 he had finally been offered a steady flying job. He would not be testing hot jet fighter planes for a manufacturer, or flying a sleek company plane. This job would put him in the cockpit of a lumbering Beech 18, a design first flown in 1937. It had two ancient piston engines and could carry six passengers at about 170 miles per hour on a good day. The job was with the Remote Sensing Institute at South Dakota State University, which had a state contract to take infrared readings of buildings from the air to determine how much heating fuel was being wasted through inadequate insulation. It was a time of great concern over energy conservation, and the venerable Beech 18 was ideal for this job because it flew slowly enough to get accurate readings from simple equipment. It was also homely enough to assure that nobody could accuse the state bureaucrats of hotdogging at taxpayer expense. When not checking heating losses, the Beech 18 was used for other state aerial chores, such as counting buffalo and geese; monitoring the spread of Dutch elm disease in trees; and photographing towns and lakes for environmental studies.

Before the Piaggio crash, Don would not have considered taking this job. Besides having to move to South Dakota, he was stepping about as far down in the professional pilot pecking order as one could go. It paid $17,000 per year, about what an experienced interstate truck driver was making at the time—a truck driver who did not have a mechanical engineering degree or 8,000 hours of flying the most sophisticated planes of the era. But from where Don sat, this job looked irresistible. He would get a steady salary with some fringe benefits, and he would have a chance to do something meaningful again. He and Helena agreed that he had to take the job, even though it meant uprooting the family when most of the kids were still in school.

Don left Ohio at the end of June 1977 to begin the new job in South Dakota. Helena followed in August with the children, and Don was just getting his teeth into his new career when the State Department called him in November. After a family celebration, Don sat down and started drafting a letter to Olympic Airways, bringing them up to date on his financial losses. He hoped they would make good on their promise to compensate him after the indictment was dismissed.

As we have seen, Don and Helena first met with Tryfon J. Koutalidis, director of the Olympic Airways legal department, in Athens on March 28, 1973. At that time Koutalidis told them that Don had been issued a passenger ticket which provided for payment of up to $18,000 as compensation for injuries and expenses; that the lawyer felt certain the entire $18,000 would be paid by the insurance company; and that Olympic itself would pay any additional expenses approved by Paul Ioannidis, Olympic's Director General, who had been very supportive of Don and Helena.

That meeting had taken place before Don was indicted. After the indictment, when Don met with Olympic Chairman Yanni Georgakis at the American Embassy on June 25, 1973, to work out his release on bail, Don reminded Georgakis of the promise Koutilidis made to him in March that his losses would be compensated by the insurance company and Olympic. Georgakis said he was aware of that promise and was in sympathy with it, but he was powerless to actually pay any money until the indictment was disposed of. So Don had to leave the question of compensation on hold for more than four years, until the indictment was dismissed on November 7, 1977.

On November 25, Don wrote to Koutilidis, reminding him of the 1973 promise of compensation and asking that his updated losses be paid now that he had been acquitted. By that time, Koutilidis had advanced from director of Olympic's legal department to chairman of the board. Don's November letter apparently got lost in the shuffle at Olympic, and he had to write two more letters, the last one on January 23, 1978. On February 2, Koutilidis sent this response on the letterhead of Olympic Airways:

Dear Mr. McCusker:

    This will acknowledge receipt of your letter dated 23 Jan 1978 in connection with which please be advised that Olympic Airways which as you may know, is owned by the Greek State since Jan 1975 has nothing to do with the case surrounding the airplane accident of Jan 1973.

    You should therefore address yourself to Messrs. Victoria Financiera Panama and Mr. C. Konialidis, to whom we are sending both your letter and our reply.

            Dr. Tryfon J. Koutalidis
            Chairman of the Board of Directors

Don assumed from this letter that "Victoria Financiera Panama and Mr. C. Konialidis" were Greek government employees to whom his claims had been referred. It required several more letters for him to learn that Financiera Panama was actually an Onassis shipping company, and that Mr. C. Konialidis could be reached at the Springfield Shipping Company's office in Athens. It turned out that Springfield was another Onassis-owned company. Unknown to Don, Mr. C. Konialidis was actually Constantine (Costa) Konialidis, Aristotle Onassis's first cousin, who fled the fires of Smyrna at the same time as Ari and then became Ari's close business associate for the rest of his life.

Thus it became apparent that when the Greek government took back the ownership of Olympic Airways in January 1975, Ari insisted that the McCusker claims be left under his control. Normally those claims would have stayed with Olympic Airways no matter who owned it, for it is not possible to shed a corporation's outstanding legal obligations by simply changing its ownership. No doubt the Greek government negotiators were happy to let Ari assume responsibility for the McCusker claims. Although Ari could have saved money by leaving the claims with Olympic, that would have deprived him of his lifeline: the ability to keep the manslaughter charges against Don McCusker alive in order to evade his own guilt. Had he left it to Olympic, the Greek government bureaucrats who now managed the airline might have disposed of the manslaughter indictment and the McCusker claims at any time, without consulting Ari.

Hence Ari retained control of "the case surrounding the airplane accident of January 1973" (as Koutalidis called it) during his lifetime, and made certain that after his death it would be referred to his most trusted aide, cousin Costa Konialidis. We have seen that Ari took his cousins Costa and Nicolas Konialidis into his

Argentine tobacco business, and that when Ari's tobacco insurance frauds were discovered, it was cousin Nicolas who went to prison in Italy. When Ari departed Argentina for London in 1932, he left the tobacco business in the hands of Costa and Nicolas. When Ari took over Olympic Airways in 1957, he put Costa in charge as president. When the Greek government took back the airline in 1975, Costa moved his Athens office to the Springfield Shipping Company, where he continued to function as Ari's right-hand man. In Ari's will, Costa was named chairman of the foundation which would carry on all of Ari's businesses.

Thus, Don's opponent in the negotiations for compensation was Ari's trusted cousin, aide, and successor, Mr. C. Konialidis. Or so Don thought. He was soon to learn that he faced an even more formidable foe: the ghost of Aristotle Onassis, in the form of his daughter Christina.

A Legacy of Deceit

When Ari died at the American Hospital in Paris on March 15, 1975, the first thing Christina did was to slash her left wrist with a surgical instrument. Some thought that in addition to demonstrating her grief, this was a sign of despair at being left with the staggering responsibility of carrying on the worldwide Onassis business empire at the age of twenty-four. She was soon to prove them mistaken.

She flew to Lausanne for a rest from the ordeal of standing by her father's deathbed for five seemingly endless weeks. By early April she was back at work, making the kind of bold moves that her father taught her so well. She was an American citizen by reason of her birth in New York in 1950. Ari had told her that when he died, she would have to renounce her American citizenship lest it cause tax complications, for the Internal Revenue Service had far stronger claims on the income of U.S. citizens than on aliens like Ari. In April she walked into the U.S. Embassy in Paris and formally renounced her United States citizenship.

Then Christina turned her attention to the typically convoluted scheme by which Ari had planned to control his empire from the grave. In January 1974, flying from Acapulco to New York in his Learjet with Jackie on board, Ari had written out his entire last will and testament by hand, pursuant to Greek custom. In the will he focused on three main goals: (1) taxation of his estate was out of the question; (2) having decided finally to divorce Jackie, he would cut her off with as little money as possible; and (3) management and control of his businesses would be concentrated in two tax-free Lichtenstein foundations to be administered by his trusted cousins and faithful retainers, allocating roughly half the profits to Christina but leaving her without any control, which could otherwise be wrested from her by a fortune-hunting husband or abused during one of her drug-induced tantrums.

Here we should note an extraordinary letter that Ari wrote to Christina a few days after drafting his will on the January 1974 flight from Acapulco, for it confirms the legacy of deceit which Ari bestowed on his daughter:

> My darling daughter Christina
>   This is my instructions as to what to do with my estate. I want the business to go on with a little more than half of my estate as a foundation for Alexander's memory. It is written in the form of "WILL" in Greek "DIATHIKI." For legal and tax and other reasons might be better not to disclose that I left a WILL in which case you just and simply do not disclose it and see that all the instructions are carried [out] fully. On the other

hand it might do no harm and on the contrary might be
advantageous to DECLARE THE "WILL." Mr.
Papandimitriou [Ari's Greek lawyer] knows all about it. A
consultation between Mummy, your mother, Cokkinis,
Papadimitriou, Costa Konialidis, Vlasopoulos and GRATSOS
with you will decide which of the two, DISCLOSE IT OR
NOT DISCLOSE IT, and just carry out the instructions is
the best course to take.

     Last Kiss   Daddy   January 14, 1974

There could be no clearer evidence that Ari had passed along to his daughter his cardinal principle: The only rules are that there are no rules, or there is no right or wrong, there is only what is possible. This letter blithely directed her to engage in obstruction of justice, perjury, and subornation of perjury, dragging along six other named conspirators, for after Ari's death it would become necessary for Christina and others to attest under oath to their knowledge of the existence of a will. This short handwritten note requiring no explanation of the direction to commit multiple felonies shows how well he had indoctrinated Christina into the life of deceit.

One of the Lichtenstein foundations was named the Alexander S. Onassis Public Benefit Foundation, and its purpose as stated in Ari's will was to "assist in the fields of medicine, education, literature, religion, the sciences, research, journalism, arts" and to establish a system of international awards similar to the Nobel prizes. On his death, Ari's assets were to be put into two roughly equal packages, A and B, with A going to the foundation for Christina's benefit and B going to the public benefit foundation named for Alexander. The gimmick was that the same set of foundation directors, consisting of Ari's alter egos, would manage and control both packages, A and B. While this would provide

Christina with roughly half the profits, it would leave her without participation in management even as to her own package. This final vote of no confidence did not suit Christina, and she immediately set about to change it.

In an ironical twist that would have amused Ari even as it trashed his elaborate scheme, the vehicle used by Christina to achieve control was to reverse Ari's shortchanging of Jackie. In his lifetime, as we have seen, Ari had contrived to cheat Jackie out of her rights as a widow under Greek law, which specified that on Ari's death she was entitled to at least 12.5 percent of his estate. He got her to sign a waiver of this entitlement, even though his lawyers told him such a waiver was prohibited by Greek law. He was confident that his control of the Greek judicial process (which he demonstrated in the fraudulent McCusker manslaughter indictment) would enable him to uphold the waiver. To make certain, he got his crooked friends in the Greek Colonels' government to enact a special provision—later called "Lex Onassis"—validating such a waiver agreement between a husband and wife signed outside of Greece, with one of the signatories (i.e. Jackie) being of non-Greek nationality.

Having used his corrupt influence on the Greek government to set Jackie up for a fleecing, Ari wrote into his will ridiculously cheap provisions for his wife of nearly seven years. Apart from a 25 percent interest in the island of Skorpios and the yacht *Christina*, she received no ownership whatsoever. She was to receive an income of $200,000 for life, and her children Caroline and John Jr. were to receive $25,000 per year until age twenty-one, at which time their payments went to Jackie. The value of these bequests was far less than the widow's minimum share of the estate under Greek law, which in Jackie's case would have been 12.5 percent of $500 million, or $62.5 million.

Knowing that Jackie was represented by highly competent American lawyers who would probably advise her to disavow the waiver as fraudulent and contest the will, Christina decided to offer Jackie a lump-sum settlement in exchange for Jackie dropping all claims as the widow. Christina conducted these negotiations herself, sometimes face to face with Jackie and sometimes with Jackie's lawyers. They finally agreed on a lump-sum settlement of $26 million. It was this payment that enabled Christina to break Ari's will in court, because under Greek law, once Jackie's claim was bought out, Christina as the sole survivor was entitled to at least 50 percent of the total estate. Since Jackie's settlement was paid out of the estate, Christina's package A, originally designed to represent 50 percent of the estate's total value, now fell short of that level. The Greek courts ruled in Christina's favor, and thus she gained control over her half of Ari's fortune, leaving his cousins and aides in control of the other half as directors of the Alexander S. Onassis Public Benefit Foundation.

Christina quickly made her position clear in a public statement carried by the media: "In the future, if anyone wants to do business with our companies, they will have to speak to me." Many of her business associates commented that she made them think they were still dealing with Ari. The foundation directors, who became known as "the Graybeards," went along with her wishes, acting more as advisors than partners. Several of the key directors felt all along that Ari's will left the businesses in an unworkable situation without one authoritative person at the helm, and were happy when Christina was able to cure this problem by breaking the will. Although confronted by a worldwide depression in the tanker business and chaotic management conditions created by Ari's one-man style, she justified the Graybeards' confidence by streamlining the shipping operations and keeping them profitable.

Stavros Niarchos probably thought he was dealing with Ari's ghost when Christina launched a nasty lawsuit against him in France in 1975. Her mother, Tina, had died in 1974 without a will, leaving assets valued as high as $270 million. As the surviving husband, Stavros would be entitled to inherit 75 percent of Tina's estate under French law, but if for any reason Stavros was found not to be the legal husband, Christina as the sole survivor would receive the whole estate. Christina asked the French courts to annul the marriage on the ground that Tina was not legally free to marry her ex-brother-in-law. Although this appeared to be a shaky legal theory, Stavros was intimidated by the prospect of airing his private affairs, and he agreed to settle for only 17.5 percent of Tina's estate. Christina received the remaining 82.5 percent, and walked away with the most satisfying Onassis victory over Niarchos.

Christina was present at Ari's bedside in the Paris hospital in 1975 when he ordered Johnny Meyer to keep the case against Don McCusker alive, as the key to proving that the C.I.A. had killed Alexander. Ari had told this to both Christina and Johnny many times before, and had repeated it on his deathbed when it was difficult for him to speak. When Christina took charge of the Onassis empire after Ari's death, she was determined to carry out Ari's wishes, provided they did not conflict with her own interests. She probably believed there was a chance that the C.I.A. sabotage theory was correct, since there is no record of anyone telling her it was a fantasy, and as we have seen, many intelligent Greeks were willing to accept it. In addition, Ari was able to use the emotional appeal that she would be desecrating Alexander's memory if she withdrew the indictment or paid money to McCusker.

Christina had no interest in the righting of a possible injustice to Don McCusker, for she had ignored all the letters that Don and Helena had written to her over the years, even though the other women close to Alex, Tina Onassis and Fiona Thyssen, had responded warmly to their letters. And she was now the sole guardian of the Onassis Rule: *There are no rules*, especially about irrelevant matters like justice.

Although the Greek government reclaimed ownership of Olympic Airways in January 1975, it was not until several months after Ari's death in March that all the contractual details were ironed out. Therefore, Christina was in charge when the final contracts were signed, and had to be aware that Ari had gone to great lengths to retain control of the McCusker claims. By going along with Ari's insistence that he or his successors deal with the McCusker claims, she was passing up the chance to save money by leaving those claims with Olympic. Therefore it is clear that she intended to make the final decision about Don McCusker's fate.

There is no record of any action taken by Christina regarding the manslaughter indictment, but it is a safe bet that she did everything she could do behind the scenes to keep it alive, as her father had done and had commanded her to do. After it was dismissed in 1977, she was faced with a stack of Don's letters, some of which were addressed to her, demanding the promised compensation. These letters were rerouted, misrouted, and ignored for over five months. Finally, after Don threatened legal action in the United States, on May 3, 1978 he got a phone call from a lawyer named Benjamin O'Sullivan, who was a partner in the New York firm of Holtzmann, Wise and Shepard, the main American legal advisors to Ari and Christina since the 1950s.

O'Sullivan said he was calling in response to Don's letters to Greece. Don asked him whom he represented, and he said "the Onassis interests." Don asked him whether Christina Onassis had received the letters addressed to her, and he replied that she had seen some letters and was "familiar with the situation." He said he was authorized to negotiate for a settlement, and asked Don what he had in mind.

Don told him that he had sent several copies of an itemized list of expenses and losses to Greece, and since it added up to $186,000, that was the figure he would settle for. O'Sullivan said that the size of this figure was "a big drawback" to reaching a settlement. He said they were thinking about something like $30,000 as a reasonable settlement.

Don said that $30,000 would not be satisfactory, and suggested that he would send O'Sullivan another copy of the itemized losses so that he could study it and come back with a more realistic offer. O'Sullivan did not sound too receptive but finally agreed that Don should send him the list.

The major categories on the itemized list were salary lost during Don's period of disability ($58,000) and the overall negative effects of the accident on his health and career ($110,000). Don reiterated his position that the total of $186,000 was a reasonable settlement for all he had been put through, and awaited O'Sullivan's response.

O'Sullivan phoned Don two weeks later and said they had carefully considered the itemized list as well as all the other factors, and concluded that they could make a final offer of $65,000. He emphasized that it was a final take-it-or-leave-it offer which would not be increased. Don said that he was disappointed, but would think it over and let O'Sullivan know his decision after he discussed it with his wife and with some people who were advising him.

Don had consulted several American lawyers about what kind of settlement he should consider. They all advised that given his excellent physical recovery, and considering the difficulties of pursuing this case in the American courts when everything happened in Greece, he would be doing well to get a settlement of as much as $50,000. There was also a problem with the statute of limitations, since it was now more than five years since the accident, and American courts usually required suit to be filed within two or three years. That made O'Sullivan's final offer of $65,000 look very tempting, especially since it would be paid immediately without any litigation or legal costs. Don and Helena talked it over and decided that they had better accept the $65,000, put the Piaggio crash behind them, and get on with their lives.

One of the people whose advice they sought was Helena's brother, the rocket scientist Herb Mehlhorn. Herb sent them a letter on May 24, 1978, enclosing a copy of a *Wall Street Journal* article which he had just read. Herb wrote, "I think this article opens several possibilities you may want to look into." The article was about recent American court cases in which victims of airplane crashes, some of which occurred in foreign countries, had recovered six-figure damages. The article mentioned my name, generously describing me as "a leading air-crash lawyer and himself a pilot in World War II."

When they received Herb's letter, Don and Helena were on the point of phoning O'Sullivan to accept the $65,000 settlement. After reading the article, they decided they had nothing to lose by phoning me.

So it was that on May 30, 1978, Don called me from South Dakota and told me his story. He asked whether I thought I could do much better than the $65,000 offered by O'Sullivan. Since I had read about the Piaggio crash and knew Don had been charged with manslaughter, I said that I thought I could top that figure, and that if I took on the case, the fee would be a percentage of any recovery over the $65,000 which was already on the table. I suggested that Don and Helena fly to New York at my expense so we could meet and make a final decision. They agreed, and the meeting was set for June 8.

I did not tell them that ever since my first lawsuit against Aristotle Onassis in 1970, I had been itching to get a second shot at him, dead or alive.

Chapter Fifteen

A Court Date for Ari's Estate

BACK IN JUNE 1970, A MAN NAMED NICHOLAS ONASSIS MADE an appointment, came to my office, and asked me to represent him in a suit to be filed against Olympic Maritime, the Monaco-based company owned by his first cousin, Aristotle.

Nicholas, then a resident of Montreal, spoke with a Greek accent. He immediately reminded me of Akim Tamiroff, one of my favorite actors. This resemblance became even more striking when I noticed that when smoking, Nicholas held his cigarette in his thumb and middle finger with his palm facing his mouth, in the same unorthodox grip that Akim Tamiroff had used on screen.

Nicholas told me that his father was the brother of Ari's father, Socrates; that he too had fled Smyrna for Greece in 1922; that he had worked with Ari in the tobacco business and had served as an apprentice captain on one of Ari's early ships in

Buenos Aires, where he lived for twenty years. After World War II Nicholas had emigrated to Montreal and had done well in real estate, but had always yearned to return to his first love, shipping. His success in real estate gave him the chance, and he chose to do so by creating a unique vehicle: The Shipowners Fund, Inc., a pool of money to be invested in diversified ownership of independent tankers and freighters. It sounded to me like a maritime version of the real estate investment trusts that were then becoming popular.

Nicholas told me that he had discussed the idea of The Shipowners Fund (SFI) with Ari, who thought it was a good project for Nicholas but was not interested in participating himself. On his own, Nicholas arranged an initial public share offering of $10 million, to be sold in the international market. He launched the offering with a large advertisement in the *International Herald Tribune*, explaining SFI's investment strategy and offering the shares at $5,000 apiece. "N. Onassis, Chairman/President, Luxembourg" appeared at the top and bottom of the ad.

A few days later, full-page ads appeared in the *International Herald Tribune*, the *Wall Street Journal*, and the *Financial Times* of London. These ads announced:

> *Olympic Maritime S.A. as general agents for the A.S. Onassis Group of Shipping companies wishes to announce that this shipping group HAS NO CONNECTION WITH "The Shipowners Fund" managed by the Shipowners Fund, Inc., N. Onassis Chairman/President, Luxembourg. That Mr. N. Onassis is not and has never been employed by or associated with the A.S. Onassis Shipping Group.*

Nicholas told me that these ads were only the tip of the iceberg. He had received more than four hundred replies from the

SFI offering ad, many of them from securities dealers who were interested in buying shares for their clients. Overnight many of the securities dealers wired and phoned Nicholas to inform him that they no longer had any interest in SFI. The reason was not merely the newspaper ads, although their size and tone clearly implied that SFI and N. Onassis were of questionable integrity. The dealers had received reports, both directly and through financial journalists, that N. Onassis was a notorious international confidence man and a complete imposter who had illegally adopted the Onassis name to cash in on its commercial value. When Nicholas sought to assure the dealers that he was actually Ari's cousin and had never been involved in criminal activities, they replied that it made no difference. The smear ads and the telephone character-assassination campaign had made it impossible for reputable dealers to put their clients into SFI ownership. The Shipowners Fund was dead in the water.

After studying his documents, I told Nicholas that I would represent him in seeking damages for destruction of the Shipowners Fund, but that it would not be easy to bring the case in the New York courts. We could probably get jurisdiction over Ari personally, but he would claim that the ads were placed by Olympic Maritime, which could not be served with legal papers in New York. There was also the problem of a Canadian citizen trying to sue Ari, another foreign citizen, in the New York courts, based on activities which took place outside New York.

In such cases, the people who are sued usually ask the court to dismiss the case under the doctrine of *forum non conveniens*, meaning that it would be far more convenient for a foreign court to hear the case. The New York courts, as always, were overcrowded with cases involving New York activities, and the judges were quick to rid their calendars of cases that could be conveniently tried elsewhere.

An example was the suit filed in New York against Ari himself by Spyridon Catapodis, claiming that Ari had agreed to compensate him for his role in procuring the 1954 Jiddah Agreement relating to Saudi Arabian oil. Catapodis claimed that Ari had signed such an agreement in disappearing ink. His lawsuit also disappeared when the New York court dismissed it because everything had happened in foreign countries and therefore New York was not a convenient forum.

My first thought was to file suit for Nicholas against Ari and Olympic Maritime in Monte Carlo, since they both had headquarters there and could hardly claim it was an inconvenient forum. There were then half a dozen lawyers with offices in Monte Carlo. I contacted every one of them to learn if any would consider representing Nicholas. All replied that they could not do so because they were under retainer to represent Olympic Maritime. I then tried lawyers in Paris, but was told that they were not permitted to appear in the courts of Monaco. That was a privilege limited to the Monte Carlo lawyers who had turned me down. So Howard Hughes was dead right: Ari's Monte Carlo setup was so perfect that he could not be sued there.

My Plan B was to arrest an Olympic ship in New York harbor, the same tactic Ari had employed in Rio de Janeiro to obtain compensation from the Norwegian government-in-exile during World War II. That was a way of obtaining jurisdiction which would give us a good chance to avoid a *forum non conveniens* dismissal. But I had to make certain we were dealing with a ship actually owned by Olympic Maritime, for the law required posting of a very large bond to indemnify the owner if a vessel was wrongfully detained. Since the ownership of Ari's ships was not easy to determine, I told Nicholas it would be necessary for me to seek a court order permitting us to conduct discovery about ownership before filing suit.

Nicholas approved this plan, and I served the necessary pre-suit discovery papers on Ari's New York office. Ari's New York lawyers, the firm of Holtzmann, Wise & Shepard, opposed the application for discovery, but the judge ordered production of the ownership records and sailing schedules of all ships in which Ari or Olympic Maritime had any interest.

As I was poring over this bonanza of records in the hope of making the arrest, I received a phone call from Nicholas's wife in Montreal. She informed me that Nicholas had suffered a heart attack, and that his doctor had advised him not to go any further with the case because the stress was too much for his heart. I offered to speak to the doctor, and to put off any further activity in the case until Nicholas recovered from his heart problem. I pointed out that we still had several years before the statute of limitations would bar the suit. But Mrs. Onassis, who spoke in a distressed tone, was adamant. I was to do absolutely nothing further on the case. Period.

I had never experienced this kind of ending, and at the time it seemed a bit peculiar. Since my hands were tied, I simply followed the client's instructions and did nothing further on behalf of Nicholas. It was not until years later, when I first read of Ari's destruction of Christina's marriage to Joe Bolker, that I began to put the pieces together. Ari's hatchet man, Johnny Meyer, had blackened Bolker's reputation by phoning journalists and business associates of Bolker, with the object of softening him up to end the marriage. That campaign was similar to the one whch destroyed the Shipowners Fund stock offering. When Bolker refused to cave in to that pressure, he received calls threatening his life, and Christina confirmed that these tactics by her father did not surprise her. As we have seen, she was aware that Johnny Meyer was in close touch with wiretappers and real-life hit men.

The Bolker intimidation occurred within a few months after the phone call from Nicholas's wife that ended the Shipowners Fund litigation.

Nicholas Onassis was a hardy character who had escaped the destruction of Smyrna at an even younger age than Ari, and had gone on to work in the rough-and-tumble world of the merchant seaman. He'd been through too many battles to let a heart problem deprive him of a multimillion dollar claim against Ari—if indeed there was a heart problem. Out of curiosity, I checked the Canadian newspapers and court records. I learned that when Nicholas was in his late sixties, years after he dropped the SFI suit against Ari, he was still energetically involved in arduous intercontinental business activities and had gone to court several times, including a trial against a major Canadian company which required him to testify in court for more than two full days. This convinced me that he had probably been threatened with bodily harm by the Ari/Johnny Meyer team, which he took seriously enough to drop the 1970 New York suit like a hot potato.

On June 8, 1978, Don and Helena McCusker sat in my office, having flown in from South Dakota the day before. In the week that had passed since Don's phone call, they had sent me a big package of documents which helped to fill in the details of their story. Within minutes of meeting them, I was satisfied that they were telling the whole truth and nothing but the truth. In fact, I would have bet a respectable sum that they wouldn't lie or exaggerate if their lives depended on it. Rather than pushing their claims aggressively, they were concerned about whether it was proper for them to sue, despite all the hardships that Ari and Olympic had imposed on them. My delight at having such admirable people as clients was quickly tempered by concern that hardened New York jurors might find them too good to be true.

The McCuskers were easy to talk to. Don was a feisty Jimmy Cagney type, while the lovely Helena seemed to have a sharper memory of details like dates and places. Since one of my duties in the Army Air Forces was a very brief stint as a test pilot, and both Don and I were airplane buffs, we had something in common other than having been cheated by Aristotle Onassis.

Before their arrival, I had taken a look at the legal problems of the case, and was not surprised to find that they were plentiful. The most obvious problem in suing on a five-year-old claim was the statute of limitations. New York had a three-year deadline for personal injury claims, but I felt we had several potential escape routes. First, settlement negotiations will sometimes extend the limitation period, and Don had received the $65,000 settlement offer only a few weeks earlier. Second, our suit would include claims for malicious prosecution, false imprisonment, defamation, and intentional infliction of emotional harm, all based on the fraudulent manslaughter indictment which had not been dismissed until November 7, 1977, and the statute of limitations would be measured from that date. Third and least promising, since the fatal Piaggio flight was scheduled to make takeoffs and landings in the Aegean sea, we could include a claim in admiralty, which has no definite limitation period but uses "laches," a vague term which permits suits to be filed within a time that is reasonable under the circumstances.

I was forced to conclude that the claims against Olympic Airways were not worth very much. Don was listed as a passenger and was issued a ticket which contained a limitation of liability to a maximum of $18,000. We could attack this limitation as being against the public policy of New York, but the outcome was uncertain. An even greater threat was the New York Worker's Compensation Law, under which Don would probably be considered an employee even though at the time of the crash he was merely auditioning for the Piaggio job. If he was held to be an employee, Olympic's liability would be limited to Don's medical expenses (already paid by Olympic) plus about $200 for each week of his physical disability, which would add up to less than $12,000. If the only defendant had been Olympic Airways, I would have told Don to follow the advice of that noted legal authority, Woody Allen: Take the money—the $65,000 on offer—and run.

From the moment Don phoned me, I felt that the important claim was against Aristotle Onassis, because he was the real culprit and also because suing his estate would solve many of our legal problems. As we have seen, the statute of limitations for malicious prosecution, false imprisonment, defamation, and intentional infliction of emotional harm had not begun to run until the Greek court acquitted Don only eight months earlier. Don could not be considered an employee of Ari, nor would the $18,000 passenger ticket limitation apply to any defendant other than Olympic Airways. But there was one major problem. After Don's call I checked the records of the New York Surrogate's Court, which administers all estates, and found that no New York estate had been opened for Ari even though he had been dead for more than three years.

Like many legal problems, this one had more than one angle to it. Lack of a New York estate would make it impossible to include claims against Ari—unless we could create an estate. Fortunately, there was an obscure provision in the Surrogate's Court rules which opened up that possibility.

In New York, the basic right to open an estate for a person leaving a will is given to those named in the will as executors. If there is no will, the close relatives who are defined as "distribu-tees"—usually the widow and children—have the right to apply for appointment as administrators. If the distributees do not apply, and there is a valid legal reason for appointment of an administrator, the Surrogate's Court can appoint the Public Administrator of New York County as the administrator. The Public Administrator (the P.A.) is a public official charged with administering estates of people who died leaving property in New York, for whom no qualified relative has opened an estate. Typically the P.A. acts as administrator for estates of foreigners who die while visiting New York, or deceased local residents who do not leave enough property to make it worthwhile for relatives to open an estate. The P.A.'s appointment as administrator often is only temporary, until the relatives get organized and take over administration of the estate.

A peculiar quirk of the law is that anyone having a legal claim against a deceased person for whom no estate has been opened may petition the Surrogate's Court to appoint the P.A. as admin-istrator. If the petition is granted, the P.A. becomes the nominal defendant, but the claim is satisfied out of the estate's assets. This provision always reminded me of the old Marx brothers gag in which Groucho says to the heavily-accented Chico, "I'll get you an interpreter so I can insult you properly!"

In our case, it was clear that our first move should be to peti-tion the Surrogate's Court to have the P.A. appointed as adminis-trator of Ari's estate. The Surrogate's Court provided a printed form of Petition for Letters of Adminisration which I had filled out, awaiting Don's signature when we met on June 8. After recit-ing Don's name and address, there were two options under "Interest of Petitioner": Distributee of decedent, which Don was not; and "Other (specify)" in which we specified "Plaintiff in lawsuit being filed against decedent's estate." Under "particulars respecting the above named decedent," we filled in the death date of March 15, 1975, in Paris, and listed Ari's domicile as 795 Fifth Avenue, New York, the address of his apartment at the Pierre Hotel. Under "Distributees" we listed Jacqueline Bouvier Kennedy Onassis, wife, domiciled at 1040 Fifth Avenue, New York, and Christina Onassis, daughter, domiciled at the Olympic Tower, 641 Fifth Avenue, New York.

The form required information about the decedent's personal property and real property in New York State at the time of death. We assumed that Ari had left some suits and shirts in his Pierre Hotel apartment, and since he was never known as a fancy dresser, we listed them as being worth less than $5,000. As to real property, we listed "Olympic Towers Office and Apartment Building located at 641 Fifth Avenue, New York. Also apartment in Pierre Hotel located at 795 Fifth Avenue, New York." The petition concluded:

> *WHEREFORE, your petitioner respectfully prays:*
>   *That process issue to all necessary parties to show cause why letters should not be issued as hereinafter requested; and*
>   *That a decree award Letters of Administration of the estate of the decedent to the Public Adminisrator of the County of New York or to such other person or persons having a prior right as may be entitled thereto.*
>   *Dated June 8, 1978. Signature of Petitioner:*
>   *Donald F. McCusker.*

This put the wheels of justice into motion. The Clerk of the Surrogate's Court sent citations to Jackie and Christina, notifying them of their right to be present at the hearing of the petition which was set for August 16, 1978. If they chose to be present or send their lawyers, they would have the right to challenge the appointment of the P.A. and get themselves appointed instead. If they did not, the P.A. would probably be appointed by default.

A copy of the petition was also sent to the P.A.'s office, where it was routed to the staff lawyer who served as counsel to the P.A. We had dealt with each other in prior cases, and when he got Don's petition, he phoned me and asked, "Is this one of your bad jokes, Speiser?" I told him that as a reward for his years of stalwart service to New York's pauper population, he was now being tapped to administer the estate of one of the world's richest men. When he pressed me, I explained Don's claims. He thought it would be very interesting to see what happened on August 16, the date set for the court hearing of Don's petition to appoint the P.A.

It would be very interesting indeed. I knew, as did the rest of the world, that Ari had never paid taxes in New York during his lifetime, and that Christina was not about to start such a disagreeable practice after his death. (By that time, Christina had arranged for Jackie to be paid $26 million to drop all her claims to the estate, so Jackie was out of it, but we had to include her name in the petition since she was legally a distributee.) Of course the Olympic Tower and Ari's other multimillion dollar holdings were not listed in his name, and Christina's lawyers would take the position that he owned no property in New York (or the United States) at the time of his death. Before Don's petition was filed, the Onassis lawyers were not required to file any estate tax returns or make any other disclosure of his holdings. By remaining silent, as was their duty to the client, apparently they had been able to insulate Ari's estate from U.S. and New York State inheritance taxes.

While I was not familiar with exactly how the P.A. conducted his office, I felt that having the estate of Aristotle Onassis dropped in his lap would probably cause him, at a minimum, to try to determine what assets it contained. There was the immediate question of how large an administrator's bond would have to be posted, which depended upon the total value of the decedent's property in the state. Presumably the P.A. would have to render some kind of accounting to the Surrogate's Court, and it would not have surprised me if he had a duty, formal or informal, to notify the New York State Tax Department of his appointment. The tax collectors have a way of cultivating other public officials who might furnish clues to hidden property. For example, relatives who seek a Surrogate's Court order for the opening of a deceased person's bank safe deposit box will usually find that the box has been sealed pending the attendance of the tax collector at the opening.

Therefore, I speculated that Christina's lawyers would advise her that they should appear in the Surrogate's Court on August 16 and oppose the appointment of the P.A. She could get herself appointed in his place automatically, but would that solve the potential tax problems? More likely, she would oppose *any* appointment on the grounds that Ari left no property in the state. But such a move would open the door to a legal donnybrook in which I would undertake to discover the precise ownership of all Ari's ships, buildings, and other personal and business assets. I would have at my disposal the liberal American discovery rules, which could be used to force production of all the ownership documents. I would have the right to obtain the sworn testimony of Christina and all the Onassis/Olympic officials who knew anything about the ownership, probably including lawyers and accountants. Finally there could be a trial of all these ownership issues in the Surrogate's Court, which might include a jury empowered to decide the facts. All of these proceedings would be conducted in public, and so the true ownership of Ari's entire empire would become fodder for the media and other interested bystanders, such as the New York State Tax Department and its bigger and better-staffed brother, the United States Internal Revenue Service.

The potential consequences of this disclosure would include the levying of estate taxes on whatever property was found to be owned by Ari which had a legal connection with New York. Depending on what was decided by the Surrogate's Court jury (typically composed of working New Yorkers who were struggling to meet their own tax bills), Ari's New York estate would probably run well into nine figures. That estate would then be subject to federal and state estate taxes (which total well over 50 percent in the upper brackets) plus interest and penalties. Beyond that, the insatiable tax collectors could allege that Ari should have paid federal and state taxes on the income produced by this property for many prior years. They could assess his estate for back income taxes, interest, and penalties for fraudulent tax evasion. In the worst case scenario, the tax collectors' bill could turn out to be larger than the total value of Ari's estate, widely estimated at $500 million. In 1965, Stavros Niarchos, never as nimble at tax evasion as Ari, had been slapped with a $25 million bill for unpaid income taxes on the profits earned by a handful of his tankers.

Thus Don's petition to appoint the P.A., a mere preliminary procedural step to open the way for Don to sue Ari's estate, could turn into a monster that would dwarf the claims for the damage done to Don. No doubt Ari would have considered this unsportsmanlike conduct, as did Al Capone when his illicit control of the Chicago courts was trumped by Eliot Ness and the Untouchables, who managed to get him convicted and jailed for income tax evasion, a white-collar crime that was hardly worthy of mention alongside his murders and racketeering.

The prospect of being called unsportsmanlike did not deter me from filing Don's petition in the Surrogate's Court. It was clear to me that Christina's lawyers should advise her to make every effort to settle Don's claims and get him to withdraw the petition prior to the August 16 hearing date in the Surrogate's Court. But I was not counting on that advice being given or taken. My decades of experience as a lawyer for the underdog had taught me that powerful defendants who are fully aware of their culpability usually do not roll over and capitulate early in the game, before they are confronted by the certain knowledge that the lowly plaintiff can actually prove the case in court.

I should point out that representing the underdog was not an ideology-driven choice, although I actually found it more enjoyable than the other side. It was the result of the selection process that governed the New York legal scene when I entered practice in 1948, under which we were most likely to be classified as plaintiffs' or defendants' lawyers, depending upon which side we represented when first making a splash. I had been fortunate enough to build a busy practice in the representation of airline passengers (and their next of kin) in accident suits, which pitted the individual passengers' families against giants like Pan American, TWA, United Airlines, Boeing, and the United States government. My partners, the first seven of whom were also former pilots, were mindful of the time-tested principle that law firms prosper most when they repeat steps they have learned well by experience. When I occasionally dabbled in representing underdogs other than aircrash victims, they would chide me with the question, "How come you always want to represent David against Goliath?" My stock answer was, "Because Goliath never phones." Thus I was not a starry-eyed crusader for the downtrodden. I would not take on any underdog client whose case I did not think I could win, not least because underdogs rarely have any money to pay lawyers, and a contingent percentage of a losing case produces a fee of zero. Nor did I believe that it was a service to the downtrodden to put them through years of fruitless litigation.

Large companies rarely settle early in the game no matter how strong the proof, simply because it requires an exercise in accountability for the decision-makers to face up to their own guilt, and accountability is easily diffused within large organizations. John DeLorean wrote of his experience with immoral decisions that were made by otherwise moral people at the top level of General Motors: "The impersonal process of business decision-making is reinforced by a sort of mob psychology that results from group management and the support of a specific system of management."

This corporate culture was confirmed by my experience in representing Ralph Nader against General Motors in the lawsuit arising out of their attempts to silence Ralph's criticism of the Chevrolet Corvair in his first book, *Unsafe at any Speed.* At first Ralph was ambivalent about suing, fearing that seeking money might tarnish his image as an advocate for the public good. Before filing the suit, I met with GM's chief New York house counsel and laid out irrefutable proof of their attempts to intimidate Ralph, hoping this would induce them to settle the case. But they turned me down, probably because they thought we would have difficulty in proving the case. Ralph overcame the image problem by announcing that the proceeds would be devoted to the consumer movement, and authorized me to file suit. We went through more than three years of bruising litigation before GM finally settled. GM's president was able to avoid accountability by testifying that he had not known of the hiring of private detectives to smear Ralph. A token accountability was achieved by the firing of some people in the GM legal department who were directly implicated in the illicit smear campaign.

One would think that moguls like Aristotle Onassis who ran their companies as one-man businesses would look more realistically at the desirability of settling early, for they have less leeway to avoid accountability. But that depends on their egos. A tycoon who achieved extraordinary business success under the Onassis Rule that there is no right or wrong is likely to be so certain of his invincibility that the concept of reimbursing a victim of his fraud is unthinkable.

For example, Aldo Gucci was the dynamo who brought the Gucci style to the United States and made the name synonymous with high fashion. Like Ari Onassis, he ran the privately-owned Gucci family business as his own fiefdom. I represented his son, Paolo, the company's chief designer, who claimed that Aldo had cheated him out of his share of company profits. At a conference with Aldo's lawyers, I laid out documentary proof that Aldo had set up a phony paper operation in Hong Kong which siphoned away profits that should have been paid to the shareholders, including Paolo and his brothers. What I did not say, but was obvious, was that Aldo's fraud had also diverted profits to Hong Kong which otherwise would have been taxable by Uncle Sam and New York State. Even after being shown the incriminating documents, Aldo would not hear of settlement talk. In fact, he angrily accused me of attempting to extort money from him. As a result of his blind egomania, his son Paolo had no choice but to put the damning Hong Kong fraud evidence into the court record, from where it was picked up by the media and later by the I.R.S. Ultimately Aldo pleaded guilty to tax fraud and was sentenced to a year in federal prison at the age of 80. He was forced to pay tens of millions in back federal and state taxes, interest, and penalties.

I knew that if Aristotle Onassis were alive, he would not have given a moment's thought to settling with Don in order to avoid the threat of taxation of his American holdings. He was supremely confident that nobody, least of all a piddling twenty-lawyer firm like mine, could trace his ownership through the maze of his hundreds of Liberian and Panamanian corporations (whose "bearer" stock certificates contained no shareholder names), dummy nominees, shadowy Lichtenstein trusts, and subleases upon subleases. He would have recalled with glee the griping report of the New York F.B.I. office to Director Hoover that no less than forty of its agents were engaged for more than two years in the exhausting effort to merely identify the nationality of the owner of Ari's war-surplus ships.

It was useless for me to speculate on whether Christina would feel equally secure about her ability to hide the ownership and the profits without Ari on the scene to move the chess pieces. I knew that Christina's lawyers would soon be drafting a motion to dismiss Don's complaint, based on *forum non conveniens*, failure to state a cause of action, statute of limitations, and half a dozen other legal grounds. After the lawsuit was commenced by serving the complaint at the Olympic Airways office in the Olympic Tower, the first order of business was to get my hands on all the available evidence relating to the Piaggio crash. That required a trip to Europe.

The first stop was London, where Mac McGregor joined me for lunch. He turned out to be a delightful old salt, a burly, affable character right out of an Ernie Gann flying novel. He had many stories of his days with the R.A.F., and he also told me that he had been the captain of the Olympic Boeing 707 that was used to fly Jackie Kennedy from New York to Athens for her 1968 wedding to Ari. It had been a regularly scheduled flight with more than ninety other passengers listed, but at the last minute all the non-Kennedy passengers were bumped so that Mac could fly Jackie and her entourage to Athens with the cabin to themselves.

Over lunch, we found a few old planes that both of us had flown. Because Don McCusker's amnesia had wiped out his entire memory of the Piaggio flight, Mac was the only survivor who would be able to testify to what had happened. He eagerly agreed to come to New York to testify at the trial. In the meantime, he gave me an animated account of the fatal crash.

Mac had been checked out in the Piaggio by Alexander, and considered him a careful pilot, except when pressure from his father caused him to cut corners. Mac believed that Ari had put everybody in Olympic Airways under intimidating pressure, including those responsible for getting the Piaggio through its major overhaul in time for Ari's February cruise. As Ari's personal pilot, he had observed at close range that Ari thought of himself as superhuman, not bound by the rules governing the conduct of ordinary men.

Mac gave me several important documents, including the pilots' checklists for the Piaggio, which were handwritten in English by Alex. None of these checklists had anything more than "full and free" as the pilots' response to checking the ailerons. That is, there was no checklist item which required the pilots to determine visually the up or down position of the ailerons when the wheel was turned. All the pilots were required to do was to make sure that the control wheel turned "full and free," all the way to the left or right without obstruction. This was a key piece of evidence because the Greek indictment (which we attached to the complaint in the New York lawsuit) had charged that Don should have checked "with his eyes the good operation of the ailerons." It showed that even if the checklist had been on board, the pilots would only have checked the free movement of the control wheel, not the position or the rigging of the ailerons.

Mac also confirmed that Alex was the sole pilot in command, which again was contrary to the indictment charging that Don was the "joint commander." The fraudulent indictment was the key to our proving Don's claims of malicious prosecution, false imprisonment, defamation, and intentional infliction of emotional harm. Mac McGregor's testimony alone could establish the basis for the jury to find that prosecution of the fraudulent indictment had to be malicious; that confining Don to Greece for six months under that indictment amounted to false imprisonment; that keeping the indictment alive for more than four years defamed Don's reputation; and that the emotional harm inflicted on Don by the indictment was both intentional and unjustifiable. As we spoke in London, I visualized Mac on the stand as a compelling witness, one of the best I had ever interviewed.

Before meeting Mac I thought Don McCusker had been the recipient of nothing but bad luck. Now I reflected on what Mac had done for Don, whom he met for the first time on the day the crash occurred. Mac and his wife Peggy had turned themselves inside out to help and comfort Don and Helena during the Athens hospital days. Mac had volunteered to fly back to Athens from his retirement in England whenever Don's manslaughter case was called for trial, thus assuring that unscrupulous prosecutors could not get away with fabricating an incriminating scenario. And he had stood by his testimony that Don was not at fault in any way, despite the fact that he and Peggy and their four children were then living in the Greece of the Colonels; that he was on the payroll of Ari's Olympic Airways; and that he depended on Olympic for his medical and retirement benefits. Don would probably have done the same thing for Mac, but Mac had no way of knowing this when he volunteered to play the Good Samaritan. Contrary to legend, there is no brotherhood of airmen that can be relied upon to produce such selfless acts of pure friendship.

I offered to pay Mac for the time he took to refresh his memory and to provide me with evidence, as permitted by the law relating to witness expenses. Despite the fact that he was far from wealthy, he would not hear of it. He even refused to accept reimbursement for the train fare between London and his home in Oxford, although he had come to London especially to meet with me.

Talking with Mac bolstered my confidence in the case, but I quickly reminded myself that we had no direct evidence that Ari himself had been involved in procuring or prolonging the fraudulent indictment or withholding Don's passport for six months, all of which was done nominally by Greek government officials. I managed to obtain copies of the suppressed reports written by the Greek Air Force investigators and Alan Hunter. I then concentrated on finding a lawyer in Greece who could help us link Ari to the trumped-up indictment and the confiscation of Don's passport.

While traveling in Europe for that purpose, I received a message from my secretary in New York. A lawyer named James Blair had phoned, saying that he was a member of Cleary Gottlieb, a large Wall Street law firm. He was calling about the McCusker suit against Olympic Airways and the estate of Aristotle Onassis. He represented the defendants, and wanted to arrange a meeting to see if the case could be settled. My first reaction to this exciting news was the thought that maybe Christina was smarter than Ari after all.

I returned to New York and arranged to meet James Blair at my office on July 13, 1978. I had rather expected that Benjamin O'Sullivan and his colleagues at Holtzmann, Wise & Shepard would be representing Christina, since they had made the $65,000 settlement offer to Don back in May. They had been the main Onassis lawyers since the 1950s and had opposed me in the Nicholas Onassis litigation of 1970. I speculated that Cleary Gottlieb, an eminent general practice firm with an excellent litigation department, might have been called in because the Holtzmann Wise lawyers thought they might be called as witnesses in the Surrogate's Court battle over ownership, which would disqualify them from acting as attorneys. While Christina could claim that Ari's dealings with his lawyers were confidential because of attorney-client privilege, the privilege does not apply to matters involving crimes or frauds—the so-called "crime-fraud exception" to privilege.

James Blair arrived with two assistants, and was polite but very businesslike. Without explaining why his client might want to settle, he put the ball in my court, noting that Don had asked for $186,000 just a few weeks ago, and that Don had never responded to O'Sullivan's $65,000 final offer. I told him that the $186,000 figure was Don's uninformed layman's estimate of the legal damages he had suffered, based mainly on his out-of-pocket losses. Now that he had the benefit of legal advice, that figure was withdrawn, and the settlement demand was one million dollars.

I watched Blair's face carefully as I made a million-dollar settlement demand for the first time in my life. I thought I saw him flinch.

I should explain here that a $1 million demand in 1978 would be the equivalent of $10 million in 2004. Apart from the effects of inflation, which would require a multiplier of 3 to equal the purchasing power of the 1970s dollar, another weighty factor is the much greater leverage enjoyed by plaintiffs and their lawyers in the twenty-first century. In the 1970s, plaintiffs' lawyers were still considered outsiders by the legal establishment, and most of the appellate courts which were the final arbiters of damage awards kept a tight lid on jury verdicts, regardless of the actual damage done. While appellate judges would readily affirm multimillion dollar verdicts for property damage if supported by the evidence, they often applied a sound-barrier treatment to large personal injury verdicts. The occasional seven-figure injury verdicts usually made newspaper headlines, and the appellate courts would almost invariably reduce them below the million-dollar level. Therefore, plaintiffs' lawyers fortunate enough to achieve million-dollar verdicts would usually rush to settle them for a lesser sum, in order to avoid the surgical knives of the appellate judges.

For example, the 1978 *Wall Street Journal* article which Herb Mehlhorn sent to Don McCusker was designed to alert the business community to the rising awards in aircrash litigation, a field already known for relatively high damages because of the strong earning power of most airline passengers. In that article, the highest jury verdict mentioned was a $900,000 award to the widow and four children of a deceased surveyor. The article noted that the case was being settled for $790,000 in order to avoid an appeal. The article did not mention punitive damages, which were hardly ever collected in the 1970s, but are more readily awarded in twenty-first century cases involving intentional or extremely reckless misconduct. Punitive damages, sometimes called exemplary damages, are designed both to punish the defendant and deter future misconduct. Usually they add up to several times the amount of the compensatory damages, which are designed to reimburse the plaintiff for his or her actual injuries and losses.

Therefore, if I were facing Christina's lawyers in 2004, I would demand not $1 million but its present-day equivalent, $10 million, to correct for inflation, for the increased likelihood of upholding fair compensatory damage awards in the appellate courts, and for the real possibility of collecting punitive damages for Ari's intentional acts—some of which were crimes as well as civil wrongs—that had cost Don McCusker his freedom and his reputation.

To justify my bravado in demanding $1 million, I voluntarily gave Blair and his assistants some details of the damage that Don and his family had suffered, and I started to sketch out some of our proof that Don was blameless. I noticed that although they were all equipped with yellow legal pads, they did very little writing. That meant one of two things: either they were so stunned or revolted by the million-dollar demand that they refused to take notes of the documentation, or they were completely focused on the Surrogate's Court proceedings which threatened to permit the Public Administrator to pry into Ari's estate. I did not mention the Surrogate's Court hearing which was coming up in four weeks, and neither did they.

Since they were not asking any questions about Don's claims, I stopped talking. This produced an offer of $275,000 from Blair. I said that it was far too low, and that I would pass it along to the McCuskers with my recommendation that it be rejected. When Blair asked me what figure I would recommend, I said that the figure of one million dollars was a realistic demand in this case, and that I saw no reason to reduce it.

When they left, I phoned South Dakota and spoke to both Don and Helena. I informed them of the $275,000 offer, and recommended that they authorize me to reject it as too low and stay at $1 million. They agreed after a slight hesitation, which was understandable in view of the fact that only six weeks earlier they had been dealing with a demand of $186,000 and an offer of $65,000.

On Monday July 17, I phoned Blair and relayed the clients' decision to reject $275,000 and stand at $1 million. After a pause, he said he would have to confer with his clients and would get back to me if they were still interested in discussing settlement. We were then exactly a month away from the August 16 Surrogate's Court hearing.

I felt that if I were in Blair's shoes, I would quickly arrange a definitive meeting with Christina, to allow as much time as possible for further negotiations before August 16. But Christina had other important matters on her mind.

Chapter Sixteen

Mrs. Kauzov Carries on Ari's Legacy

ON AUGUST 1, 1978, KLARA YERNSHEKOVA, A MARRIAGE registrar, addressed the couple standing before her in the former mansion of Czarist Russia's Prince Felix Yussupov, now Moscow's Palace of Weddings. As she collected $2.15 for the wedding, the fanciest available, she said to the beaming newlyweds:

> *The Executive Committee of the Soviet of Working People's Deputies of the City of Moscow has empowered me to register your marriage. This is the most important and honorable event in your lives. The Soviet government wishes you the greatest success in your marriage. You will not achieve happiness without working at it.*

The bridegroom, Sergei Kauzov, late of the K.G.B., kissed the bride, Christina Onassis, of the Olympic Tower, Avenue Foch in Paris, and Skorpios, to complete what had to be the strangest wedding of the year. As they left the hall to the strains of Mendelssohn's "Wedding March," they brushed past the long line of other couples waiting to be married.

Sergei and Christina first met in October 1977 (two and a half years after Ari's death) when she flew to Moscow with Costa Gratsos, the New York major-domo of Onassis operations, to negotiate leases of five Olympic tankers to Sovfracht, a tanker department of the Soviet Ministry of the Maritime Fleet. Sergei was in charge of that department and handled the negotiations for his side. After an agreement in principle was reached, Christina returned to Paris, where she was spending much of her time. In November she was asked to visit the Paris office of Sovfracht to iron out some final details of the leasing agreements. On arriving there, she was pleasantly surprised to find that Sergei had been transferred from Moscow to take charge of the Paris office. After concluding the business of the leases, they embarked on a torrid love affair, despite the fact that Sergei had a wife and nine-year-old daughter back in Moscow.

For the rest of 1977 and into early 1978, they carried on the affair in small hotels and in Christina's Paris apartment, doing their best to keep it secret because Sergei warned he would be recalled to Moscow if it became public. Christina confided to a few friends that she was ecstatically happy with Sergei, who exquisitely fulfilled her sexual desires. In February 1978 they slipped away to Rio de Janeiro, celebrating the Carnival for two weeks in a penthouse suite at the Copacabana Palace Hotel. It was in that romantic setting that Christina proposed marriage. Sergei said they both should think it over.

Shortly after they returned to Paris from their Brazilian frolic, Sergei was abruptly recalled to Moscow. Christina tried frantically to phone him but the Sovfracht officials in Paris and Moscow refused to reveal his whereabouts. Christina used some of Ari's high-level international contacts to obtain Sergei's unlisted home phone number in Moscow. She was warned not to phone him from Paris, where the call would be made by an operator and might be recorded or intercepted. Instead she was advised to use IDD, the International Direct Dialing system that linked London and Moscow. So Christina flew to London and dialed Sergei's number, hoping that his wife would not answer.

To Christina's delight, Sergei picked up the phone. He told her he had been recalled to run a new tanker division, and hadn't phoned because he thought it best that they never see each other again. But after these weeks of separation, he realized that he missed her too much to break off, and he had asked his wife for a divorce.

During the spring of 1978, Christina commuted between Paris and London for weeks so she could stay in phone contact with Sergei. She was beside herself with frustration and worry about their future. She began to concoct desperate schemes to spirit Sergei out of the Soviet Union. She offered one of her Olympic captains $500,000 to smuggle Sergei out in a tanker, but the captain told her it was too risky.

Finally in May they arranged for Christina to meet Sergei in Moscow, under security precautions which he said were necessary. She took the train from Paris, and was to be met at the Moscow station by a man who would take her to Sergei. But the mysterious guide did not show up, and the distraught Christina, unable to reach Sergei and fearing a kidnapping plot, caught the next train back to Paris. She holed up in her Avenue Foch apartment for a week, refusing to answer her phone or speak to anyone. Then with the help of her ever-present drugs, she pulled herself together and flew to London so she could phone Sergei.

Christina dropped her plans to scold Sergei about the aborted Moscow meeting when she heard his thrilling news. Sergei's wife had agreed to a divorce, accepting the financial incentives provided by Christina. He would be free to marry her within six weeks, but because of his K.G.B. background, he could not leave the Soviet Union. Therefore they would have to live in Moscow.

Christina was not surprised by the restrictions on Sergei's travel. She immediately agreed to marry him even though it meant living in Moscow. She wanted to bring along her long-time personal maid, Eleni Syros, but Eleni would have none of living in Moscow. Eleni saw Christina off at the Paris railroad station on June 24, 1978. During their tearful farewell, Christina handed Eleni a parting gift of $200,000 in cash.

On Sunday June 25, Christina's train arrived at the Moscow station, and this time Sergei was there to meet her. Sergei had begun the divorce proceedings, but they still had more than five weeks to wait before they could be married. Her presence in Moscow had been discovered by the media, and although the Soviet papers remained silent, she was besieged by Western journalists who demanded to know her wedding plans. For most of the remaining five weeks of required waiting, she steadfastly denied that she was in Moscow to get married. She said she was just a tourist, and that the marriage rumors were preposterous.

During the waiting period, which encompassed the entire month of July 1978, Christina was bombarded by messages and visits from relatives, friends, and business associates, all of them urging her not to marry Sergei. Her aunts in Athens refused to believe that the twenty-seven-year-old Christina, who could have had her pick of international socialites, was actually going to marry the forty-year-old Soviet spy whose most prominent features were gold teeth and a glass eye. Her friends told her she would be miserable in Moscow, living in a spare bedroom of her mother-in-law's small apartment, missing all the luxuries to which she had become accustomed. Her shipping executives warned her that it would not be good for business if she were perceived to be coming under Soviet influence. Christina reacted with her usual remedy: she stopped taking their calls and messages.

Costa Gratsos was delegated to get through to Christina. She had great respect for Ari's old colleague, and he could talk to her like a loving father. Gratsos flew from New York to Moscow to speak with her privately. He told her there were widespread rumors that after the marriage, she planned to move her business headquarters to Moscow, putting Sergei in charge. Gratsos implored her to reconsider the marriage, but when she insisted on going ahead, he asked her to make a public statement denying any changes in the business.

In deference to Gratsos, on July 27 Christina held a private press conference in her Intourist Hotel suite with the English journalist Denis Blewett of the London *Daily Mail*. She handed Blewett a scoop which made the world's front pages that day. With Sergei at her side, she announced that they would be married on August 1; they would make their home in Moscow, living with Sergei's mother until they could buy a cooperative apartment; and they planned to start a family right away. She made certain that Blewett got her final punchline:

> *I want the world to know—and this is very important—that the Onassis business will continue to be run by my father's old associates. There will be no changes. All this speculation I*

have read about the headquarters being moved to Moscow is
quite wrong.

The wedding came off as planned on Tuesday August 1, 1978.
The newlyweds were scheduled to begin a Lake Baikal honeymoon
on the weekend, but instead on Saturday August 5, Christina flew
alone to Athens. She left it to Sergei to explain to the media that
she had been "called to Athens on urgent business."

After I informed James Blair on July 14, 1978, that the
McCuskers had rejected the $275,000 offer, I heard nothing from
him for nearly a month. Then on Friday August 11, just three
business days before the scheduled hearing in the Surrogate's
Court, Blair phoned. He said that after careful consideration, his
clients were willing to offer $500,000. Since that sum was far
above what any New York judge would allow a jury to award as
damages for Don's injuries and loss of income, I was convinced
that the Onassis forces were seeking to settle the case in order to
avoid facing potential tax problems in the Surrogate's Court.

I said that I did not consider $500,000 a satisfactory settle-
ment, and would report it to the McCuskers with my recommen-
dation that they reject it.

Blair then said that he personally would recommend to his
clients that they pay $600,000, and asked if I would recommend
that figure for acceptance.

I said that I would not, but again I had to report these figures
to the clients and would call him back on Monday August 14.

I phoned Don and Helena in South Dakota and recounted the
conversation with Blair. They said that it sounded like we had
achieved a very good settlement, and asked me whether we ran

any risk by rejecting it. I said I had the feeling that Blair might go as high as $700,000, and since they did not want me to prolong the negotiations, I suggested that they authorize me to settle the case for any sum over $600,000 that I could get. They agreed, and I said I would call Blair back on Monday.

On Monday August 14 I phoned Blair and told him I had talked to the McCuskers. I left the door open by saying simply that they were not satisfied with the $600,000 offer. I had never departed from the one-million-dollar demand, but this time I said nothing about sticking to it.

That moved Blair to ask what it would take to settle the case. I said that if he were prepared to pay $800,000, I would recommend that the clients accept it.

He agreed almost before I had finished speaking.

It occurred to me that $800,000 was the price Ari paid for his first big tanker, the *Ariston*, in 1938. If he were still alive, he would probably comfort himself by saying that he had settled the case for the price of one old tanker.

I stopped myself from thinking like Ari, and quickly phoned Don and Helena. They seemed to think I was kidding when I told them the case was settled for $800,000. They were delighted when I told them it was for real.

I told them there would probably be a wait of several weeks before they got the money. I would sign the necessary papers to dismiss the lawsuit and also to withdraw Don's petition for appointment of the Public Administrator, so that it would not come up for hearing in the Surrogate's Court on August 16 as scheduled. But there was another document, called a general release, which Don and Helena had to sign, releasing Christina, Ari's estate, and Olympic Airways from any further liability. Blair would be sending the general release form to me, and I would send it on to South Dakota for their signature and notarization. When they returned it to me, I would send it to Blair, with the understanding that he would be holding it in escrow until he delivered the $800,000 check to me. Normally the check does not arrive until several weeks after the general release is delivered to the defendants' lawyer, especially when the money is coming from a foreign country.

In fact, at that time we had been experiencing delays as long as three months in getting settlement payments from Lloyd's of London in other cases, probably because they were trying to retain the interest income for as long as possible, and also because they were said to be playing the foreign exchange markets to get as many American dollars as possible for their English pounds. So I wanted to condition Don and Helena not to become impatient if it took a few weeks to get the settlement money.

I had no sooner finished talking to them when my secretary walked in and handed me an envelope that had just been delivered by a messenger. It was from Cleary Gottlieb, and it contained one small piece of paper: a cashier's check for $800,000. Blair was taking no chances that the McCuskers might change their minds and go ahead with the August 16 Surrogate's Court hearing. He had my oral commitment to settle for $800,000, but he made the cheese more binding by paying the money immediately, thereby completing the settlement.

So it was that for the first and last time in my legal career, the settlement was paid in full before the defendants' lawyer had even sent me the general release that formalized the acceptance of the final offer. That left no doubt in my mind that the case of *McCusker v. The Estate of Aristotle Onassis, deceased and Olympic Airways, S.A.* had been settled for an unprecedented amount because of the defendants' need to avoid the meddling of the

Surrogate's Court and the Public Administrator—to say nothing of the tax collectors—in the secret affairs of Aristotle Onassis, deceased.

On Monday, August 14, 1978, the day of the $800,000 settlement, Christina Onassis, having spent the previous ten days in Athens, flew back to Moscow to rejoin her husband and embark on the honeymoon which she had been forced to abort.

Christina never explained the nature of the "urgent business" that required her to fly to Athens on August 5 instead of beginning the Lake Baikal honeymoon. But she left enough circumstantial evidence for us to reasonably conclude that the unscheduled flight was made because she needed to meet in Athens with her lawyers and the Graybeards, her father's old colleagues, to make the final decision on the McCusker settlement.

We begin with Christina's emotional state, always a weighty factor in her decisions. At age twenty-seven, she had already been through two disastrous marriages. We have seen how Ari and Johnny Meyer destroyed her short marriage to Joe Bolker in 1971. Four months after Ari's death in March 1975, Christina had married Alexander Andreadis, whose father Stratis was a Greek entrepreneur of the Onassis school. Soon after the wedding, Christina's new father-in-law was charged with fraud in three of the five banks he controlled. Then came a desperate plea from her new husband to hand over $20 million needed to keep the Andreadis banks afloat. Christina, insecure about her ugly duckling image since childhood and wary of fortune hunters, was completely disillusioned with her husband. She refused to give him any money, and decided to terminate the marriage as quickly as possible without revealing the reason, to avoid further embarrassment to herself and the Andreadis family. Pregnant at the time of the $20 million demand, she underwent an abortion.

The ink was hardly dry on her divorce from Alexander Andreadis when Christina fell in love with Sergei Kauzov. When she married Sergei, she was desperate to prove to herself and to the world that she could sustain a real marriage. It was a long shot at best, given their cultural and financial differences. She had taken him away from an apparently satisfactory marriage and a young daughter. She could hardly have relished endangering the new marriage by walking out right after the wedding, leaving Sergei to explain to the voracious journalists that she had been called to Athens for unspecified business matters which took precedence over their honeymoon.

So Christina's business in Athens had to be crucially important to bring her there on August 5, 1978. We have seen that Ari's estate was divided roughly in half, between Christina and the Alexander S. Onassis Public Benefit Foundation, run by the Graybeards in Athens. The August 16 hearing date for the Public Administrator petition in the New York Surrogate's Court was of equal concern to the Graybeards. If the P.A. administered the estate and the tax collectors became involved, there was no way of calculating how big a bite they might take out of Ari's estate. Whatever that bite was, half of it would come from the assets of the foundation administered by the Graybeards. Apart from concern about their vows to carry on Ari's businesses, the Graybeards enjoyed handsome salaries and expense accounts which could go up in smoke if Ari's estate and income taxes finally had to be paid in full.

Therefore, it is likely that the Graybeards convinced Christina she had to come to Athens for discussion of the grave threat posed by the McCusker litigation. This was not something that could be discussed in Moscow, where they had to assume that Christina's phones were tapped and her residence bugged. When Christina's lawyers received the McCusker suit papers on June 8, she was totally immersed in her frantic efforts to establish contact with Sergei. After the aborted rendezvous in Moscow, she had shut herself off from all communications in Paris. By the time her New York lawyers learned on July 13 that the McCuskers were demanding a million-dollar settlement, Christina was in Moscow counting down the days to the August 1st wedding. As we have seen, in Moscow she was besieged by demands from relatives, friends, and business associates that she abandon her wedding plans, and again she shut off these unpleasant communications. If James Blair or another of her lawyers had been sent to Moscow and they had found a secure place to discuss the estate's problems, it is doubtful that he alone could have convinced her of the threat posed by the August 16 hearing. Even to arrange such a meeting would have required more telephone conversation than was discreet. The safest and surest strategy was for the Graybeards to inform Christina that she needed to fly to Athens to discuss with all of them and the Onassis legal team a serious problem that had to be solved before August 16.

Christina arrived in Athens on Saturday August 5. It could well have taken the next four business days for the Graybeards and the lawyers to convince Christina that a settlement had to be reached even though it flew in the face of Ari's wishes and his explicit deathbed instructions to her. It was on Friday August 11 that James Blair phoned me to offer $600,000, and not until the following Monday, August 14, when the case was settled for $800,000, did Christina fly back to Moscow.

The only other conceivable reason for aborting the honeymoon was to reassure the shipping world that the Onassis empire would carry on business as usual despite Christina's wedding to a former K.G.B. agent. If that had been the purpose of the trip, Christina would have flown to Saudi Arabia rather than to Athens, for at that time 85 percent of the oil carried in Onassis tankers came from that country, and its rulers were more touchy about doing business with the Soviets than most governments. As we have seen, Costas Gratsos's mission to Moscow in July had produced Christina's well-publicized statement of July 27 that the marriage would not cause any changes in the Onassis business. There is no record of any meetings or talks between Christina and Saudi officials during her August trip to Athens. Nor was there any immediate danger of losing the Saudi business, since most of it was on long-term charters.

It should be noted that 1978 was a time of continued depression in the worldwide tanker business, with many large tankers being laid up for lack of cargoes. Therefore, the threat of the Onassis fleet (or the portion of it owned by Christina) ultimately falling under Soviet domination would have been of little security concern to the Western nations, given the glut of readily-available tanker capacity. Indeed, as we have seen, Christina had first met Sergei when she flew to Moscow in 1977 with Costas Gratsos to seek out Soviet business, resulting in the lease of five Olympic tankers to Sovfracht. Whatever the Soviets might learn about Olympic tanker movements was hardly an intelligence prize, since this information was available to the world in the daily shipping press.

On August 10, 1978, Christina flew in her Learjet from Athens to London for a luncheon meeting with officials of British Petroleum, an important Olympic customer. She returned to Athens the same day. One purpose of the meeting was for Christina to personally reassure the BP management that her marriage would not result in K.G.B. or Soviet domination of Olympic Maritime affairs. Since the Brits themselves were actively pursuing trade with the Soviet Union at the time, this half-day devoted to meeting with BP officials could hardly have been the main purpose of Christina's ten-day trip to Athens which took the place of her honeymoon.

From her past attitude toward the McCusker claims, we can safely assume that Christina was not of a mind to pay the McCuskers anything more than a token amount in settlement. Imbued with the oft-demonstrated financial invincibility of Ari, she could not readily accept the need to consider a million-dollar settlement demand, especially while under siege in Moscow as she fought her lonely battle to keep the highly controversial wedding plans alive.

Certainly Christina's agreement was needed to pay a substantial sum to settle the McCusker case. The Graybeards had no legal power to settle the case without her consent. She alone controlled the outcome of the August 16 Surrogate's Court hearing, since she was named in the petition as a distributee who could supplant the Public Administrator. She was present in Athens when the decision was made to treat the million-dollar demand seriously, and finally to pay $800,000. It can hardly be argued that her presence in Athens rather than in the Lake Baikal honeymoon cottage during those decisions was a mere coincidence.

We have seen that Don McCusker had been advised by previous lawyers that a pre-litigation settlement of $50,000 would have been satisfactory, given the problems of the case. That was certainly sound advice before the litigation began and the Public Administrator came into the picture. Christina and her public relations people could probably have portrayed a settlement of perhaps $50,000 to $75,000 as a mere nuisance payment, to avoid legal fees and the loss of time by Christina and other high-priced executives. But $800,000 was much higher than any appellate court would have allowed as damages, even if we had been able to muster proof that Ari was behind the indictment.

In itself, the amount of the settlement sent a strong message to the aviation community that Don could not have been at fault. It was tantamount to a public admission that Don had been framed by a fraudulent manslaughter indictment, since Ari was the only person who publicly supported the indictment and proclaimed that Don had been responsible for the crash.

Therefore, it is not surprising that several days of face-to-face argument with Christina would be required before the Graybeards could convince her to make such a damning admission, especially since Ari had repeated on his deathbed the order that she keep the McCusker indictment alive at all costs.

In the end, Aristotle Onassis's life of fraud, deceit, and tax cheating forced his daughter to undo his diabolical plot to transfer the blame for killing his son from Ari's own shoulders, where it belonged, to those of the hayseeds from Ohio—Don McCusker and the Central Intelligence Agency.

Chapter Seventeen

The Aftermath of the Fall

As we have seen, Aristotle Onassis died in 1975, and the case of *McCusker vs. Onassis* was settled in 1978. Here is what happened to the main characters after that.

Christina Onassis weathered the storms that followed in the immediate wake of her 1978 Moscow marriage, which did not damage the Onassis businesses. She quickly tired of life in the Soviet Union and separated from Sergei Kauzov five months after the marriage. In May 1979 she divorced him in a Swiss court, throwing in a 78,000-ton tanker as part of Sergei's settlement, which he used as the cornerstone of a successful new career as a capitalist entrepreneur. Christina lived mostly in Paris and New York, using Skorpios for summer holidays. Despite the persistent weight problem that sometimes made her balloon to over two hundred pounds, she had many lovers.

In March 1984 she married Thierry Roussel, heir to a French pharmaceutical fortune. On January 29, 1985, at the American Hospital in Paris where Ari had died ten years earlier, she gave birth to a daughter, Athina. Despite Christina's gifts to Thierry, which were estimated to total $75 million, they were divorced in May of 1987. They shared custody of Athina.

On November 19, 1988, while staying at a hotel in Buenos Aires, Christina was found slumped in the nearly empty bathtub by her maid Eleni, who had rejoined her service after Christina's return from the Soviet Union. Christina was pronounced dead, the result of an acute pulmonary edema of the lung which produced a heart attack, the same cause given for her mother's death. The autopsy reports were inconclusive as to the cause of the edema, but those close to Christina were certain that she had continued to overdose on upper and downer pills—amphetamines and barbiturates—despite warnings that they could weaken her heart and cause her lungs to fill with fluid. She was thirty-seven.

Christina was buried in the Chapel of the Little Virgin on Skorpios. Thus Aristotle rests on his private island alongside the two children whom he never gave a chance to live. Their combined life spans were less than his sixty-nine years.

After Christina's death, her ex-husband Thierry Roussel assumed full custody of the three-year-old Athina, now called the last Onassis. In the course of seeking to administer his daughter's property during her childhood, Thierry found that the ownership of many assets (which were supposed to be divided evenly between Christina and Alexander's foundation) had been scrambled, with four of the fifteen foundation directors also serving as administrators of Athina's inherited property. The foundation directors—the Graybeards—resisted Thierry's efforts to assume control of Athina's property. This touched off a legal battle-royal in the Greek and

Swiss courts which is now in its second decade. When Athina turned eighteen in January 2003, the media reported that she came into legal control of her half, estimated at $700 million to $1 billion. They also reported that when she turns twenty-one in 2006, she will be in a position to take control of Alexander's foundation from the Graybeards, who can be counted on to continue their fierce opposition to such a move. She was raised in Switzerland by Thierry, along with his three children by his present wife Gaby, who was his mistress before and during his marriage to Christina.

Jacqueline Kennedy Onassis resumed her life in New York after Ari's death in 1975, devoting herself to her children and grandchildren, to many charitable and public service causes, and to a new career as a book editor at Viking and Doubleday. She never remarried. Her closest companion in her later years was the financier Maurice Tempelsman, who helped her to multiply the $26 million settlement she had received from Ari's estate. She died of cancer on May 19, 1994, at the age of sixty-four. After her death, her son *John F. Kennedy Jr.* violated the pledge she had extracted from him at the time of Alexander Onassis's fatal 1973 plane crash that he would not get a pilot's license. On July 16, 1999, he was killed when the single-engine plane he was flying crashed into the Atlantic Ocean near Martha's Vineyard, Massachusetts, along with his wife, Carolyn Bessette Kennedy and her sister, Lauren Bessette. He was thirty-eight.

At Jackie's funeral in Manhattan's St. Ignatius Loyola Church, where she had been baptized, Senator Ted Kennedy said in his eulogy that she will be remembered most for those four days after the assassination of President Kennedy "when she held us together, as a nation and as a family."

At Jackie's burial alongside President John F. Kennedy in Arlington National Cemetery, President Clinton said:

330 The Deadly Sins of Aristotle Onassis

*She taught us by example about the beauty of art, the meaning
of culture, the lessons of history, the power of personal courage,
and most of all, the sanctity of the family.*

The Alexander S. Onassis Public Benefit Foundation was created
as a Lichtenstein trust, Ari's favorite tax-evasion tool since it did
not require disclosure of the trustees, the beneficiaries, or the
source of its assets. During his lifetime, Ari managed to abstain
from assistance to charities and other forms of "public benefit,"
and did nothing to enhance the monumental Greek contribution
to Western culture. But the Public Benefit Foundation that
emerged from his will, although designed to cheat Jackie out of
her widow's inheritance and keep the hapless tax collectors grasp-
ing at smoke, has honored Alexander's memory by distributing
over $250 million to such worthy causes as badly-needed Greek
hospitals, merit scholarship funds for Greek students to study
abroad, Greek Studies chairs in Europe and the United States,
and prizes of up to $250,000 for lifetime achievement in cultural
and environmental pursuits throughout the world. Prize recipients
include Bishop Desmond Tutu of South Africa, President Jimmy
Carter, Prime Minister Harold Macmillan, Senator J. William
Fulbright, and U.N. Secretary General Boutros Boutros-Ghali.
On September 24, 2001, the foundation announced the gift of
$500,000 to the fund benefiting the relatives of firefighters and
police officers who died in the World Trade Center disaster.

Maria Callas became a virtual recluse in her Paris apartment
after Ari's death in 1975. Dependent on prescription drugs, she
died there of a heart attack on September 16, 1977. She was fifty-
three. She is considered one of the greatest opera singers of all
time, both for her voice and her ability to dramatize her roles. In
2004, twenty-seven years after her death, her recordings are still

selling in the hundreds of thousands each year, at a far higher rate than during the last year of her life.

The yacht *Christina* was discarded by Christina soon after Ari's death in favor of her own smaller yacht which she named after Alexander. She gave the *Christina* to the Greek government, which used it as the presidential yacht for a short time until the nation's leaders concluded it was too ostentatious for a socialist government. It was left to rot in a Greek naval shipyard until 1998, when it was purchased by Greek shipping magnate John Paul Papanicolaou, who first set foot on it as a twelve-year-old guest of Ari. Papanicolaou and a group of investors spent over $45 million to restore the yacht to its former grandeur. In 2001 they renamed it *Christina O* and made it available for luxury charters at a reported rate of $70,000 per day. It no longer carries an airplane aboard.

Johnny Meyer continued to serve Christina during the transition period after Ari's death in 1975, and then retired to Florida. On October 17, 1978, while driving home from a Palm Beach dinner party, he stopped by the roadside to relieve himself. As he stood behind the car to do his business, the car somehow slipped out of "park" and into "reverse." It made straight for Johnny, knocking him down and then running over him. He died at the scene. He was seventy-two.

The Baroness Fiona Thyssen-Bornemisza, who prefers to be called Fiona Thyssen, never remarried. Despite the pressures of international society, she maintained sole custody of her two children and raised them successfully. Now enthralled with her three grandchildren, she lives in Switzerland and in Greece, and continues to carry a heavy calendar of charitable work, especially for her daughter's ARCH Foundation, which restores bombed-out buildings.

Fiona is a survivor and a woman of great spirit. I cannot help thinking that she and Alexander would have made a go of it, either in marriage or a continuing relationship that would have given Alex a far better life than he could have lived under Ari's domination.

Stavros Niarchos, relieved of the rivalry burden when Ari died in 1975, shifted gears and began to fulfill Helen Vlachos's prophecy that he "had it in him" to become a great benefactor if he did not have to compete with Onassis. In his final twenty years he was content to give up his worldwide leadership in ownership of tankers (shrinking his fleet from eighty to eight) so that he could devote more time and resources to charity and art. When he died in 1996 at age eighty-six, he was reported to be worth $4 billion. But he could not entirely escape Ari's shadow, since his obituary in the *New York Times*, which featured headlines of "The archrival of Onassis" and "Two industrial giants in a game of one-upmanship," contained nearly as much history of Ari as of Stavros.

Don and *Helena McCusker* celebrated the 1978 settlement by taking a cruise to Bermuda with their lifelong friends from Maine, *Rob* and *Rowena Nelson*, who had helped them get through the tough years after the Piaggio crash. They paid off all their obligations, splurged for new box springs and mattresses, put away enough money to complete the college education of their six children, and invested the balance in four apartment buildings in Sioux Falls, South Dakota. With his reputation in the aviation community rehabilitated, Don was offered a job as a flying boat captain for Antilles Air Boats, the local passenger airline in the U.S. Virgin Islands. Don and Helena flew to St. Thomas to evaluate the offer, but decided against relocating again while they still had children in school.

Back at South Dakota State University, Don had added to his flying duties the responsibilities of data collection manager. He found this environmentally important work more rewarding than anything else open to him, so he continued to fly the old Beech 18 until the state contract ran out in 1984. By then he was sixty, too old to start a new flying job. He and Helena spent their time managing and improving their apartment houses and helping the children complete their education. In 1986, with the children all living on their own, they moved back to their old house in Ohio, which they had rented out when they left for South Dakota. Retired from full-time work, Don served as a volunteer at a local hospital.

Meanwhile the six McCusker children, who were also victims of Ari's fraudulent Greek indictment, achieved their versions of the American Dream. They built their own successful lives and careers, some in public service and others as executives in leading business companies.

The McCuskers' ability to weather the storms created by the Onassis empire was aided in no small part by their religious faith and their dedication to traditional American values. In stark contrast to the Onassis doctrine of "there are no rules, no right or wrong," which eventually destroyed Ari's family, the story ended happily for the McCuskers, who followed Don's principle: "Do what you know is right."

In 1995, Don experienced loss of memory which was finally diagnosed as Alzheimer's disease. He passed away on June 23, 2000, at the age of seventy-six.

Helena lives with her bright memories in the Ohio home which she and Don built in 1963, savoring visits from her eight grandchildren.

Mac McGregor retired to an Oxfordshire farm in 1973, where he and *Peggy* raised their four children successfully and doted on their eight grandchildren. Mac died in 1992 at age seventy-seven, and Peggy passed away in 2000. Their son *Ian,* who wrote an essay on Alexander Onassis's Olympic Aviation air-taxi service as a school project in Greece, carries on the family flying tradition as a captain for British Airways.

The November 17 Group, a Greek terrorist organization, took its name from the violent crushing of a student protest by the U.S.-backed military junta on November 17, 1973. The Group was widely believed to have carried out the 1975 murder of Richard Welch, C.I.A. station chief in Athens, and at least twenty-two other politically-motivated killings, but there were no arrests for more than a quarter of a century. Finally, with the 2004 Olympic Games on the horizon, a Greek court found fifteen members of the Group guilty of terrorism in December 2003.

A few words about the American legal system...

The settlement that secured the financial future of the McCusker family and helped to clear Don's name could not have been achieved anywhere but in the United States. In all other countries, wealthy crooks like Aristotle Onassis were virtually immune from lawsuits by ordinary people like the McCuskers in 1978. As Ambrose Bierce defined it in his 1911 classic, *The Devil's Dictionary,* "*wealth (n.)*: impunity." Ambrose was actually writing about the United States, which in 1911 would also have protected Aristotle from a suit by the McCuskers. Today the American legal system is still far from perfect, but it no longer supports Ambrose Bierce's definition of wealth—at least not in civil cases brought by underdogs.

The McCuskers were able to achieve justice at Ari's expense because of four unique features of the American legal system: (1) jury trials available in all civil (as well as criminal) cases; (2) contingent legal fees, payable only if the plaintiff wins; (3) protection of losers against "fee-shifting" (having to pay the winner's legal fees); and (4) the plaintiffs' specialist lawyers—whom I call the Equalizers—who provide legal services equal to those enjoyed by the affluent, without any cash outlay by the plaintiffs. These features support each other like the legs of a table. Without contingent fees and the Equalizers, the right to jury trial would be meaningless. Legal rights are useless without access to the courts, and access means the ability to get a lawyer who can make the system work even if you don't have the money to pay the fees that his training and experience would bring in the legal marketplace. And without protection against fee-shifting, a Don McCusker could not afford to sue an Aristotle Onassis to enforce his legal rights, for he would be risking financial ruin if he lost the case.

Apart from the United States, the United Kingdom came closer to providing such access than any other nation. So let's assume that Don and Helena McCusker were residents of England in 1978, and that they were able to sue Olympic Airways and the Estate of Aristotle Onassis there. What would have happened?

For purposes of this comparison, it doesn't really matter what legal rights the McCuskers had. The American law of torts—civil wrongs—developed from the English common law, and the tort laws of both nations are still virtually identical in spelling out legal rights. For example, the McCuskers sued Ari's estate for five torts: negligence, malicious prosecution, false imprisonment, defamation, and intentional infliction of emotional distress. Each of these American torts evolved from the earlier English common law, and each of them provides virtually the same rights of redress in both nations today. The difference lies in *access*, the ability of victims to enforce those rights against powerful defendants. Without enforcement, these rights become as meaningless as those memorialized by Anatole France in 1894: "The law, in its majestic equality, forbids the rich as well as the poor to sleep under bridges, to beg in the streets, and to steal bread."

In 1978, no English lawyer would have been permitted to take Don McCusker's case on a contingent basis, i.e., no fee unless the case was won or settled. Those who controlled the English legal system were aware that contingent fees would expose members of the establishment to troublesome lawsuits brought by people who could not afford to pay lawyers. Also, many English lawyers at that time thought it was beneath their professional dignity to make their services available without assurance of payment. To fill this gap, Legal Aid was provided in both civil and criminal cases, unlike the system in the United States, where the government pays only for defense of criminal cases because the contingent fee takes care of representation in civil cases. But the McCuskers would not have qualified for English Legal Aid, because they owned their house, which would have put the value of their assets above the very low Legal Aid disqualification threshold. Also, their claim would have been pre-screened for prospects of success by the Legal Aid Board, which probably would have denied them Legal Aid because of lack of documented proof that Ari was behind the fraudulent indictment.

England took an important step toward the broader access afforded by the American system when "conditional fees" were introduced in 1995. Under this new procedure, English lawyers can take civil cases on a no-win, no-fee basis. If the case is won or settled, the lawyer does not get a percentage of the amount recovered as in the U.S., but instead is allowed to add a "success fee" which raises the hourly fee that he would have charged a paying client by as much as 100 percent, thereby doubling the usual hourly fee. This would make it possible for the McCuskers to get an English lawyer today, provided they could find one who was willing to assume the risk of investigating, preparing, and trying such a case without receiving a percentage of the recovery.

Even today, if the McCuskers convinced an English lawyer to take the case on a conditional fee, they would still be liable for the defendants' legal fees and other expenses ("costs") if they lost the case, under the English fee-shifting rule. English legal fees are the highest in the world. Defendants like Onassis typically retain a high-priced firm of solicitors (lawyers), who assign a team of two or three solicitors to investigate and prepare the case for trial by an equally pricey team of barristers, led by a senior barrister with the title of QC (for Queen's Counsel). The QC must always be assisted by a "junior" who may well be fifty or sixty years old and is usually quite expensive. In all, the defendants' legal team would be likely to run up fees of $10,000 or more *per day*.

This means that an average person suing a large company or a wealthy defendant in England is betting the farm—his home, his savings, his entire fortune—that he will not lose the case. Even the strongest of cases can be lost for unforeseeable reasons, such as a witness failing to show up or a legal technicality arising from a forgotten document. Indeed, the plaintiff doesn't even have to lose the case. A wealthy defendant can make a series of pre-trial motions, each carrying an award of costs to the winner, and thereby bankrupt the plaintiff long before the case ever gets to trial.

In an attempt to mitigate this obvious injustice, British underwriters recently made available legal expense insurance policies, paid for by the plaintiff, which undertake to reimburse defendant's costs if plaintiff loses the case. My reading of these policies indicates that they are designed for routine accident claims, the great majority of which are settled without extensive litigation. All the policies I was able to obtain required pre-screening of claims by the insurers for

338   The Deadly Sins of Aristotle Onassis

prospects of success. Such screening often puts the plaintiff in the Catch-22 situation of trying to prove the merits of her case without benefit of the discovery that can be obtained only after filing the suit, which she dare not file without the insurance protection. Some of these policies limit the coverage to as little as $150,000, which would be of practically no use to a Don McCusker facing the millions of dollars in costs likely to be billed by an Onassis-style legal team. Unless plaintiffs can count on full coverage at nominal cost, this insurance will be nothing more than a fig leaf designed to cover up the unfairness of the fee-shifting rule.

There are only two possible reasons for fee-shifting: (1) protecting defendants, the court system, and the public from frivolous claims, and (2) shielding wealthy defendants from meritorious claims of impecunious plaintiffs. Assuming that the second reason is no longer considered valid in England, it would appear that protection against frivolous claims could best be achieved by allowing defendants to purchase insurance to reimburse their costs in cases that they win. The insurance cost would be exactly the same as in the present system if the coverage were limited to those defendants who actually prove the plaintiff's claims to be unfounded, because the identical risk is being insured. If there are a handful of unfounded claims in every one hundred filed, it would be far more appropriate to put the insurance coverage on the defendants' side, instead of burdening the majority of plaintiffs whose claims are not frivolous. Those defendants who lose in court should expect to pay their own legal costs, as they do now under both the English and American systems.

Proponents of the present English system may argue that such a shift would bring many more frivolous claims into court, for the claimants would have nothing to lose, not even the nominal insurance cost. But English conditional fees, like the American contingent fees, provide a natural filter against frivolous claims. When an English lawyer is offered a conditional fee case, she must engage in a meticulous screening process to make certain she is not taking on a frivolous claim which will leave her holding the bag for thousands of dollars worth of legal work and expenses. This is particularly important when the claim is against a large company or wealthy person who will retain a powerful team of lawyers to defend vigorously. Having practiced law on a contingent-fee basis for more than half a century, I can assure you that there is no money to be made in frivolous claims, and even committing one's time and capital to suing wealthy defendants on claims which are merely uncertain (rather than frivolous) is a prescription for professional disaster. Indeed, even meritorious cases can be lost in the unpredictable free-for-all of a trial.

If England really wanted to level the playing field for litigation, it would seem simpler and more appropriate to eliminate fee-shifting entirely in conditional fee cases, providing cheap insurance to defendants who are concerned about the costs of opposing unfounded claims. In any event, it appears that England is now officially espousing the principle of equal access to the courts, and eventually will find its way to that goal by removing the fee-shifting roadblock.

As we have just seen, the English legal system in the time of Onassis arbitrarily shielded powerful defendants from the enforcement of valid claims against them. It also enabled them to use the legal system as a sword, to thwart justice and suppress the truth. As a case in point, let's take Robert Maxwell, an English tycoon who patterned himself after Aristotle Onassis in some important respects. (Maxwell is an example of the insidious fallout from Ari's glamorization of fraud, which inspired other people at high levels of business to emulate him.)

Bob Maxwell was a London publishing and printing mogul who built a maze of Lichtenstein trusts to camouflage the ownership of his major business holdings. He tapped the telephones of his own associates and employees. His yacht, the *Lady Ghislaine,* named after his daughter, was more than a hundred feet longer than the *Christina,* and was elaborately equipped for use as his floating office. He verbally bullied and publicly humiliated his children, especially the three who were unfortunate enough to work in his businesses. Nick Davies, a long-time editor of one of Maxwell's newspapers, described Maxwell's methods of child abuse in his 1992 biography, *Death of a Tycoon*:

> *To me it was yet another example of Maxwell's pathological need to demonstrate his power over people. He exercised it over everyone who worked for him and more so over his own family. For some extraordinary reason Maxwell had to know that he was in control over everyone at all times.*

Unlike Ari, Maxwell generally did not create new jobs or profit-making enterprises. His usual game was to take over a losing company with bank financing, and then fire a lot of employees and manipulate the books to make the company appear profitable. He also illegally controlled the employee pension funds, which were required to be administered by independent trustees. This enabled him to secretly plunder the pension funds, using that money (which belonged to his employees) to shore up his money-losing and ego-feeding businesses. He was a world-class swindler who eventually stole hundreds of millions of dollars from his employees' pension funds in the desperate effort to keep his fraudulent empire of four hundred companies afloat.

This thievery was not exposed until he disappeared from his yacht in 1991 and his body was found floating in the Atlantic Ocean off the Canary Islands. Then the roof caved in, and in the process his employees' pension funds were virtually wiped out. Yet as far back as 1971, the U.K.'s Department of Trade and Industry had issued a report branding him as "a person who cannot be relied on to exercise proper stewardship of a publicly quoted company." For the next twenty years, Maxwell managed to avoid being closed down by government regulators because he used Ponzi-like tactics to keep insolvent companies afloat and to pay pension benefits as they accrued.

Many of Britain's highly-skilled investigative reporters were aware of Maxwell's larcenous tactics, but when they wrote their stories, the editors killed them on the advice of their libel lawyers. As Roy Greenslade, another former Maxwell editor, wrote in his 1992 biography *Maxwell*:

> *There can be little doubt that Maxwell did successfully intimidate the press, launching (and usually abandoning) more court actions than any other individual in newspaper history. While this added to the public perception of him as a malevolent business mogul, probably with something to hide, it did largely prevent the truth from coming out.*

The investigative reports that could have exposed Maxwell much earlier were not published because of the legal risks. If they contained the slightest mistake or inaccuracy, Maxwell, aided by England's lack of constitutionally-guaranteed freedom of the press, could use the English courts to collect nominal damages plus millions of dollars for his own legal fees. As we have seen, Onassis kept himself above the law largely by bribery, as in Greece and Saudi Arabia, or by owning the country and retaining all the lawyers, as in Monaco. Bob Maxwell could not have pulled off such tricks in England. But he didn't have to. He only needed to hide behind the protection of wealthy crooks that is built into the English civil legal system.

Thus Maxwell was able to use the English legal system as an offensive weapon to suppress the truth and keep his fraudulent businesses in operation. If anyone had dared to sue him for any of his numerous frauds, he would have used the legal system defensively, running up millions of dollars in legal fees which would have to be paid by the plaintiff if Maxwell won.

The fee-shifting or loser-pays rule also has had a chilling effect on the development of Equalizers among English lawyers. There are many excellent English lawyers who are fully capable of equalizing the scales of justice just as American plaintiffs' lawyers have done. But they do not have the same opportunity to develop the special skills, organizations, and financing needed to take on powerful wrongdoers in court, because many English cases present serious risks of bankrupting the plaintiffs. Thus, until the United Kingdom and other nations abolish the unjust fee-shifting rule, American courts will have to stand alone as the haven for underdogs like Don and Helena McCusker.

I'll never forget a meeting I had in London with an Englishman who had lost his son, an only child, in an accident that was caused by a large American company. The father had pulled himself up from menial jobs to a lower-rung management post, and had acquired a house and a respectable nest egg for retirement. He said that he had consulted his regular solicitor and was informed that while he could get jurisdiction over the American company in the English courts, he would be foolish to sue in England because losing the case would consume his house and all his savings to pay the defendants' legal costs. Although the solicitor felt there was at least a 50-50 chance of winning the case, he told the client, "Suing them in England is quite out of the question." As the father told me how hard he had worked to raise his son, the first in the family to attend a university, and how callous the American company had been in covering up the causes of the fatal accident, there was no hint of a tremor in his voice. I wondered how he had the strength to tell that story without breaking down. But when I told him that I would file the case for him in an American court on a contingent-fee basis and that if we lost the case he would not have to pay the defendants' costs, I noticed that tears formed in his eyes.

In 1978, when Don and Helena McCusker decided to sue in the United States, they could have chosen from hundreds of Equalizers capable of doing the job at least as well as I did. In 2004, there are thousands of Equalizers, better trained and equipped than we were. This cannot be comforting to the spirit of Aristotle Onassis or to those who live by his rule that there is no right or wrong. The last thing they want to face is accountability for their conduct, frauds and all.

In the colorful words of Kurt Vonnegut, "There is no reason goodness cannot triumph over evil, so long as the angels are as organized as the Mafia." The Equalizers are as well organized as the Mafia, but they don't need to use Mafia tactics because they have learned how to help goodness triumph over evil through the strengths of the American legal system.

Chapter Eighteen

Assessing Ari's Life

LIKE ALL OF US, ARISTOTLE ONASSIS HAD HIS GOOD AND bad traits, his strengths and weaknesses.

On the Plus Side

Throughout his life, Ari was loyal and generous to many relatives and friends. The sixteen-year-old Ari demonstrated this in 1922 when he was largely responsible for saving the lives of at least seventeen relatives under the Turkish guns at Smyrna. Then he risked his life again by sailing to Turkey to buy his father's release from the Smyrna prison, even though his father had not shown much interest in him as a child.

In later years, Ari shared his wealth liberally with his sister Artemis, his half-sisters Kalliroe and Merope, and various other relatives who were in need of financial assistance. During the tempestuous long-running affair with Maria Callas, Ari showered her with generous gifts of money and jewelry. Two fellow Greeks whom Ari befriended during his early business years in Argentina, Costa Gratsos and Ari's cousin Costas Konialidis, remained in his employ throughout their lives, and he tapped them to carry on his business after his death as directors of the Lichtenstein foundations. The same was true of Professor Yanni Georgakis, whom Ari plucked from academia to head Olympic Airways, and Paul Ioannidis, its long-time director-general, both of whom stayed on after Ari's death to help run the foundations. In fact, the foundation directors became known as the Graybeards because their attachment to Ari went back so many years.

While Ari did not share his wealth with charities or public benefit organizations during his life, the Alexander S. Onassis Public Benefit Foundation established after his death has used half his fortune for such worthy purposes.

I consider it a plus that Ari had a rollicking sense of humor and went out of his way to amuse people even if it made him seem unrefined. Despite his identification with Maria Callas, he made no pretense of appreciating grand opera, saying that it sounded to him "like a lot of Italian chefs shouting risotto recipes at each other." When he assigned Yanni Georgakis to make the arrangements for his Skorpios wedding to Jackie Kennedy, he told Yanni to try to find a priest who "speaks English and doesn't look like Rasputin."

Ari's extraordinary business vision, creativity, and imagination were important factors in his success, and here we must give him credit for using these talents to create a new tanker industry which eventually benefited many people through expansion of employment and trade, starting with the building of the tankers in previously moribund shipyards. And what other business owner in need of office space would have bought control of the whole country and restored its former grandeur, as Ari did in Monaco?

Ari was widely admired by members of the Jet Set that he helped to found, and also by a lot of people lower on the economic ladder, who saw him as an amusing relief from the stuffy business establishment, a high-school dropout who made it to the top and thumbed his nose at the conventions that bound most tycoons.

If we accept the premise that Ari chose to end his life to escape the burden of guilt for the killing of Alexander, we must credit him with enough character and conscience to hold himself accountable for the fatal frauds, even though he was not willing to admit them to anyone else.

The Minus Side: The Deadly Sins

Deceitfulness was the defining trait of Ari's character and the hallmark of his life.

This conclusion is inescapable when the evidence in the preceding chapters is weighed, even if Ari is given the benefit of any doubts about the nature of his many deceptions. Indeed, Ari's Rule, "There are no rules, there is no right or wrong, there is only what is possible," precludes any other conclusion because he not only proclaimed this principle—he lived by it and it was the major lesson he taught to his children.

As we have seen, Ari demonstrated his devotion to deceit throughout his life, in these serial frauds:

- Argentine tobacco, insurance, and Black Market currency swindles that produced the money with which he began building his shipping empire.
- Acquisition of war-surplus ships by defrauding the U.S. government through falsification of ownership documents, to which he pleaded guilty.

- Bribing Saudi Arabian government officials to gain control of most of that nation's oil under the Jiddah Agreement.
- Illegally slaughtering thousands of whales in violation of international whaling regulations.
- Evading taxes globally on most of his income throughout his life, by controlling Monaco, bribing Greek dictatorship officials, registering his ships under flags of convenience, filing false documents in the United States and other nations to which taxes were owed, and other devices.
- Ordering Johnny Meyer to destroy Christina's marriage to Joe Bolker by intimidation and character assassination; ordering Meyer to collaborate with Roy Cohn in similar tactics to get favorable divorce terms from Jackie.
- Ordering Christina to lie about the existence of his will, to help him cheat Jackie Kennedy out of her legal share of his estate.
- Creating and perpetuating the Myth of the Sea-Going Piaggio in order to convey the false impression of control and invincibility; lying to Alexander about switching to a helicopter; insisting that the Piaggio be overhauled in the Olympic Airways shops for his own tax-cheating benefit; and putting intimidating pressure on Alexander and Olympic to complete the overhaul and pilot checkout in time for the February 1973 cruise of the *Christina*.
- Procuring a false indictment which blamed Don McCusker for the killing of Alexander, and refusing to allow it to be dismissed even after reports from the Greek Air Force and his own investigator completely cleared McCusker and placed the blame on Ari's Olympic Airways mechanics who were unfit to perform the overhaul.

Note that every one of these frauds was committed in pursuit of a selfish and evil goal. Some powerful people have used deceit to achieve laudable purposes. For example, Lyndon Johnson used deceit and intimidation to secure passage of civil rights legislation, as chronicled by Robert A. Caro in *The Years of Lyndon Johnson: Master of the Senate*. But given Ari's extreme egocentrism and machismo and his penchant for total control of the people in his life, it was almost inevitable that he would use deceit for self-aggrandizement rather than for some meritorious purpose. Clearly, he was as selfish and greedy as he was deceitful.

Ari's extraordinary charisma, charm, and conversational skills were universally acknowledged. Like some other major con men, Ari had enough talent and drive to succeed legitimately. Indeed, the principal source of his fortune was the profits from legitimate tanker charters to major oil producers. But he could not resist the temptation to make it bigger and faster by using deceit.

Some may argue in mitigation that Ari was forced into the practice of bribery and trickery by the pressure of the Turkish sacking of Smyrna. Certainly he cannot be faulted for the steps he took there to save himself and his family. But he was never again under such pressure. The steady stream of commissions from sales of his father's tobacco exports provided him with a subsidy during his formative business years in Argentina. Yet the more successful he became, the more brazen were his frauds, escalating from the petty sabotaging of tobacco shipments with sea water to paying multimillion-dollar bribes for control of Saudi Arabia's oil output. Deceit was his first choice even when he didn't need it, because it was in his nature and character, and he enjoyed making it his way rather than the honest way.

His hiring of Johnny Meyer is a case in point. Ari enjoyed the full-time services of Nigel Neilson, a highly-regarded professional public relations counselor who could handle any legitimate communications. But Ari employed Johnny under the phony title of public relations consultant because he knew that Johnny gave him access to corruptible journalists and policemen, wire-tappers, and hoodlums who could expedite the dishonest practices Ari used in his business and personal affairs—even in relations with his children, as in the destruction of the Bolker marriage.

The deadly effects of Ari's deceitful nature are seen most vividly in his children—what he did to them and how their lives turned out. Alexander knew he could not believe anything Ari told him, and he became a lost soul, clinging to his girlfriend Fiona Thyssen for parental support and ending his tragic life at twenty-four because of Ari's deceitful manipulation of his yacht, his airline, and his private airplane. Christina, an emotional cripple throughout her life, died at thirty-seven from the effects of the amphetamines and barbiturates she required to cope with life as Ari's daughter and designated successor in deceit.

The women Ari loved also suffered blighted lives as he used them to enhance his mystique: Inga, Tina, Maria. Only the indomitable Jackie survived intact—perhaps even stronger—no thanks to Ari or his henchmen, Johnny Meyer and Roy Cohn.

Here we should take note of the 2004 book *Nemesis: The True Story of Aristotle Onassis, Jackie O, and the Love Triangle that Brought Down the Kennedys*, written by the distinguished British author Peter Evans. Evans also wrote the 1986 biography *Ari: The Life and Times of Aristotle Socrates Onassis,* in which he skillfully recounted the then known historical facts without attempting to judge Ari. In the 2004 *Nemesis*, Evans brands Ari a business crook, noting his use of intrigue and corruption in all his big deals, and alleges that Ari began building his fortune in Argentina through drug dealing, returning to that trade near the end of his life by smuggling heroin into the United States aboard his tankers. Evans goes on to accuse Ari of paying a Palestinian terrorist to hire Sirhan Sirhan to assassinate Bobby Kennedy.

Since Evans is a highly-regarded investigative reporter who spent more than thirty years researching Ari's life, including many interviews with Ari himself, Christina, Alexander, and other Onassis intimates, it is tempting to add the fruits of his work to the historical reservoir we are drawing upon to assess Ari's life. But because *Nemesis* goes well beyond the evidence of Ari's deceit, greed, fraud, and hubris to charge him with drug-smuggling and murder, it would be unfair to accept Evans's conclusions without examining the supporting evidence he cites.

Evans says that after publication of his 1986 *Ari* biography, he was told by Christina Onassis and Yanni Georgakis (then chairman of Olympic Airways) that he had missed the really big story, but neither was willing to be more specific. Continuing to interview them and other Onassis colleagues (such as Johnny Meyer, Roy Cohn, and Costa Gratsos), Evans pieced together what he considers to be the true story of Ari's involvement in the killing of Bobby Kennedy, as follows.

In the spring of 1968, Ari had several meetings in Paris with Mahmoud Hamshari, a member of the Palestinian guerilla group Fatah, whose military commander was Yassir Arafat. Hamshari told Ari that he had been approached by a Palestinian terrorist group which was demanding payment of $350,000, failing which they were prepared to plant a bomb on an Olympic passenger flight. Ari took this threat seriously because there were rumors that Palestinian terrorists were targeting western airlines for hijacking or bombing. Ari decided to pay Hamshari this protection money, ordering Yanni Georgakis to provide $200,000 in cash from the Olympic Airways coffers to cover the down payment.

Christina Onassis confirmed the Hamshari payment story to Evans, adding that Ari later learned that Hamshari had used the money to finance the shooting of Bobby Kennedy, but claiming that Ari himself was not involved in the murder plot and did not know how the money would be used. Evans's final piece of evidence is his 2003 interview with Helene Gaillet, the New York socialite who had visited Ari on Skorpios a few months before his death. She told Evans that when they were alone together during that visit, Ari had shocked her by saying, "I put up the money for Bobby Kennedy's murder."

Bobby Kennedy was shot and killed in the kitchen of the Los Angeles Ambassador Hotel on June 5, 1968 by Sirhan Sirhan, a displaced Palestinian who shouted, "I did it for my country!" He was tried in Los Angeles and convicted of first degree murder. Neither his lawyers (who argued mental illness as a defense to premeditation) nor the prosecutors claimed that he was acting in concert with others, and none of the extensive government investigations of the assassination revealed evidence of a conspiracy or any payment to Sirhan. Neither Fatah nor any other organization claimed credit for the killing. In fact, Evans reports that Hamshari's 1967 suggestion that Fatah assassinate a prominent American was rejected by that group's leadership as counter-productive if not insane, and Hamshari was later executed by Fatah for embezzling funds.

Evans's 2004 book is the first published claim that Ari had paid to have Bobby murdered. Why would Ari become involved in such a bizarre and risky plot?

In the spring of 1968, Ari and Jackie Kennedy were discussing the possibility of marriage, while Bobby was fighting his way through the primary elections in pursuit of the Democratic presidential nomination. When Jackie revealed to Bobby the seriousness of her Onassis affair, he was alarmed that such a marriage would harm his campaign. As he put it, if she married Ari before the election, "it could cost me five states." By Evans's own account, Bobby did not seek to obstruct the marriage, but only asked Jackie to postpone it until after the November election. Jackie said that her plans were not that far along anyway, so she would gladly avoid any public mention of the potential marriage before the election, and even volunteered to end her retirement from public life to campaign actively for Bobby. Therefore, Bobby's distaste for the Onassis marriage did not furnish any motive for Ari to have him murdered. In fact, Ari would have been in a much more powerful position if Bobby had lived to become president, for as Jackie's husband, Ari's mystique would have been enhanced by appearing to have a direct pipeline to the White House.

Evans does not claim that Ari had a valid or logical reason for having Bobby killed, but rather ascribes the motivation to Ari's alleged pathological hatred of Bobby and his paranoid fear that Bobby might do him harm. Thus he paints a picture of the 1968 Ari—then at the height of his powers and unencumbered by the later burden of Alexander's death—as one prone to allow emotions to govern his conduct, leading him to do the opposite of what was good for his image and his business. Evans argues that this explains why Ari procured the murder of a United States senator who happened to be the beloved brother-in-law of his intended trophy wife, employing for this daunting task a terrorist who was already extorting money from him and a mentally-disturbed amateur assassin.

Assuming that Helene Gaillet's recollections of a twenty-nine-year-old conversation are accurate, why would Ari make such a confession to her unless it was the truth? At that moment, four months before his death, he had lost much of his mystique. Monaco,

Olympic Airways, and the Greek Colonels whom he could control by bribery were gone. The grandiose plans for oil refineries in Greece and New Hampshire had come to nothing. He no longer dominated the tanker business, and apartment sales at New York's Olympic Tower were not going too well. The death of Alexander had transformed him into a figure of pity, and now he was in the process of shedding Jackie. What he had left would more than fulfill the ambitions of most successful businessmen, but Ari did not give up power gracefully. What more could he have done to restore the legend of that power than to make up a story that he had taken out an Olympian figure like Bobby Kennedy, who had the bad judgment to challenge the Golden Greek?

To support the allegation that Ari and his New York partner Costa Gratsos used Olympic tankers to smuggle heroin into the United States, Evans cites interviews with people in Florida (unrelated to Ari's business) who told him that Ari had met with Paul Helliwell, a Miami attorney who was rumored to be involved in drug trafficking. Evans does not assert that this busy Miami lawyer met only with people who were involved in drug trafficking.

To me these stories of murder and heroin smuggling appear improbable, and the evidence supporting them is speculative hearsay at best. This is not a putdown of the job Peter Evans did in pursuing the facts, because the deaths of the principal witnesses left him without access to first-hand evidence by the time he got on the trail. I believe that readers interested in making their own assessment of Ari's life should consider both of Evans's Onassis books.

The Lessons of Ari's Media Hype

Ari has served as the role model for financial manipulators seeking to operate beyond the rules while leading glamorized, highly-publicized lives. Ari's extravagant life style, combined with his seemingly effortless financial success and his ego-driven rivalry with Stavros Niarchos, furnished the media with an irresistible story. It was not only the gossip columnists who bought into Johnny Meyer's Onassis hype. The staid *Lloyd's List*, bible of the shipping industry, posthumously named Ari shipping's Man of the 20th Century, turning a blind eye to his monumental frauds and extolling the virtues of the flag of convenience (now adopted by virtually the entire shipping industry) which Ari perfected in order to avoid accountability for those frauds.

Following in Ari's wake were such mystique-manipulating rogues as Robert Maxwell, the British swindler who copied Ari's style down to the ostentatious sea-going office named after his daughter; Leona Helmsley, jailed for falsely claiming the costs of renovating her luxurious estate as business expenses, whose famous statement that "only the little people pay taxes" qualifies as a sub-tenet of Ari's "no rules" principle; and Marc Rich, "pardoned" in the closing hours of the Clinton administration, who carried Ari's defiance of the rules to new levels of arrogance from the sanctuary of his palatial Swiss manor.

The 2001 Enron collapse is another case in point. The perpetrators of the biggest financial swindle in American history copied the Byzantine corporate structure pioneered by Ari, using more than three thousand partnerships and subsidiary companies to camouflage their fleecing of shareholders, employee pensions, and the public. Their unscrupulous public relations hype deceived not only the business press but high-salaried financial analysts who controlled billions of investment dollars. And as in Ari's case, Enron was not only about making money—it was about flaunting it and trashing the rules that restrained ordinary mortals. As one of Enron's former officials put it:

It was insane. There were no rules for people, even in our personal lives. Everything was about the company and everything was supposed to be on the edge—sex, money, all of it.

Today there are many more investigative journalists than in Ari's time, and sometimes they succeed in exposing potential Enrons before it is too late. Perhaps the lesson is that when extraordinary financial success is accompanied by a profligate lifestyle in the Onassis pattern, the media, the accountants, and the regulators should take a careful second look to determine if there is a hyping exercise under way to so glamorize the perpetrator's mystique that he will be able to operate outside the rules.

There is another lesson in Ari's downfall, one so simple and straightforward that some may consider it corny. Ari's story shows that ultimately there is a price to pay for a life lived beyond the rules, in which there is no right or wrong. The price for Ari was the destruction of his son Alexander. That he was not prepared to pay such a price is evident from the way in which he gave up his own life.

Given Ari's superstitious nature, it is surprising that he chose to flaunt his disdain for the rules governing ordinary mortals despite the clear warning in Greek tradition against the sin of *hubris*:

> *...it is accordingly significant that, in Greek thought, hubris was distinguished as the capital sin; for it meant that the gods were relentless in striking down a man who, confident in his own achievement or good fortune, tended to forget his human status.*

The editors of *Encyclopedia Britannica* explain *hubris* as "impious disregard of the limits governing men's actions...suggestive of the overconfidence that the gods find offensive." They go on to say that *hubris* is the "sin to which the great and gifted are most susceptible, and in Greek tragedy it is usually the basic flaw of the tragic hero."

The no-rules principle which led to Ari's downfall stands in stark contrast to the one that Don McCusker laid down for himself and his family. At the lowest point in his life, jobless and out of money, confined to a Greek hospital with painful injuries and shackled by Ari's fraudulent manslaughter indictment, Don took his pen in his shaky hand and wrote to his six young children: "Do what you know is right."

We can only wonder how much more inspirational the story of Aristotle Onassis would have been if he had lived by that principle and had given Alexander and Christina the chance for such a life.

Note: Neither the Greek police nor the Civil Aviation Authority had the facilities or personnel to conduct a full-scale technical investigation of the Piaggio accident. Only the Greek Air Force had this capability. Therefore, the Greek police lieutenant in charge of determining the cause of the Piaggio accident appointed a five-member commission to conduct the technical investigation and submit a report. All five members of the commission were personnel of the Greek Air Force and their report became known as the Greek Air Force Report. It was written in Greek and was submitted to the police on April 20, 1973. The following English translation is the first publication of this report.

Findings under the Evidence as Regards the Accident of the Piaggio 136 Aircraft SX-BDC of Olympic Airways on January 22, 1973

I. COMMISSION

President: Group Captain M. Tsingris (Pilot)

Members: Squadron Leader D. Papageorgiou (Pilot)

Squadron Leader M. Saharides (Engineer)

Flight Lieutenant D. Mpiniaris

Sergeant-Major M. Katsikis

II. INVESTIGATION ORDER

On January 25, 1973, the members selected by Police Lieutenant A.P.D. Kakouli were instructed to proceed with the investigation.

III. SEQUENCE OF EVENTS

1. On January 22, 1973, at approximately 15:00 (3 p.m.) local time, the Piaggio 136 amphibian aircraft of Olympic Airways, with Alexandros Onassis as the pilot, had been scheduled for flight from the Athens Airport to the area of Poros Isle. The aircraft was scheduled to make a number of water takeoffs and landings before it returned to the airport.

2. The pilot of the aircraft submitted the flight schedule in accordance with the regulations before the flight. In this schedule, among other things, were the names of two people reported as passengers. These two people were the foreigners McGregor and McCusker.

3. The pilot in command entered the aircraft and sat on the right-hand side of the cockpit. McCusker sat in the left seat, and the third person, McGregor, sat in the back seat.

4. After the engines were started and the aircraft was ready to take off, the pilot received via radio the relevant clearance from the control tower. The aircraft slowly moved towards the runway where they stopped to perform the necessary procedures and final checks before taking off. After this, the pilot was permitted to enter the runway from the taxiway. Once the aircraft was on the runway, the pilot set the engines to full power and the aircraft accelerated to takeoff. The control tower gave them information regarding wind velocity and direction. It also informed the pilot about other aircraft traffic on the airport.

5. After the aircraft accelerated for approximately 570 meters it left the ground and immediately it turned to the right. This sudden turn caused the aircraft's right wing to strike the runway surface, thus causing the aircraft to crash between the runway and the taxiway. The time of the crash was estimated at 15:20 (3:20 p.m.) local time.

6. The control tower immediately ordered the rescue teams into action for immediate assistance of the passengers and crew of the crashed aircraft. The pilot and the two other occupants of the aircraft were taken out badly injured and were immediately transported to the hospital. After a few days the pilot of the aircraft died due to his serious injuries.

IV. <u>INVESTIGATION</u>

1. The commission, which was organized three days after the crash, went to the scene of the accident on January 25, 1973. They found the following facts:

2. The aircraft crashed within the airport about 84 meters away from the runway. The aircraft's engines were still running at full power.

3. In examining the aircraft's remains, the commission came to the conclusion that once the plane was off the ground and at a right angle to the runway, the right wing came in contact with the ground, forcing the plane to crash nose-first. Then the plane spun to the right for about 300 degrees, because the engines were still at full power. Due to the fast spinning motion, the aircraft's left wing also hit the ground, forcing it to fold in half.

4. The plane's cabin was completely destroyed at both the front and rear end. This was due to the repeated contacts with the ground during the final phase of the crash.

5. Due to the severe impact at the front of the aircraft, the cockpit and the passenger seats were also crushed, thus causing the serious injuries of the pilot and passengers.

6. It was also observed that the wheels of the landing gear were in the landing position, and only the steel legs holding the wheels appeared to be damaged. The right leg indicated harsh contact with a rough surface. The tail wheel was locked in the

neutral upward position as it is supposed to be according to the takeoff procedures. This wheel also showed contact but with a dirt surface.

7. The aircraft's doors were cut and removed by the rescue team in order to extricate the trapped occupants.

8. Both the aircraft's wings were destroyed at the ends, but the propellers were completely undamaged.

9. Although the wings were mostly destroyed, the wing flaps were in perfect condition and were found in the "up" position.

10. The right aileron was also destroyed, while the left aileron was undamaged but not functioning due to damage to the part of the wing to which it is attached.

11, The elevators were found in the aircraft's horizontal tail section, but were also badly damaged from the crash and spinning of the plane.

12. The surface of the rudder, found in the vertical tail section, was damaged in the upper left section, also as a result of the crash.

13. The left wingtip float of the aircraft was still on the wing, sustaining minor damage due to contact with the cement surface of the runway, while the right one was detached and was found close to the aircraft.

14. Although the cockpit was badly damaged by the crash and by the rescue team's efforts, the experts were still able to study the instrument panel and the positions of the levers and switches. The seat belt mechanisms were in the locked position but the belts were cut by the rescue team in order to free the three occupants. The instrument panel and the pilot's seats had been compressed and moved to the right due to the angle of the contact with the ground.

15. The lever controlling the landing gear was found in the "landing gear-down" position. The lever controlling the wing flaps was in the "up" position. The wing flaps, in accordance with the

position of the lever, were up, and this is not the proper position for takeoff procedure.

16. Both the aircraft's control columns were found in the leftward position, the last position they were in before the crash. This was worthy of note since the whole structure of the plane was distorted completely to the left.

17. The elevator trim tabs were observed to be in the "6 degrees up" position. Again this position is not appropriate for taking off.

18. The levers controlling power and fuel were found in the position appropriate for full engine power, in accordance with takeoff procedure.

19. The fuel tanks were undamaged and full.

20. Inside the aircraft were various documents, logbooks, maintenance manuals, fuel reports, and the aircraft's Certificate of Airworthiness.

21. A tape containing the live conversation between the aircraft and the control tower was also given to the commission.

22. Based on the tape, the commission came to the conclusion that the pilot, Alexandros Onassis, was the one handling the radio throughout the flight.

23. From both the control tower's records and the tape, it was apparent that an Air France Boeing 727 had taken off shortly before the Piaggio did. The accident took place approximately two minutes later.

24. An identical Piaggio aircraft was furnished to the commission by Olympic Airways for the purpose of testing and studying the aircraft's engines. The commission transferred the engines of the crashed aircraft to the second Piaggio for testing purposes. They were found to be in perfect condition and operated normally in all respects.

25. The laboratory reports stated that the hydraulic, electronic, and fuel systems were in good condition and there were no indications of malfunction.

26. From the study of the aircraft's controls the following observations were made:

a. The rudder's pulley, cables, and the rest of the rudder's gear were tested and found in good condition and without any kind of malfunction.

b. The elevator assembly was also found to be in good condition and responded correctly to all tests. It was observed that the elevators, responsible for causing the aircraft to climb, were in the completely "up" position due to the final impact of the plane's tail section. The elevator trim-tab lever was found at a position of 6 degrees up, which was not in accordance with the aircraft manual's instructions for takeoff procedure.

c. The aileron control system and all its parts were in good condition. But the tests showed that its last position was the opposite of the correct one. The commission and the specialized technicians made this observation; they came to the conclusion that the reason for this was the fact that the control cables were connected wrongly in a reverse manner. These control cables begin from the floor of the cockpit and transmit the movement through pulleys to the ailerons on the aircraft's wings.

d. It was further noted that the control cables were made of 5/32 carbon, but the one connected to the right aileron was of 3/16 stainless steel.

27. The prevailing weather conditions at the airport when the accident occurred were good. The pilot received all relevant information regarding wind and current runway traffic from the control tower. Wind velocity and direction were clearly within safety limits for the safe takeoff of the Piaggio aircraft.

28. The occupants of the crashed aircraft were Alexandros Onassis (pilot), foreigner McCusker occupying the left-hand seat, and the second foreign passenger McGregor in the back passenger seat. The commission came to the following conclusions based on the evidence:

a. The pilot of the aircraft, Alexandros Onassis, was an authorized "B" class license holder (serial no. 719). He had been submitted to the proper medical testing and was granted a medical certificate which was valid until May 9, 1973. By the order E1/A/19899/3557/6-7-72 of the Civil Aviation Authority, he had been granted the authorized license to examine pilots to qualify them to fly amphibious aircraft like the Piaggio 136. His total flying time was 896 hours, 51 hours of which were in the Piaggio aircraft. His last flight in this kind of aircraft prior to the accident was on August 27, 1972. In his personal file there is a reported incident regarding a regulation violation, as to which he submitted an apology to the Civil Aviation Authority. Further details are unknown.

b. As regards McCusker, who was sitting in the left front seat, no information was found concerning his flying experience or medical certificate.

c. As regards the third person on board, McGregor, evidence was supplied by Olympic Airways that he was a certificated airline pilot. However, his pilot certificate had expired as of November 9, 1972, due to the expiration of his medical certificate. He had been originally recruited by Olympic Airways as a Boeing 707 pilot, but later transferred to the amphibian section of Olympic Airways as a pilot of the Piaggio 136. He had 166 hours of flight time on that type of aircraft.

29. According to the flight schedule, the flight was local and the estimated time of flight was 2 hours and 30 minutes.

30. According to the records of Olympic Airways, the purpose of this flight was to familiarize McCusker with this type of aicraft by making a number of takeoffs and landings on the water in the vicinity of Poros Isle.

31. According to the statement of McGregor, the following was reported:

a. All the relevant pre-flight checks were done by Alexandros Onassis. He then started the aircraft's engines and made further checks, while simultaneously explaining the procedures to McCusker.

b. McCusker taxied the aircraft from the parking lot to the beginning of the runway.

c. All further testing of the engines, up to the point of taking off, was done entirely by Alexandros Onassis.

32. From examination of the aircraft's log books it appears that the load being carried was within limits, and that the fuel and other fluids were adequate for this scheduled flight.

33. Further examination of the aircraft's records shows that permits were granted for its operation by both Olympic Airways and the airport authorities.

34. The aircraft was acquired by Olympic Airways on December 22, 1967. It bore manufacturer's serial number 97.

35. The previous Certificate of Airworthiness of the amphibian aircraft had expired on November 29, 1972. The new certificate, which was issued on January 18, 1973 by the Civil Aviation Authority, had an expiration date of January 18, 1974.

36. From the time the aircraft was built to the moment of its destruction it had been flown for a total of 1081 hours. It had undergone a general overhaul on December 1, 1970.

37. The last flight prior to the accident took place on October 2, 1972, from Skorpios to the Athens Airport.

38. During the aircraft's stay at the Athens Airport, considerable maintenance and overhaul work was done to it. The following were reported:

a. Some parts were replaced with new ones according to the instructions in the aircraft manual, and some test flights took place, according to the aircraft's logbook.

b. On November 15, 1972, again according to the aircraft's logbook, the ailerons were removed along with their control systems since they had exceeded the estimated life period (5 years).

c. Ten days later, on November 25, 1972, the records of additional work noted that a re-installation of the ailerons and their control systems was made.

d. On November 11, 1972, the aircraft was taken out of operation because of the expiration of the Certificate of Airworthiness, and this was noted in the daily service forms from that time on until January 19, 1973.

e. In the daily service form 000/A16-9/5/69 of January 17, 1973, apart from the repeated observation that the aircraft was out of operation due to expiration of the Certificate of Airworthiness, it was noted that the Certificate of Airworthiness had been renewed.

f. However, in the daily service form of January 19, 1973 as well as in the daily service form of January 21, 1973, the observation continued to be noted that the aircraft was out of operation due to expiration of the Certificate of Airworthiness, without any other comment or observation.

g. Apart from the above, the Certificate of Airworthiness itself showed that it was renewed on January 18, 1973. Therefore the observation about renewal of the Certificate of Airworthiness entered in the daily service form of January 17, 1973 was not correct, although that observation was correct for January 18, 1973.

39. Through document No. TD/1-3030/2622/3-11, Olympic Airways applied to the Civil Aviation Authority (C.A.A.) for renewal of the Certificate of Airworthiness of the Piaggio on November 29, 1972. This document noted that the said aircraft was fit for safe flight under the responsibility of Olympic Airways.

40. The C.A.A., through its message No. 6617/10.11.72 on November 10, 1972, informed Olympic Airways that for the renewal of the Certificate of Airworthiness, two aeronautical engineers were appointed: G. Papademetropoulus (3rd Grade) and E. Mavroforos (5th grade), both employees of the C.A.A.

41. Then, Olympic Airways, through its message to the C.A.A. dated December 4, 1972, applied for the granting of a special license to carry out test flights for the renewal of the Certificate of Airworthiness.

42. Through a message dated December 14, 1972, the C.A.A. approved the carrying out of the requested flight tests, on condition that under the responsibility of Olympic Airways, said aircraft would be fit for safe flight.

43. By document dated January 18, 1973 addressed to the C.A.A. Department of Aircraft Airworthiness, one of the appointed airworthiness inspectors, E. Mavroforos, submitted an inspection report of the aircraft SX-BDC according to which the aircraft was considered "fit for flight." The Certificate of Airworthiness of that aircraft was renewed for one year, from January 18, 1973 to January 18, 1974.

44. Please note here that the test flight requested by Olympic Airways was not carried out.

45. From investigation of the form relating to daily inspection of the aircraft on January 22, 1973, which was the day of the accident, it emerged that this document carried the signatures of the authorized maintenance technicians who confirmed that the aircraft

was in good condition and had been cleared for flight, despite a noted observation that the Certificate of Airworthiness had expired.

46. The maintenance of Olympic Airways' aircraft as well as the inspection and control of the maintenance work carried out by technical personnel was the responsibility of Olympic Airways.

V. ANALYSIS

1. Before the takeoff from Athens Airport for a domestic flight of 2 hours and 30 minutes on January 22, 1973, the pilot of the aircraft, Alexandros Onassis, had submitted a flight plan and was briefed on the prevailing weather conditions. The meteorogological conditions of that day were suitable for flight.

2. The purpose of the flight was to familiarize McCusker with this type of aircraft, by making water landings in the area of Poros Isle.

3. Before the flight, the required briefing of McCusker was made by the pilot, Alexandros Onassis, according to McGregor's statement.

4. The technical check of the aircraft before the flight was made by the authorized maintenance personnel of Olympic Airways, who signed the appropriate inspection documents confirming the fitness and readiness of the aircraft for flight; however, the investigation showed that the aircraft was not at all fit for flight.

5. The pilot, together with the two foreign nationals, took possession of the aircraft and boarded, with the pilot taking the seat on the right. McCusker took the left seat while McGregor sat behind McCusker. The pilot started the engines and carried out the checks and the taxiing process from memory, given the fact that no checklist was used, nor found, as required. At this point

one of the items on the checklist is the check of the ailerons for free and correct movement.

6. Then, in accordance with the instructions of the control tower, the aircraft taxied to the second connecting taxiway of Runway 33. At this point a test of the engines was made, which confirmed their proper functioning (according to McGregor's statement). At this point the pre-takeoff checks were carried out, also from memory. In accordance with the checklist, the first of these is a test of the ailerons. The flaps were positioned at 20 degrees down (according to McGregor's statement) and the other levers and controls were positioned at the proper settings.

7. Around 15:12 hours (3:12 pm.) local time, the pilot of the aircraft told the control tower that he was ready for takeoff. The control tower instructed him to wait.

8. At 15:18 hours (3:18 p.m.) the Air France aircraft took off from Runway 33.

9. At 15:19 hours (3:19 p.m.) the pilot of the Piaggio requested permission to enter the takeoff runway. The control tower granted permission and also gave the latest information on air traffic and wind velocity, which at that time was at 8 knots from 240 degrees, that is, from the left side of the aircraft. The pilot acknowledged reception and understanding and began to taxi for takeoff at 15:20 hours (3:20 p.m.).

10. The time lapse between the takeoff of the Boeing 727 and of the Piaggio, measured with the assistance of the control tower tape recorder, was estimated at about 2 minutes.

11. Here it should be clarified that in the case of successive takeoffs, the control tower grants takeoff permission, but it is up to the pilot in the command of the aircraft about to take off to decide whether it will take off and with how much separation, in order to avoid entering air turbulence caused by the preceding aircraft.

12.The commission cannot determine with certainty who was handling the aircraft at the critical time of the takeoff. If what is reported by the passenger McGregor is correct, the takeoff was executed by McCusker, sitting in the left seat, under the supervision of Alexandros Onassis.

13. The aircraft accelerated normally on the runway and took off at a speed of about 100 miles per hour. At takeoff, the aircraft banked to the right. As a consequence of this bank to the right, the right-hand wingtip float came into contact with the runway, with the result that the aircraft veered to the right of the takeoff point. As a result of the increasing bank, the right tire came into skidding contact with the runway. This caused a short bounce, and the aircraft exited from the right side of the runway, maintaining a bank to the right while climbing.

14. At this point, it is presumed that the flaps were retracted. It is highly probable and reasonable to assume that the pilot of the aircraft at that moment presumed that the continuous and intense bank to the right was due to a disparate position of the flaps. This action, however, resulted in further loss of stability and climbing ability of the aircraft, the right wing of which impacted rough ground outside the runway.

15. At this point, the banking increased further, and due to the contact of the wing with the ground, the nose of the aircraft came down and followed a circular motion of about 300 degrees to the right, in which the nose, affected by the movement to the right on the one hand and the propulsion of the engines on the other hand, crashed to the ground. The cockpit and passenger cabin were crushed and as a consequence those on board were severely injured, particularly those sitting in the front, McCusker and Alexandros Onassis.

16. The latter, Onassis, due to the fact that he was sitting on the right side, and due to the fact that the impact of the crash was from the left to the right, came under the greatest force of impact, and suffered the most serious injuries.

17. After the collision of the nose of the aircraft with the ground, with the nose coming down low and the right wing banked, the aircraft crashed and came to a stop on the ground resting on the left wing and tail section of the fuselage.

18. From the investigation that followed, it appeared that the functioning of the ailerons was the opposite of the correct function, due to the reverse connection of the aileron control cables. This work was conducted on November 25, 1972 (see Technical Section, Part V).

19. If the ailerons were correctly connected and the aileron control system were operating correctly, the correct position for a turn to the left is that when the control wheel is turned by the pilot to the left, the left aileron rises while the left wing declines, and thus the aircraft makes a turn to the left. In this case, with the turning of the control wheel to the left, the left aileron, instead of rising, was declining, with the natural result that the aircraft performed a move opposite from the normal, that is, a right turn. Therefore the continuous right turn of the aircraft after takeoff, under the above-mentioned circumstances of the reversed connection of the ailerons, is fully explained.

20. It is here judged by the commission as appropriate to note the quality of the maintenance work carried out by the personnel of Olympic Airways on the aircraft in question.

a. The whole process of replacing the aileron control system of the aircraft, that is, its removal on November 15, 1972 and its reinstallation on November 25, 1972, during which operation the movement axis of the aileron pulleys and the separation ring were found in improper positions and the aileron links were found in the reversed positions; and

b. the presence of wrongly connected aileron control cables; and

c. the preparation and inspection for flight of the aircraft in question by the maintenance personnel despite the written observation on the daily service forms of November 21 and 22 concerning the expiration of the Certificate of Airworthiness, and also the signed certification of the authorized technicians that the aircraft was fit and cleared for flight;

indicated that in the execution of maintenance on the aircraft in question, the necessary attention and care due to such work was not duly paid.

21. The technique of takeoff under cross-wind conditions, as in this case, requires for all types of aircraft the turning of the control wheel toward the side from which the wind is blowing, at the start of taxiing for takeoff until the point of leaving the ground. This is done for the purpose of counteracting the tendency of the wind to tilt the wing into the ground. When the aircraft is in flight and after it gains airspeed, the ailerons become active and the turning of the control wheel into the wind is gradually reversed by the pilot.

22. During the takeoff run, the Piaggio aircraft encountered the effect of the wind from the left, and immediately after its takeoff, because of the reversed connection of the ailerons, instead of finding itself in the position of correcting for the wind drift, it was turned the wrong way, with the result that the right wing dropped and turned the aircraft even further to the right, followed by the striking of the right wing float, the forceful contact of the right wheel, the right wing striking the ground, and finally the crash.

23. The persistent increase of the bank to the right was due to the reaction of the pilot, who, when he first realized the bank to the

right, attempted to correct with a left turn of the control wheel. This action increased the bank to the right and evidently created the impression of an irregular deployment of the wing flaps, which he raised. The bank to the right increased, the pilot turned the control wheel completely to the left and at the same time pulled the control wheel back to gain altitude. Due however to the excessive increase of the bank to the right, the loss of lift from the raising of the wing flaps, and the contact of the right wing with the rough ground, it became impossible to maintain altitude despite the continuous operation of the engines at full power.

24. The commission examined and ruled out the suggestion that the accident was caused by the effect of the turbulence created by the preceding takeoff of the Boeing 727 aircraft, because the phenomenon of turbulence by a preceding aircraft begins to appear from the moment that an aircraft takes off from the ground. The Boeing 727, which was larger and heavier, took off at a longer distance from the take-off point of the Piaggio, and therefore the Piaggio, at the point of take-off at least, was not inside the area of the turbulence of the preceding aircraft and was not affected by it.

25. Also ruled out was the suggestion of failure or malfunction of an engine, given that the engines were not damaged during the accident, and when tested they operated normally. Moreover, both engines operated at full power even after the crash and immobilization of the aircraft on the ground. Additionally, the passenger McGregor, who is experienced on this type of aircraft, testified to the normal operation of the engines.

26. Finally, also ruled out was the loss of sufficient airspeed of the aircraft at takeoff, given that the aircraft was at an airspeed of about 100 miles per hour at takeoff, which is within the safe level for takeoff.

27. The commission believes it is its obligation at this point to refer to the actions of the pilot of the aircraft in the takeoff phase. The actions taken by him were the appropriate and required actions assuming that the ailerons were properly connected, and not connected in reverse as was the case here. However, as the fact of the reverse connection of the ailerons was not known to the pilot, and because the aircraft was flying at low ground speed in the takeoff phase, it was not possible for him to react otherwise.

VI. CONCLUSIONS

Following the investigation and analysis it carried out, the commission came to the following conclusions regarding the circumstances and cause of the accident.

1. The accident was not the result of poor technique or mistake of the pilot of the aircraft at the time of the accident.

2. The main cause of the accident was the mistakes of the maintenance personnel of Olympic Airways which consisted of:

a) The reversed connection of the ailerons during the work for the replacement of the controls of the aircraft, and

b) The inadequate inspection by the inspector of Olympic Airways of the work which had been carried out on the aircraft.

3. Contributory causes of the accident are believed to be the following:

a) The faulty operational check of the aircraft by the authorized official of the Civil Aeronautics Authority for the renewal of the Certificate of Airworthiness.

b) The omission by the pilot to use the checklist and as a result the omission by the pilot to carry out the required check of the ailerons before takeoff, which resulted in the failure to notice the reverse connection and operation of the ailerons.

Signed at Athens on April 20, 1973, by the President and each Member of the commission:

President:
Group Captain M. Tsingris

Members:
Squadron Leader D. Papageorgiou
Squadron Leader M. Saharides
Flight Lieutenant D. Mpiniaris
Sergeant–Major M. Katsikis

Photos

Photo Credits

1. Camera Press
2. Corbis
3. Corbis
4. Desmond O'Neill Features
5. Camera Press
6. TV Picture Life Magazine
7. Piaggio Aero Industries S.p.A.
8. Piaggio Aero Industries S.p.A.
9. Pan American World Airways
10. Helena McCusker
11. Helena McCusker

1 Father and son, Aristotle and Alexander Onassis

2 Aristotle Onassis at the head table of the 1960 Monaco Rose Ball, with Princess Grace on his right and Prince Rainier opposite. Ava Gardner is on the prince's right. Ari bought control of Monaco and manipulated it as his private country, to globally avoid taxation, government regulation, and accountability.

3 The Onassis yacht *Christina* with the Piaggio amphibian carried on board, so that Aristotle could "use it in all the seas of the world."

4 Aristotle Onassis and Maria Callas's husband, Giovanni Battista Meneghini, jointly embracing her during the supper party in London's Dorchester Hotel hosted by Onassis to celebrate her 1959 performance of *Medea* at Covent Garden. The party was the prelude to the 1959 *Christina* cruise which ended the marriages of Onassis and Callas.

5 Alexander Onassis and Fiona, the Baroness Thyssen-Bornemisza, in Switzerland.

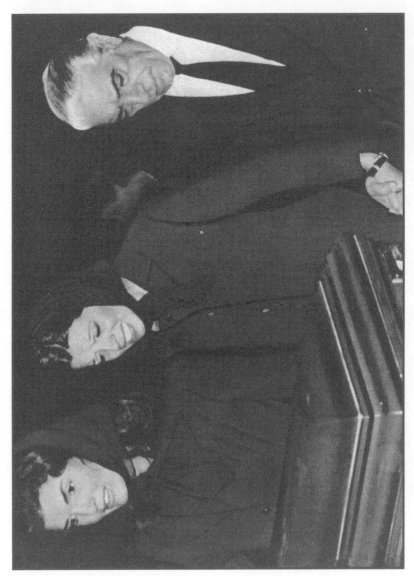

6 Jacqueline Kennedy Onassis, Christina Onassis, and Aristotle Onassis at the casket of Alexander Onassis.

7 Excerpts from Piaggio literature, showing the Onassis amphibian, license SX-BDC in top photo, "that Aristotle Onassis kept aboard his yacht as a tender."

The versatility of this robust amphibian is shown in these photos of an example in the hands of an American private operator: from water to land, and vice versa, with complete nonchalance.

The P.136L that Aristotle Onassis kept aboard his yacht as a "tender" was used also for air-taxi service: its generous avionics fit is shown by its numerous antennas.

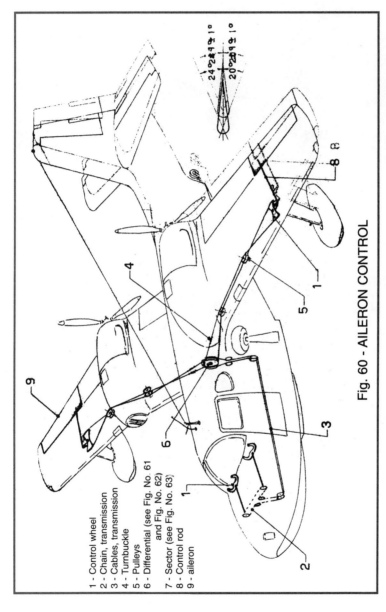

Fig. 60 - AILERON CONTROL

1 - Control wheel
2 - Chain, transmission
3 - Cables, transmission
4 - Turnbuckle
5 - Pulleys
6 - Differential (see Fig. No. 61 and Fig. No. 62)
7 - Sector (see Fig. No. 63)
8 - Control rod
9 - aileron

8 Diagram of the aileron control system of the Piaggio, as shown in the Piaggio 136 L Maintenance Manual. The right aileron is shown at "9." When properly rigged, turning the pilot's wheel ("1") to the left for a left turn would cause the left aileron to go up and the right aileron to go down.

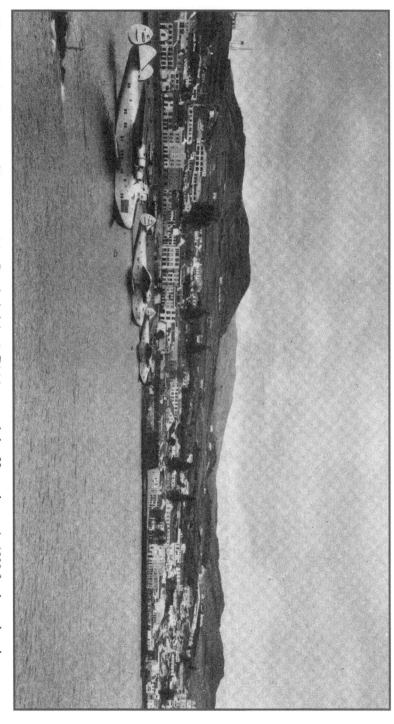

9 Three of the five Boeing 314 Clippers comprising Pan Am's Atlantic Division stranded at Horta, Azores, in 1939 for eleven days due to wave heights above three feet.

10 Don McCusker (center), legendary test pilot Scott Crossfield (left) who was the first to fly at twice the speed of sound, and Jack Swigert (who later piloted the Apollo command module safely back to earth after a catastrophic inflight explosion) preparing for Don to flight-test North American-Rockwell's recovery system for space vehicles, 1966.

11 The McCusker family shortly before the time of their Grecian adventure. Standing in rear, left to right: Karen, Tom, Mike. Seated, left to right, Don, Helena. In front, left to right, Jean, Mary, John.

Acknowledgments

THE MAIN SOURCE MATERIAL FOR THIS BOOK WAS ACQUIRED from my interviews with the surviving participants, whom I cannot thank enough.

They include:

Don and Helena McCusker, my clients, who suffered from the effects of Ari's Rule for more than five years but held their family together and triumphed in the end;

Mac McGregor, the third man aboard the Piaggio, who served Aristotle Onassis as his last personal Piaggio pilot;

Peggy McGregor, Mac's wife, who (along with Mac) gave extraordinary support to the McCuskers in Greece;

Alan Hunter, the British aviation accident investigator who was called in by Aristotle Onassis and was given access to the witnesses as well as the physical and documentary evidence;

Herb Mehlhorn, Helena McCusker's brother, who worked tirelessly to get the U.S. Department of State to rescue Don McCusker from his Greek confinement;

Rob Nelson, Don's lifelong friend, who marshaled the modest financial resources of Don's relatives and friends (including his own) to relieve Don's predicament; and

Fiona Thyssen, the person closest to Alexander Onassis during the last five years of his life.

I also benefited from documents and information which I obtained during the litigation against Onassis in which I represented Don and Helena McCusker.

Other sources, including the works of other authors and records of the U.S. Department of State, the Federal Bureau of Investigation, and the Hellenic Republic (Greece), are identified in the text, in the notes, and in the bibliography.

Notes

Publishing information on works cited in the notes will be found in the bibliography. The bibliography also lists the biographies of Aristotle Onassis, Christina Onassis, and Jacqueline Kennedy Onassis consulted by the author.

Chapter 1

Page 9: The portions of the F.B.I. file on Aristotle Onassis which are available to the public under the Freedom of Information Act may be accessed on the Internet at *http://foia.fbi.gov/aonassis.htm*.

Page 10: Publishing information on the biography of Aristotle Onassis written by the London *Sunday Times* investigative reporters will be found in the bibliography under Fraser, Nicholas et al.

Chapter 3

Pages 49-52:The Maheu quotations are from chapter 1 of Maheu's book, *Next to Hughes*.

Chapter 4

A principal reference source for the relationship between Maria Callas and Aristotle Onassis was *Maria Callas: The Woman Behind the Legend*, by Arianna Stassinopoulos (now Huffington), particularly her chapter 11 covering the years 1960-1963.

Chapter 6

Pages 104-105: The Vlachos quotations appear at pages 118, 119, 121, and 122 of *House Arrest*.

Pages 106-107: The Vlachos quotations appear at pages 118, 119, and 120 of *House Arrest*.

Page 112: The Lilly quotation appears at page 119 of *Those Fabulous Greeks*.

Page 113: The Frischauer quotation appears at page 16 of *Onassis*.

The Brady quotation appears at page 135 of *Onassis: An Extravagant Life*.

The Wright quotation appears at page 170 of *All the Pain that Money Can Buy*.

Chapter 8

Page 138: The French Ministry of Transport Report on the Kouris brothers' Learjet crash was issued on November 15, 1972.

Chapter 9

Pages 160-161: Aristotle Onassis's speech at the press conference of January 24, 1973, was reported verbatim in English in the *Athens Daily Post* of January 25, 1973, pp. 1 and 4, under the headline "ONASSIS SPEAKS ABOUT HIS SON'S DEATH."

Chapter 12

Page 218: The Thurston quotation appears at page 235 of *Design for Flying*.

Page 218: The De Remer statement appears at page 11-5 of *Seaplane Operations*.

Page 219: The Mees quotation appears at pp. 13-14 of *Notes of a Seaplane Instructor*.

Page 219: Clarke's ocean charts for the Atlantic Ocean appear at pp. 10-11 of *Atlantic Pilot Atlas,* and those for the Mediterranean appear at page 73 thereof.

Page 220: The World Meteorological Organization definition of moderate waves appears in *Guide to Meteorological Instruments and Methods of Observation,* Section 4.2.12.5, "Terminology for Sea and Swell Waves."

Page 221: The Lindbergh quotations appear at pages 107 and 113 of *Autobiography of Values.*

Page 221: The Davies quotation appears at page 28 of *Pan Am: An Airline and Its Aircraft.*

Page 221: The Foxworth quotation appears at page 66 of *Skyways,* April 1999.

Page 222: The Richardson quotation appears at page 3 of the *New York Times,* January 24, 1939.

Page 223: The Watson quotation appears at page 3 of the *New York Times,* January 24, 1939.

Page 223: The Spurr quotation appears at page 2 of the *New York Times,* January 24, 1939.

Page 223: The *Life* quotation appears at page 11 of the February 6, 1939 number.

Page 224: The quotations from the British Air Ministry *Cavalier* Report appear at pages 11 and 18.

Page 226 The quotation about the Catalina rescue missions appears at Volume VII, page 493 of Craven, Wesley F. et al.

Page 228: The maritime definition of "tender" appears at page 183 of Dear, Ian et al.

Chapter 13

Page 248: The Greek parliament's approval of a bill "to establish a major overhaul and repair facility for military and commercial aircraft in Greece" was announced in *Aviation Week & Space Technology*, August 4, 1975, at page 23.

Page 249: The Maheu quotations are from pp. 137-140 of Maheu's book, *Next to Hughes*.

Pages 253: The Callas quotations are from *Maria Callas: The Woman Behind the Legend*, by Arianna Stassinopoulos (now Huffington), page 323.

Page 254: The Papanikolaou quotations in this chapter were obtained by interviews conducted by Nicholas Gage, first published in chapter 21 of his 2000 book, *Greek Fire*.

Page 257: The Rosenfeld quotations in this chapter were obtained by interviews conducted by Nicholas Gage, first published in chapter 21 of his 2000 book, *Greek Fire*.

Page 263: The *Lloyd's List* quotations appear in the March 30, 2000 number, Special Feature, "Onassis and his Legacy," pp. 1-4.

Chapter 14

Page 269: The quotation from *Greece: A Country Study* appears at page 76 of Curtis, Glenn E., ed.

Pages 272: The Woodhouse quotation appears at page 170 of *The Rise and Fall of the Greek Colonels*.

Pages 280-281: The letter of January 14, 1974 from Ari to Christina was first published in Nicholas Gage's 2000 book, *Greek Fire*, at p. 342. In addition to the crimes described in the text, the concealment of a will is also a felony in many jurisdictions. For example, §190.30 of the New York Penal Code provides, "Unlawfully concealing a will is a class E felony."

Page 287: The article that Herb Mehlhorn sent to the McCuskers was "Gambling Lawyer: The stakes are huge in the competitive world of air-crash lawsuits" by Roy J. Harris Jr., *Wall Street Journal*, May 22, 1978, page 1.

Chapter 15

Page 303: The DeLorean quotation appears at page 53 of Wright, J., *On a Clear Day You Can See General Motors*.

Chapter 17

Page 332: The obituary of Stavros Niarchos appears in the *New York Times* edition of April 18, 1996.

Page 340: The Davies quotation appears at page 83 of *Death of a Tycoon*.

Page 341: The Greenslade quotation appears at pp. 48-49 of *Maxwell*.

Chapter 18

Pages 350-354: The Evans statements from his 2004 book *Nemesis* appear at pages 155-156, 164, 170-171, 195, 212, 236-237, 256-257, 282, and 304. The 1995 book by Dan E. Moldea, *The Killing of Robert F. Kennedy*, contains a detailed investigation of the assassination, including interviews with the police and F.B.I. officers involved and analysis of the relevant documents. While finding fault with the manner in which the Los Angeles Police Department handled the case, Moldea concludes that Sirhan Sirhan acted alone and was not paid for the assassination.

Page 356: The Enron quotation was reported in the London *Telegraph* of January 28, 2002, in an article by Philip Delves Broughton entitled "Enron cocktail of cash, sex, and fast living."

Page 356: The quotation about *hubris* appears in volume 4 of *The Dictionary of the History of Ideas* at page 228.

Bibliography

Anderson, Christopher P. *Jackie After Jack: Portrtait of the Lady.* New York: William Morrow, 1998.

Bradford, Sarah. *America's Queen: The Life of Jacqueline Kennedy Onassis.* New York: Viking, 2000.

Brady, Frank. *Onassis: An Extravagant Life.* Englewood Cliffs, N.J.: Prentice-Hall, 1977.

British Air Ministry. *Report by the Chief Inspector of Accidents on the Loss of the Aircraft G-ADUU "Cavalier" on the 21st January, 1939.* London: HMSO, 1939.

Caro, Robert A., *The Years of Lyndon Johnson: Master of the Senate.* New York: Knopf, 2002.

Clarke, James. *Atlantic Pilot Atlas.* Camden, Maine: International Marine Division of McGraw-Hill, 1997.

Craven, Wesley F.; and James L. Cate. *The Army Air Forces in World War II.* Chicago: University of Chicago Press, 1958.

Curtis, Glenn E., ed. *Greece: A Country Study.* Washington, D.C.: Library of Congress, 1995.

Davies, Nick. *Death of a Tycoon.* New York: St. Martin's, 1992.

Davies, R.E.G. *Pan Am: An Airline and Its Aircraft.* New York: Orion,1987.

Davis, L.J. *Onassis: Aristotle and Christina.* New York: St. Martin's, 1986.

Dear, Ian; and Peter Kemp, *An A-Z of Sailing Terms.* New York: Oxford, 1997.

Dempster, Nigel. *Heiress: The Story of Christina Onassis.* London: Weidenfeld & Nicholson, 1989.

De Remer, Dale. *Seaplane Operations.* Como, Italy: Edizioni Newpress, 1998.

Evans, Peter. *Ari: The Life and Times of Aristotle Onassis.* New York: Summit, 1986.

— *Nemesis: The True Story of Aristotle Onassis, Jackie O, and the Love Triangle that Brought Down the Kennedys.* New York: ReganBooks, HarperCollins, 2004.

Fraser, Nicholas; Philip Jacobson; Mark Ottaway; and Lewis Chester. *Aristotle Onassis.* New York: J. B. Lippincott, 1977.

Frischauer, Willi. *Onassis.* New York: Avon, 1968.

Gage, Nicholas. *Greek Fire: The Story of Maria Callas and Aritstotle Onassis.* New York: Knopf, 2000.

Greenslade, Roy. *Maxwell.* New York: Carol, 1992.

Heymann, C. David. *A Woman Named Jackie.* New York: Lyle Stuart, 1989.

Hutchins, Chris; and Peter Thompson. *Athina: The Last Onassis.* London: Blake, 1999.

Klein, Edward. *Just Jackie: Her Private Years.* New York: Ballantine, 1998.

Lenzner, Robert. *The Great Getty.* New York: Crown, 1986.

Lilly, Doris. *Those Fabulous Greeks: Onassis, Niarchos and Livanos.* New York: Cowles, 1970.

Lindbergh, Charles A. *Autobiography of Values.* New York: Harcourt Brace Jovanovich, 1977.

Maheu, Robert, with Richard Hack. *Next to Hughes.* New York: HarperCollins, 1992.

Mees, Burke. *Notes of a Seaplane Instructor.* Newcastle, Washington: Aviation Supplies & Academics, 1998.

Moldea, Dan E. *The Killing of Robert F. Kennedy: An Investigation of Motive, Means, and Opportunity.* New York: Norton, 1995.

Stassinopoulos, Arianna. *Maria Callas: The Woman Behind the Legend.* New York: Simon and Schuster, 1981.

Spoto, Donald. *Jacqueline Bouvier Kennedy Onassis: A Life.* New York: St. Martin's, 2000.

Thurston, David B. *Design for Flying.* New York: McGraw-Hill, 1978.

Vlachos, Helen. *House Arrest.* Boston: Gambit, 1970.

Woodhouse, C. M. *The Rise and Fall of the Greek Colonels.* London: Granada, 1985.

World Meteorological Organization. *Guide to Meteorological Instruments and Methods of Observation.* Geneva: World Meteorological Organization, 1997.

Wright, J. *On a Clear Day You Can See General Motors.* Grosse Point, Michigan: Wright Enterprises, 1979.

Wright, William. *All the Pain That Money Can Buy: The Life of Christina Onassis.* New York: Simon & Schuster, 1991.

Index

About the Author

STUART M. SPEISER IS THE AUTHOR OF 53 BOOKS ON LAW
and business, including *Lawsuit,* which was favorably reviewed by
*The New York Times, New York Review of Books, Los Angeles Times,
Chicago Tribune,* and NBC's *Today* show. A World War II bomber
pilot and later a commercial pilot, he was a pioneer in air crash litigation, successfully representing victims of most of the major air
disasters of the twentieth century. He represented plaintiffs in
many famous cases, including Ralph Nader's suit against General
Motors, the war of the Guccis, the Entebbe hijacking, the death
of Roberto Clemente, the Pan Am Lockerbie bombing, and the
suit against the estate of Aristotle Onassis which is described in
this book.

For his work in spreading American legal principles to other
nations, he was honored by creation of the Stuart Speiser Chair at
Britain's Nottingham Law School. He is a member of the Honorary
Board of Editors of the *Journal of Post Keynesian Economics,* and was
awarded the James Smithson medal for his art contributions to the
Smithsonian's National Air and Space Museum.